Advances in Game-Based Learning

Series Editors
Dirk Ifenthaler
Scott Joseph Warren
Deniz Eseryel

More information about this series at http://www.springer.com/series/13094

Joke Torbeyns • Erno Lehtinen • Jan Elen
Editors

Describing and Studying Domain-Specific Serious Games

 Springer

Editors
Joke Torbeyns
Education and Training
KU Leuven
Leuven, Belgium

Erno Lehtinen
Department of Teacher Education
University of Turku
Turku, Finland

Jan Elen
Education and Training
KU Leuven
Leuven, Belgium

Advances in Game-Based Learning
ISBN 978-3-319-20275-4   ISBN 978-3-319-20276-1   (eBook)
DOI 10.1007/978-3-319-20276-1

Library of Congress Control Number: 2015950631

Springer Cham Heidelberg New York Dordrecht London

Printed on acid-free paper

Springer International Publishing AG Switzerland is part of Springer Science+Business Media (www.springer.com)

Preface

In 2014, a new International Research Network entitled "Developing competencies in learners: From ascertaining to intervening" was established. This network, which is coordinated by the Center for Instructional Psychology and Technology (CIP&T) of the KU Leuven, Belgium, and funded for a 5-year period by the Research Foundation—Flanders (FWO), involves 14—mainly European—research teams. As the network's title indicates, it addresses a theoretically and methodologically major theme of instructional sciences, namely how to make the difficult step from results of ascertaining studies to intervention studies, or, stated differently, from models or theories of (stimulating) cognition, development, and learning to models or theories of instruction, with a particular attention to the role of instructional technology. Arguably, addressing this complex and fundamental issue requires the confrontation and integration of insights and approaches from various subdomains of instructional sciences, including instructional psychology, instructional technology, instructional design, subject-matter didactics, and teacher education.

For its first meeting, which took place in the Autumn of 2014 in the Irish College, Leuven, a theme was chosen that is in the heart of the network's research agenda, namely domain-specific serious (computer) games.

The present volume is based on that meeting, during which the theme of domain-specific serious games was addressed in different domains, at different educational levels, and from the distinct above-mentioned subdisciplinary perspectives reflected in the network.

The volume is quite unique in its conception and structure. Compared to most other scientific volumes on serious games, this publication does not only comprise scientific reports of the effects of these games on the development of various aspects of learners' competencies, or on how these games are effectively implemented and used in learners' educational settings. This book also pays ample attention at and provides a revealing insight into the conception, design, and construction of these games under investigation, their underlying theoretical assumptions, their developers' struggles with trying to balance and integrate the (domain-specific) learning and gaming elements, the contextual and pragmatic affordances and constraints that co-determined their architecture and outlook, etc. Moreover, the volume contains unusually detailed descriptions of the domain-specific serious games being used in implementation and intervention studies being reported. By providing such an unusually rich and vivid view on (the making of) these serious games, this volume constitutes a nice complement to the available research literature on (domain-specific) serious games.

I would like to congratulate and thank the organizers and sponsor of the meeting and the editors of the volume that resulted from it. I am sure that this book will be informative and inspiring to researchers and other professionals active in the design, implementation, and evaluation of domain-specific serious gaming.

Leuven, Belgium   Lieven Verschaffel
March 2015

Contents

Contributors

Vero Vanden Abeele e-Media Lab, KU Leuven, Leuven, Belgium

Lieven Van den Audenaeren e-Media Lab, KU Leuven, Leuven, Belgium

Boglárka Brezovszky Department of Teacher Education, Centre for Learning Research, University of Turku, Turku, Finland

Véronique Celis Parenting and Special Education Research Unit, KU Leuven, Leuven, Belgium

Theodore Chao College of Education and Human Ecology, The Ohio State University, Columbus, OH, USA

Jason A. Chen School of Education, The College of William and Mary, Williamsburg, VA, USA

Frederik Cornillie ITEC—iMinds—KU Leuven—Kulak, Interactive Technologies, Kortrijk, Belgium

Chris Dede Graduate School of Education, Harvard University, Cambridge, MA, USA

Piet Desmet ITEC—iMinds—KU Leuven—Kulak, Interactive Technologies, Kortrijk, Belgium

Franitalco, Research on French, Italian and Comparative Linguistics, KU Leuven, Kortrijk, Belgium

Elke Desmet Faculty of Psychology and Educational Sciences, Campus Kortrijk @ Kulak, KU Leuven, Kortrijk, Belgium

Wim Van Dooren Center for Instructional Psychology and Technology, KU Leuven, Leuven, Belgium

Kelley Durkin Department of Psychological and Brain Sciences, University of Louisville, Louisville, KY, USA

Jan Elen Center for Instructional Psychology and Technology, KU Leuven, Leuven, Belgium

Hedwig Gasteiger Department of Mathematics, Ludwig-Maximilians-Universität München, Munich, Germany

Luc Geurts e-Media Lab, KU Leuven, Leuven, Belgium

Pol Ghesquière Parenting and Special Education Research Unit, KU Leuven, Leuven, Belgium

Ann Goeleven Department of Speech Language Pathology (MUCLA), University Hospitals Leuven Belgium, Leuven, Belgium

Minna M. Hannula-Sormunen Department of Teacher Education, Turku Institute for Advanced Studies, University of Turku, Turku, Finland

Jelle Husson e-Media Lab, KU Leuven, Leuven, Belgium

Tomi Jaakkola Department of Teacher Education, Centre for Learning Research, University of Turku, Turku, Finland

Ton de Jong Department of Instructional Technology, University of Twente, Enschede, The Netherlands

Erno Lehtinen Department of Teacher Education, Centre for Learning Research, University of Turku, Turku, Finland

Sarah Linsen Parenting and Special Education Research Unit, KU Leuven, Leuven, Belgium

Leen Loyez Department of Speech Language Pathology (MUCLA), University Hospitals Leuven Belgium, Leuven, Belgium

Bieke Maertens Faculty of Psychology and Educational Sciences @ KULAK, Kortrijk, Belgium

Marie Maertens ITEC—iMinds—KU Leuven—Kulak, Interactive Technologies, Kortrijk, Belgium

Jake McMullen Department of Teacher Education, Centre for Learning Research, University of Turku, Turku, Finland

Andreas Obersteiner TUM School of Education, Technische Universität München, Munich, Germany

Herre van Oostendorp Department of Information and Computing Sciences, Utrecht University, Utrecht, The Netherlands

Gabriela Rodríguez Padilla Department of Teacher Education, Centre for Learning Research, University of Turku, Turku, Finland

Nonmanut Pongsakdi Department of Teacher Education, Centre for Learning Research, University of Turku, Turku, Finland

Kristina Reiss TUM School of Education, Technische Universität München, Munich, Germany

Bert Reynvoet Faculty of Psychology and Educational Sciences, KU Leuven, Leuven, Belgium

Faculty of Psychology and Educational Sciences @ KULAK, Kortrijk, Belgium

Bert De Smedt Faculty of Psychology and Educational Sciences, KU Leuven, Leuven, Belgium

Jon R. Star Graduate School of Education, Harvard University, Cambridge, MA, USA

Megan W. Taylor Sonoma State University, Rohnert Park, CA, USA

Joke Torbeyns Center for Instructional Psychology and Technology, KU Leuven, Leuven, Belgium

Sylke Vandercruysse Center for Instructional Psychology & Technology, KU Leuven, Leuven, Belgium

Mieke Vandewaetere ITEC—iMinds—KU Leuven—Kulak, Interactive Technologies, Kortrijk, Belgium

Center for Instructional Psychology and Technology, KU Leuven, Leuven, Belgium

Koen Veermans Department of Teacher Education, Centre for Learning Research, University of Turku, Turku, Finland

Lieven Verschaffel Faculty of Psychology and Educational Sciences, KU Leuven, Leuven, Belgium

Judith ter Vrugte Department of Instructional Technology, University of Twente, Enschede, The Netherlands

Jeroen Wauters e-Media Lab Group T, Leuven Engineering College, Leuven, Belgium

Pieter Wouters Department of Information and Computing Sciences, Utrecht University, Utrecht, The Netherlands

Jan Wouters ExpORL, Department of Neurosciences, KU Leuven, Leuven, Belgium

Describing and Studying Domain-Specific Serious Games: Introduction

Joke Torbeyns, Erno Lehtinen, and Jan Elen

Abstract The past decade witnessed increasing interest and extremely positive beliefs in the use of games, and especially so-called "serious" games, as educational tools. This AGBL-book on "Describing and studying domain-specific serious games" aims at complementing our current insights into the effectiveness of games as educational tools. In this introductory chapter, we discuss the general scope and outline of the book, with special attention for the content of and relation between the chapters included in Part 1 (game descriptions) and Part 2 (empirical studies on serious games).

Keywords Game descriptions • Empirical studies on serious games • Outline of the book

The past decade witnessed increasing interest and extremely positive beliefs in the use of games, and especially so-called serious games, as educational tools. However, up to now, empirical evidence on the effectiveness of games as potential learning tools is limited and inconclusive due to weaknesses in both the conceptual framework and the methodology in the available research literature (e.g., Girard, Ecalle, & Magnan, 2013; Papastergiou, 2009; Sitzman, 2011; Vogel et al., 2006).

A first weakness of empirical studies on (serious) games as educational tools relates to the definition of a (serious) game. Although researchers generally agree

J. Torbeyns (✉) • J. Elen
Center for Instructional Psychology and Technology, KU Leuven,
Dekenstraat 2, Box 3773, Leuven 3000, Belgium
e-mail: joke.torbeyns@ppw.kuleuven.be; jan.elen@ppw.kuleuven.be

E. Lehtinen
Department of Teacher Education, Center for Learning Research,
University of Turku, Assistentinkatu 7, Turku 20014, Finland
e-mail: erno.lehtinen@utu.fi

© Springer International Publishing Switzerland 2015   1
J. Torbeyns et al. (eds.), *Describing and Studying Domain-Specific Serious Games*,
Advances in Game-Based Learning, DOI 10.1007/978-3-319-20276-1_1

on broad definitions of serious games as "games primarily focused on education rather than entertainment" (Miller, Chang, Wang, Beier, & Klisch, 2011, p. 1425) or "digital games, simulations, virtual environments and mixed reality/media that provide opportunities to engage in activities through responsive narrative/story, gameplay or encounters to inform, influence, for well-being, and/or experience to convey meaning" (Marsh, 2011, p. 63), the concrete operationalization of these broad definitions into the core mechanisms of the serious games under study significantly varies across studies.

Second, on top of the unclear and diverse concrete definitions of serious games, the major characteristics of the games under study are only loosely described in the available research literature. One of the major arguments for using game-based learning environments is that games and gaming activities are more engaging and lead to more active learning processes than conventional pedagogical classroom practices. However, more detailed analysis is needed of the specific features of games which are supposed to be engaging and the nature of the activities students are engaged in during gameplay. Recent meta-analyses show that in school contexts serious games are not always as motivating as expected (e.g., Wouters, van Nimwegen, van Oostendorp, & van der Spek, 2013). From the point of view of goal-oriented learning, the mere engagement in an intensive activity is not sufficient; the activity should involve focusing on meaningful content in a way that is beneficial for learning (Engle & Conant, 2002).

A third major problem refers to the scope and methodologies of current studies on serious games, characterized by a rich variety in both major aims and materials used. It is difficult to get a convincing overview of the educational effectiveness of games because most published articles are descriptive or only loosely demonstrate learning outcomes without controlled empirical designs (Young et al., 2012).

This book aims at complementing our current insights into the effectiveness of games as educational tools. Different from previous work, the contributions to this book do not merely focus on "serious games" but discuss the characteristics and the potential effectiveness of "game-based learning environments" or GBLE, defined as learning environments that contain (serious) games as potential learning tools. By doing so, the essential interplay between game features and context is highlighted and brought to the front as an important research issue. Moreover, the different contributions all address the potentials of such game-based learning environments for students' learning and motivation in the domain of Science, Technology, Engineering, and Mathematics (STEM). As outlined below, there is only one exception in terms of definition and scope, focusing on the potential of serious games as diagnostic tools in the domain of reading and as such nicely complementing the other contributions to the book.

Taking into account the importance of clear and complete descriptions of the games under study, the first part of this book focuses on the core mechanisms of six recently developed game-based learning environments in the domains of STEM and reading.

In the first chapter, Linsen, Maertens, and colleagues describe the GBLE "Dudeman & Sidegirl: Operation clean world," specifically designed to stimulate Kindergartners' and lower elementary school students' numerical magnitude processing skills.

The second chapter, by Vandercruysse, Maertens, and Elen, focuses on the core mechanisms of the commercially available GBLE "Monkey Tales," aiming at improving elementary school students' mathematical competencies.

The GBLE described in the third chapter by Lehtinen and colleagues, namely "Number Navigation Game," is specifically designed to stimulate upper elementary school students' number knowledge and problem-solving skills.

In the fourth chapter, Vandercruysse and colleagues describe the GBLE "Zeldenrust," a mathematical GBLE for prevocational secondary school students, aiming at promoting these students' motivation for and understanding of proportional reasoning problems.

In the fifth chapter, Star, Chen, and Dede discuss the design process and the core characteristics of a GBLE that was designed on the basis of Eccles and Wigfield's (2000) expectancy-value theory of motivation. The authors refer to this GBLE as an Immersive Virtual Environment (IVE), specifically aimed at promoting upper elementary and secondary school students' interest in and motivation for STEM careers.

The sixth chapter, by Geurts and colleagues, focuses on the design principles and rationale behind DIESEL-X, a serious game for detecting a high risk for developing dyslexia in Kindergartners.

Following the concrete and extensive GBLE descriptions in the first part of the book, the second part of the book discusses recent empirical investigations on the learning and motivational effectiveness of (most of) these GBLEs. Table 1 provides an overview of the GBLEs described in the first part of the book and the empirical studies on these GBLEs in the second part of the book.

As demonstrated in Table 1, the seventh and eighth chapters focus on two recent studies with the GBLE Monkey Tales. In "Performance in Educational Math Games: Is it a Question of Math Knowledge?", Maertens, Vandewaetere, Cornillie, and Desmet focus on the contribution of both mathematical knowledge and gaming skills to elementary school students' learning processes within this GBLE. In "Integration in the Curriculum as a Factor in Math-game Effectiveness," Vandercruysse, Desmet, Vandewaetere, and Elen address the issue of game integration in the curriculum and its influence on students' learning, perception, and motivation using Monkey Tales.

In "Developing Adaptive Number Knowledge with the Number Navigation Game-based Learning Environment" Chapter 9 and "Number Navigation Game Experience and Motivational Effects," Chapter 10 Brezovszky and colleagues and Rodríguez Padilla and colleagues report on the learning and motivational effectiveness of the GBLE Number Navigation Game, respectively. "Developing Adaptive Number Knowledge with the Number Navigation Game-based Learning Environment" mainly focuses on the effectiveness of Number Navigation Game in terms of learning outcomes, whereas "Number Navigation Game Experience and Motivational Effects" also addresses the important assumptions regarding the motivational effectiveness of GBLEs in general and Number Navigation Game in particular.

Table 1 Overview of GBLE descriptions (Part 1) and empirical studies (Part 2)

GBLE	Domain	Age	Description (Part 1)	Empirical study (Part 2)
Dudeman & Sidegirl: Operation clean world	STEM	Kindergartners, lower grades elementary school	"Design of the Game 'Dudeman & Sidegirl: Operation Clean World,' A Numerical Magnitude Processing Training"	–
Monkey Tales	STEM	Elementary school	"Description of the Educational Math Game 'Monkey Tales: The Museum of Anything'"	"Performance in Educational Math Games: Is it a Question of Math Knowledge?"
				"Integration in the Curriculum as a Factor in Math-game Effectiveness"
Number Navigation Game	STEM	Upper grades elementary school	"Number Navigation Game (NNG): Design Principles and Game Description"	"Developing Adaptive Number Knowledge with the Number Navigation Game-based Learning Environment"
				"Number Navigation Game Experience and Motivational Effects"
Zeldenrust	STEM	Prevocational secondary school students	"'Zeldenrust': a Mathematical Game-based Learning Environment for Prevocational Students"	"The Role of Curiosity-Triggering Events in Game-based Learning for Mathematics"
Immersive Virtual Environment	STEM	Upper grades of elementary school; lower grades of secondary school	"Applying Motivation Theory to the Design of Game-based Learning Environments"	"Evaluating Game-based Learning Environments for Enhancing Motivation in Mathematics"
DIESEL-X	Reading	Kindergartners	"DIESEL-X: A Game-based Tool for Early Risk Detection of Dyslexia in Preschoolers"	–
Conventional board games	STEM	Kindergartners	–	"Formal and Informal Learning Environments: Using Games to Support Early Numeracy"

"The Role of Curiosity-triggering Events in Game-based Learning for Mathematics," Chapter 11 by Wouters and colleagues, focuses on the effectiveness of including extra curiosity-triggering events to the GBLE Zeldenrust for increasing prevocational secondary students' motivational and learning outcomes.

In "Evaluating Game-based Learning Environments for Enhancing Motivation in Mathematics," Chapter 12 Star and colleagues critically discuss the motivational effectiveness of the GBLE designed on the basis of Eccles and Wigfield's (2000) expectancy-value theory of motivation with a view to stimulate upper elementary and secondary school students' interest in and motivation for STEM careers (see Part 1, "Applying Motivation Theory to the Design of Game-based Learning Environments").

The book closes with the contribution of Gasteiger, Obersteiner, and Reiss ("Formal and Informal Learning Environments: Using Games to Support Early Numeracy") Chapter 13 on the effectiveness of using conventional board games for enhancing Kindergartners' early mathematical development. Prior to the report of their own intervention study, the authors critically review (the definition of) conventional board games and previous work on the use of these games in educational contexts.

Taken together, the contributions to the book at first sight display the rich diversity in the current research literature on (serious) games, given the clear focus on either the design process (contributions to Part 1) or the learning and/or motivational effectiveness of GBLEs (contributions to Part 2), as well as the various GBLEs that are described and studied in the different chapters. However, the common GBLE starting point and definition, the detailed descriptions of the core mechanisms of the GBLEs under study, and the concrete focus and sound design of the different empirical studies provide building blocks for empirically addressing the positive claims and expectations regarding the potential of serious games as educational tools in future studies. As such, this book does not only significantly add to our understanding of the core mechanisms of different GBLEs and their design and effectiveness in educational contexts, but also offers interesting and timely avenues for future studies on these topics.

References

Engle, R. A., & Conant, F. R. (2002). Guiding principles for fostering productive disciplinary engagement: Explaining an emergent argument in a community of learners classroom. *Cognition and Instruction, 20*, 399–483. doi:10.1207/S1532690XCI2004_1.

Girard, C., Ecalle, J., & Magnan, A. (2013). Serious games as new educational tools. How effective are they? A meta-analysis of recent studies. *Journal of Computer Assisted Learning, 29*, 207–219. 10/1111/j.1365-2729.2012.00489.x.

Marsh, T. (2011). Serious games continuum: Between games for purpose and experiential environments for purpose. *Entertainment Computing, 2*, 61–68.

Miller, L. M., Chang, C.-I., Wang, S., Beier, M. E., & Klisch, Y. (2011). Learning and motivational impacts of a multimedia science game. *Computers & Education, 57*, 1425–1433.

Papastergiou, M. (2009). Digital game-based learning in high school computer science education: Impact on educational effectiveness and school motivation. *Computers & Education, 52*, 1–12. doi:10.1016/j.compedu.2008.06.004.

Sitzman, T. (2011). A meta-analytic examination of the instructional effectiveness of computer-based simulation games. *Personnel Psychology, 64*, 489–528.

Vogel, J. J., Vogel, D. S., Cannon-Bowers, J., Bowers, C. A., Muse, K., & Wright, M. (2006). Computer games and interactive simulations for learning: A meta-analysis. *Journal of Educational Computing Research, 34*, 229–243. doi:10.2190/FLHV-K4WA-WPVQ-H0YM.

Wigfield, A., & Eccles, J. S. (2000). Expectancy-value theory of motivation. *Contemporary Educational Psychology, 25*, 68–81.

Wouters, P., van Nimwegen, C., van Oostendorp, H., & van der Spek, E. D. (2013). A meta-analysis of the cognitive and motivational effects of serious games. *Journal of Educational Psychology, 105*, 249–265.

Young, M. F., Slota, S., Cutter, A. B., Jalette, G., Mullin, G., Lai, B., … Yukhymenko, M. (2012). Our princess is in another castle: a review of trends in serious gaming for education. *Review of Educational Research, 82*, 61-89.

Part 1
Game Descriptions

Design of the Game-Based Learning Environment "Dudeman & Sidegirl: Operation Clean World," a Numerical Magnitude Processing Training

**Sarah Linsen, Bieke Maertens, Jelle Husson,
Lieven Van den Audenaeren, Jeroen Wauters,
Bert Reynvoet, Bert De Smedt, Lieven Verschaffel, and Jan Elen**

Abstract Numerical magnitude processing has been shown to play a crucial role in the development of mathematical ability and intervention studies have revealed that training children's numerical magnitude processing has positive effects on their numerical magnitude processing skills and mathematics achievement. However, from these intervention studies, it remains unclear whether numerical magnitude processing interventions should focus on training with a numerical magnitude comparison or a number line estimation task. It also remains to be determined whether

S. Linsen (✉)
Faculty of Psychology and Educational Sciences, KU Leuven, Leuven, Belgium

Parenting and Special Education Research Unit, KU Leuven,
L. Vanderkelenstraat 32, 3765, Leuven 3000, Belgium
e-mail: sarah.linsen@ppw.kuleuven.be

B. Maertens (✉) • B. Reynvoet
Faculty of Psychology and Educational Sciences @ KULAK, Kortrijk, Belgium

Brain and Cognition, Etienne Sabbelaan 53, Kortrijk 8500, Belgium
e-mail: bieke.maertens@ppw.kuleuven.be; bert.reynvoet@kuleuven-kulak.be

J. Husson • L. Van den Audenaeren • J. Wauters
e-Media Lab, KU Leuven, Leuven, Belgium
e-mail: jelle.husson@kuleuven.be; lieven.vandenaudenaeren@kuleuven.be;
jeroen.wauters@kuleuven.be

B. De Smedt • L. Verschaffel • J. Elen
Faculty of Psychology and Educational Sciences, KU Leuven, Leuven, Belgium
e-mail: bert.desmedt@ppw.kuleuven.be; lieven.verschaffel@ppw.kuleuven.be;
jan.elen@ppw.kuleuven.be

© Springer International Publishing Switzerland 2015
J. Torbeyns et al. (eds.), *Describing and Studying Domain-Specific Serious Games*,
Advances in Game-Based Learning, DOI 10.1007/978-3-319-20276-1_2

there is a different impact of training symbolic versus nonsymbolic numerical magnitude processing skills. In order to answer these two questions, we developed four game-based learning environments, using the storyline of "Dudeman & Sidegirl: Operation clean world". The first two game-based learning environments comprise either a numerical magnitude comparison or a number line estimation training and the last two game-based learning environments stimulate either the processing of symbolic or nonsymbolic numerical magnitudes.

Keywords Game-based learning environment • Numerical magnitude processing • Mathematical achievement • Educational intervention • Design principles

Mathematical skills are of great importance in everyday life. We use them, for example, when we measure ingredients for cooking, read the timetables to catch a train, or pay in the supermarket. In the last decade, there has been an increasing research interest in the cognitive processes that underlie these mathematical skills, which points to numerical magnitude processing, or people's elementary intuitions about number and quantity, as an important factor in explaining individual differences in mathematical ability in children as well as adults (Bugden & Ansari, 2011; De Smedt, Verschaffel, & Ghesquière, 2009; Halberda, Mazzocco, & Feigenson, 2008; Sasanguie, Van den Bussche, & Reynvoet, 2012; see De Smedt, Noël, Gilmore, & Ansari, 2013, for a review). For this reason, the development of interventions to improve children's numerical magnitude processing skills is very relevant and would provide opportunities for early intervention of children at-risk for mathematical difficulties. Furthermore, choosing a game-based learning environment might provide a motivating environment for the children, given the combination of learning and playing (Garris, Ahlers, & Driskell, 2002). We therefore developed two game-based learning environments to train children's numerical magnitude processing skills. In this contribution, we will first discuss the concept of numerical magnitude processing and its association with mathematical skills. Afterwards, we will elaborate on previous research that investigated the effects of interventions that aim to improve numerical magnitude processing. Finally, we will explain in detail the four game-based learning environments that were developed.

Numerical Magnitude Processing

Numerical magnitude processing has been shown to play a crucial role in the development of mathematical ability (see De Smedt et al., 2013, for a review). The understanding of numbers is rooted in a very basic sense of numerosities and number symbols. This numerical magnitude processing has often been described using the metaphor of a "mental number line" (Bailey, Siegler, & Geary, 2014; Dehaene, 1992; Gallistel & Gelman, 1992; Laski & Siegler, 2007). The mental number line is characterized as a number line for which the numerical magnitudes are represented by distributions around the true location of each specific value. Because the representations of numerical magnitudes that are adjacent overlap, the closer two numerical magnitudes are, the harder it will be to distinguish them.

There are two common ways to measure numerical magnitude processing skills, namely with a numerical magnitude comparison task and a number line estimation task. In the *numerical magnitude comparison task* (Sekuler & Mierkiewicz, 1977), children are instructed to indicate the numerically larger of two presented numerical magnitudes, which can be presented in either a symbolic (digits) or a nonsymbolic (dot patterns) format (Holloway & Ansari, 2009). A second classic task is the *number line estimation task* (Booth & Siegler, 2006). In this task, children are typically shown a horizontal number line, for example, with 0 on one end and 10, 100, or 1000 on the other. In the number-to-position variant, children are instructed to position a given number on this number line, and in the position-to-number variant, children have to estimate which number is indicated on the number line (Ashcraft & Moore, 2012; Booth & Siegler, 2006, 2008). This task can also be presented in a symbolic or a nonsymbolic format (Sasanguie, De Smedt, Defever, & Reynvoet, 2012). The numerical magnitude comparison task and the number line estimation task are generally assumed to rely on the same underlying magnitude representation (Dehaene, 1997; Laski & Siegler, 2007), but this idea has recently been questioned (Barth & Paladino, 2011; Sasanguie & Reynvoet, 2013). Sasanguie and Reynvoet (2013), for example, compared the performance in the numerical magnitude comparison task and the number line estimation task directly in one study and observed no significant association between both tasks, which suggests that different processes might play a role in both numerical magnitude processing tasks.

Research on these two kinds of tasks has revealed that children who perform better on them also showed higher mathematics achievement at that time (Bugden & Ansari, 2011; Halberda et al., 2008; Holloway & Ansari, 2009; Sasanguie, Van den Bussche & Reynvoet, 2012; Siegler & Booth, 2004). More specifically, studies revealed that children who were faster or more accurate in indicating which of two numbers or quantities was the larger, showed higher achievement in mathematics (e.g., Bugden & Ansari, 2011; De Smedt et al., 2009; Halberda et al., 2008; Holloway & Ansari, 2009; Lonnemann, Linkersdörfer, Hasselhorn, & Lindberg, 2011; Mundy & Gilmore, 2009; Sasanguie, De Smedt et al., 2012; see De Smedt et al., 2013, for a review). A similar association with mathematics achievement has been observed in studies with number line estimation as a measure for numerical magnitude processing, showing that individual differences in number line estimation were strongly correlated with their mathematics achievement test scores (e.g., Sasanguie, Van den Bussche & Reynvoet, 2012; Siegler & Booth, 2004). More specifically, children with more linear estimation patterns, resulting in more precise estimations, showed higher mathematics achievement.

In the literature on numerical magnitude processing, there has been an ongoing debate on whether the representation of numerical magnitudes per se, or its access via symbolic digits, is important for mathematical achievement (De Smedt & Gilmore, 2011; Rousselle & Noël, 2007; see also De Smedt et al., 2013, for a review). This question is typically approached by comparing children's performance on symbolic and nonsymbolic tasks. If both symbolic and nonsymbolic tasks predict individual differences in mathematical achievement, this indicates that numerical magnitude processing per se is crucial for mathematical achievement. On the other hand, if only symbolic, but not nonsymbolic tasks, predict general mathematical skills, the hypothesis of the access to numerical meaning from symbolic digits is favored. Correlational evidence favoring the first hypothesis (Halberda et al., 2008; Libertus, Feigenson, & Halberda, 2011; Lonnemann et al., 2011; Mussolin, Mejias, & Noël, 2010) and the second one (De Smedt & Gilmore, 2011; Holloway & Ansari, 2009; Landerl & Kölle, 2009; Rousselle & Noël, 2007; Sasanguie, De Smedt et al., 2012; Vanbinst, Ghesquière, & De Smedt, 2012) has been reported, and it remains to be determined whether these associations are causal or not (see De Smedt et al., 2013, for a review).

Although many studies have examined the association between numerical magnitude processing and mathematical skills, the major part of these studies are cross-sectional in nature and therefore do not allow us to establish causal connections. De Smedt and colleagues (2009) provided longitudinal evidence that the speed of comparing numbers assessed at the start of formal schooling is predictively related to subsequent general mathematics achievement in second grade. Halberda and colleagues (2008) demonstrated this longitudinal evidence for nonsymbolic processing, showing that individual differences on a nonsymbolic magnitude comparison task in the present correlated with children's past scores on standardized math achievement tests, extending all the way back to kindergarten. In the same way, individual differences in number line estimation are predictive for math achievement, measured using a curriculum-based standardized test (Sasanguie, Van den Bussche & Reynvoet, 2012). These longitudinal studies suggest that symbolic and nonsymbolic processing may have a causal role in determining individual math achievement, although this possibility needs to be verified by means of experimental research designs, that is, intervention research.

Educational Interventions

There are a few studies that have examined the effect of educational interventions on the development of numerical magnitude processing (see De Smedt et al., 2013, for a review) and such intervention studies are a good way to explore causal associations. These intervention studies trained on a broad range of numerical activities, such as number recognition, playing board games, counting, and had significant effects on children's numerical magnitude processing and mathematical abilities (Griffin, 2004; Jordan, Glutting, Dyson, Hassinger-Das, & Irwin, 2012). There are also studies that have specifically focused on training numerical magnitude processing as conceived and operationalized in this contribution. For example, a set of various studies have investigated the effects of playing with linear number board games on preschoolers' symbolic number line estimation and numerical magnitude comparison skills, counting abilities, and numeral identification knowledge (Ramani & Siegler, 2008, 2011; Ramani, Siegler, & Hitti, 2012; Siegler & Ramani, 2009; Whyte & Bull, 2008). These studies comprised two conditions, that is, a numerical board game and a color board game, the latter being a control condition. Findings revealed stable improvements in performance on number line estimation and symbolic comparison after playing with the numerical board game, but not with the color board game. Another example is the study of Kucian et al. (2011), which used the game "Rescue Calcularis," which involves symbolic number line estimation tasks in combination with addition and subtraction problems. They showed that the symbolic number line estimation skills of children improved after playing this game, just like their arithmetic skills. Finally, another set of studies used the game "The Number Race," which involved symbolic and nonsymbolic numerical magnitude comparison and number board games (Obersteiner, Reiss, & Ufer, 2013; Räsänen, Salminen, Wilson, Aunio, & Dehaene, 2009; Wilson et al., 2006; Wilson, Dehaene, Dubois, & Fayol, 2009; Wilson, Revkin, Cohen, Cohen, & Dehaene, 2006) and led to positive effects on comparison skills and mathematics achievement.

From these intervention studies, it remains unclear whether numerical magnitude processing interventions should focus on training with a numerical magnitude comparison or a number line estimation task (=question 1). It also remains to be determined whether there is a different impact of training symbolic versus nonsymbolic numerical magnitude processing skills (=question 2). In order to answer these two questions, we developed four game-based learning environments[1] (see Fig. 1).

The first two game-based learning environments, which are designed and used to answer the first question, comprise either a numerical magnitude comparison or a number line estimation training (Fig. 1). Both games involve symbolic as well as nonsymbolic stimuli. With these two game-based learning environments, it is feasible to appraise the effect of both interventions on children's numerical magnitude processing skills and on their mathematical skills. These games are developed to be played by children in the last (third) year of kindergarten or the first year of elementary school, and therefore only Arabic digits up to 9 are used. We will refer to these game-based learning environments as K-games (i.e., kindergarten games).

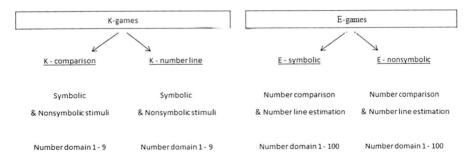

Fig. 1 Overview of the four games

---

[1] Learning environment is used in the broad sense of the term in this contribution. The games described in this contribution are just one type of learning environment, namely a training environment.

To address question 2, we designed two other game-based learning environments that stimulated either the processing of symbolic or nonsymbolic numerical magnitudes. By developing and contrasting two interventions that either focus on symbolic or nonsymbolic numerical magnitude processing (Fig. 1), we are able to examine whether symbolic or nonsymbolic numerical magnitude processing is causally associated with mathematical achievement. This will allow us to evaluate whether one of these interventions has a larger effect on children's numerical magnitude processing and mathematical skills, than the other. Both game-based learning environments involve a numerical magnitude comparison and number line estimation task. These games focus on children in the first years of elementary school and use numbers in the number domain 1–100. We will refer to these game-based learning environments as E-games (i.e., elementary school games).

All interventions are game-based to increase the richness and appeal of the mathematical task, hoping to provide a motivating environment to play in. Especially for young children, combining learning with playing might be an important motivational aspect (see Connolly, Boyle, MacArthur, Hainey, & Boyle, 2012, for a review). The game-based learning environments are designed to be played on tablets and computers, and taking into account the popularity of these multimedia devices, this also offers opportunities to practice the numerical magnitude processing skills at home.

All four game-based learning environments are developed in a similar environment, using the same storyline of "Dudeman & Sidegirl: Operation clean world". Although the game-based learning environments are developed for children of specific age groups, the number domains can be adapted for different age groups.

Dudeman & Sidegirl: Operation Clean World

Story Line

Children are presented with the story that the world is polluted. They have to make the world beautiful again by finding the animals that are hiding. There is a small superhero, Sidegirl, who needs to help the ill superhero, Dudeman. As a player of the game, he/she needs to look for animals in three different parts of the world, that is, under water, on land, and in the air.

Game Elements

Instructions during the game. At the start of the game, children are shown a short movie that explains the purpose of the game, that is, to collect as many animals as possible. From this point on, children have a shared control over their game progress. They can start the game and go through the levels by controlling their own pace, which can be defined as a type of learner control (Scheiter & Gerjets, 2007). Every child has a unique user-id to game-login. Thereby, it is possible to take a break and start again later at the level they ended. However, the learner control is limited because the computer program makes decisions about the amount of instruction (Lee & Lee, 1991), which is identical for all children.

At the beginning of each level, a voice-over explains the goal of the task to the player. This instruction is adapted to the specific characteristics of the level, that is, the instruction depends on the specific task (comparison or number line estimation), the format of the stimuli (symbolic or nonsymbolic), and the number domain. The number of levels and their content differ for each game and are explained in greater detail below.

Instructional design principles. Our game-based learning environments rely on the idea that one can enhance specific skills by part-task practice. This part-task practice involves repeated practice of recurrent constituent skills in the learning tasks and is one component of the 4C/ID-model (Van Merriënboer, Clark, & de Croock, 2002). Part-task practice is mainly used to promote the automatization of a specific skill. Therefore, it comprises simple tasks or skills, which are repeatedly practiced, and feedback on the quality of performance is provided during practice, immediately after performing a particular step in a procedure. Comparison and number line estimation skills are considered to be part-task practices and we assume that the practice of both skills can contribute to enhance magnitude processing skills. Other components of the 4C/ID-model are learning tasks, supportive information, and just-in-time information. However, given the focus of our intervention, that is, training on the accuracy and the speed of execution of simple tasks, these components are not included in our game-based learning environments.

Content. We use numerical magnitude comparison tasks and number line estimation tasks as a basis for the game-based learning environments. To train numerical magnitude comparison processing, children need to navigate with their vehicle through the world and they are shown two groups of animals (i.e., nonsymbolic), two animals carrying an Arabic numeral (i.e., symbolic), or a group of animals and an animal carrying an Arabic numeral (i.e., nonsymbolic and symbolic) (Fig. 2). They are instructed to collect as many animals as possible and therefore need to tap the larger group of animals or the animal with the numerically larger number.

Fig. 2 The *left* figure shows a screenshot of the nonsymbolic numerical magnitude comparison task at the beginning of a trial. The *middle* figure shows a screenshot of the symbolic numerical magnitude comparison task. The *right* figure shows a screenshot of a mixed comparison trial

Fig. 3 The *left* figure shows a screenshot of the symbolic number line estimation task with anchor point on the units at the beginning of a trial. The *middle* figure shows a screenshot of the nonsymbolic number line estimation task with only an anchor point in the middle of the number line. The *right* figure shows a screenshot of a mixed number line estimation trial without anchor points

To train children's number line estimation skills, children need to navigate with their vehicle through the world and are shown an empty number line (Fig. 3). This number line is bounded with digit "0" (i.e., symbolic) or an empty array (i.e., nonsymbolic) on the left side and with digits "10" or "100" or an array of 10 or 100 dots on the right side. Children need to position a numerosity (i.e., nonsymbolic or symbolic), shown on the right of the screen, on the empty number line. When children tap on the correct position on the number line, that is, within the allowable range of the correct answer, the vehicle collects the animal. If the player taps on a position outside the allowable range, the animal appears on the correct position but is not collected.

Starting from this common structure four games are developed each focusing on a specific skill and age group.

K-games. The two K-games are developed to examine the differential effect of comparison versus number line training. Both game-based learning environments contain tasks in which nonsymbolic and symbolic representations are used. The two game-based learning environments consist of different levels, presented in a fixed order and characterized by increasing difficulty. For each game-based learning environment, there are specific criteria to go to the next level, which will be explained below. If the children do not reach these criteria, they have to replay the level until the target score is reached.

K-comparison game. The K-comparison game consists of 14 different levels and each level comprises 24 trials, resulting in a total of 336 trials for all levels. The levels are designed to vary in difficulty based on the *numerosities* (i.e., 1–4, 1–9, and 5–18), the *display duration* (i.e., until response and 1500 ms), and the *type of stimuli* (i.e., nonsymbolic notation, symbolic notation, and mixed notation) used in the tasks. A detailed overview of the characteristics of the levels in this game-based learning environment can be found in Table 1.

A trial is considered as correct when the player selects the larger out of two numerosities. Children need to correctly answer at least 80 % of the trials to succeed the level. This minimum score is based on several empirical studies in young children (e.g., De Smedt et al., 2009; Holloway & Ansari, 2009; Mazzocco, Feigenson, & Halberda, 2011; Sasanguie, De Smedt et al., 2012; Soltész, Szücs, & Szücs, 2010).

Table 1 Details of the K-games

K-comparison game

Level	Numerosities	Display duration	Characteristics of the stimuli
1	1–4	UR	NS–NS
2	1–4	1500 ms	NS–NS
3	1–9	UR	NS–NS
4	1–4	1500 ms	NS–NS
5	5–18	UR	NS–NS
6	5–18	1500 ms	NS–NS
7	1–4	UR	S–S
8	1–4	1500 ms	S–S
9	1–9	UR	S–S
10	1–9	1500 ms	S–S
11	1–4	UR	NS–S
12	1–4	1500 ms	NS–S
13	1–9	UR	NS–S
14	1–9	1500 ms	NS–S

K-number line game

Level	Benchmarks	Display duration	Characteristics of the stimuli
1	9	UR	NS–NS
2	9	1500 ms	NS–NS
3	1	UR	NS–NS
4	1	1500 ms	NS–NS
5	9	UR	S–S
6	9	1500 ms	S–S
7	1	UR	S–S
8	1	1500 ms	S–S
9	9	UR	NS–S
10	9	1500 ms	NS–S
11	1	UR	NS–S
12	1	1500 ms	NS–S
13	/	UR	NS–NS
14	/	1500 ms	NS–NS
15	/	UR	S–S
16	/	1500 ms	S–S
17	/	UR	NS–S
18	/	1500 ms	NS–S

Note. UR = until response, NS = nonsymbolic, S = symbolic

K-number line game. The K-number line game consists of 18 different levels and each level comprises 18 trials, which resulted in a total of 324 trials for all levels. Again, the levels depend on three aspects to vary in difficulty: the number of *anchor points*, the *display duration* (i.e., until response and 1500 ms), and the *type of stimuli* (i.e., nonsymbolic notation, symbolic notation, and mixed notation). A detailed overview of the levels in this game-based learning environment can be found in Table 1.

A correct answer is set to 12.5 % of the number line range on both sides of the to-be-positioned numerosity (e.g., if the child has to position the number 4 on a 0–10 number line, any answer between 2.75 and 5.25 is considered to be correct). To avoid that children get stuck up in a level because they perform too low, the cut-off score to move to the next level is set at 50 %. This criterion is based on other empirical studies (e.g., Berteletti, Lucangeli, Piazza, Dehaene, & Zorzi, 2010; Booth & Siegler, 2006; Siegler & Booth, 2004; Siegler & Ramani, 2009).

E-games. The two game-based learning environments that will be explained below are developed to examine the differential effect of symbolic versus nonsymbolic numerical magnitude processing training in second grade children. Both game-based learning environments comprise a set of tasks that are variants of the numerical magnitude comparison task and the number line estimation task. One version of the game-based learning environment uses the symbolic format and the other version uses the nonsymbolic format. Each game-based learning environment comprises 32 different levels (16 levels with the numerical magnitude comparison task and 16 levels with the number line estimation task) starting with the easiest and going to the most difficult level. Each level comprises 28 trials, resulting in a total of 896 trials for all levels within a game-based learning environment. The levels are designed to vary in difficulty based on the *numerosities* in each task, the *time pressure* that is used, and the *anchor points* that are added to the number line. A detailed overview of the levels can be found in Table 2.

Each game-based learning environment starts with numbers up to 10 and becomes increasingly more difficult with numbers up to 100. In the E-games we add time pressure, as a competition element, in order to enhance automatization of children's skills and as a motivational aspect in the game. Competition is a gaming characteristic that influences motivation in the game, which might in turn influence one's performance in the game (Wilson et al., 2009). This time pressure element is an extra reward mechanism in which children received positive feedback when they are fast enough. Within each game-based learning environment children play each level first without and then with time pressure. This allows us to first train children on their accuracy and then to focus on their speed. This is done by having a shark, a rhino, or an eagle to follow them. If children are not fast enough, the animal catches them, which means that they have to start at the beginning of the level again. Children are instructed to answer each trial as fast as possible and need to avoid that the dangerous animal catches them. To indicate how close this animal is, a red bar is added to the progress bar in the middle of the screen (Fig. 2). If this red bar catches up with the blue progress bar, the child is not fast enough and is caught by the animal.

In the number line estimation task, children firstly need to succeed the levels comprising a number line with anchor points on the units (in number domain 1–10) or decades (in number domain 10–100). After this, the difficulty increases by firstly only showing an anchor point on the number 50, in the middle of the number line, followed by the most difficult levels which comprises number lines without any anchor points.

Table 2 Details of the E-games

E-symbolic game			
Level	Task	Numbers presented	Time pressure
1	NMC	Numbers up to 10	No
2	NLE	Numbers up to 10, with anchor points on units	No
3	NMC	Numbers up to 10	Strong
4	NLE	Numbers up to 10, with anchor points on units	Strong
5	NMC	One number up to 10, other up to 100	No
6	NLE	Numbers up to 10, without anchor points	No
7	NMC	One number up to 10, other up to 100	Strong
8	NLE	Numbers up to 10, without anchor points	Strong
9	NMC	Numbers from 10 to 100, same decade	No
10	NLE	Decades up to 100, anchor points on decades	No
11	NMC	Numbers from 10 to 100, same decade	Strong
12	NLE	Decades up to 100, anchor points on decades	Strong
13	NMC	Numbers from 10 to 100, different decade, compatible	No
14	NLE	Decades up to 100, anchor point on 50	No
15	NMC	Numbers from 10 to 100, different decade, compatible	Strong
16	NLE	Decades up to 100, anchor point on 50	Strong
17	NMC	Combination of levels one to eight	No
18	NLE	Decades up to 100, without anchor points	No
19	NMC	Combination of levels one to eight	Strong
20	NLE	Decades up to 100, without anchor points	Strong
21	NMC	Numbers from 10 to 100, different decade, incompatible	No
22	NLE	Numbers up to 100, anchor points on decades	No
23	NMC	Numbers from 10 to 100, different decade, incompatible	Strong
24	NLE	Numbers up to 100, anchor points on decades	Strong
25	NMC	Combination all levels	No
26	NLE	Numbers up to 100, anchor points on 50	No
27	NMC	Combination all levels	Strong
28	NLE	Numbers up to 100, anchor points on 50	Strong
29	NMC	Combination all levels	Strong
30	NLE	Numbers up to 100, without anchor points	No
31	NMC	Combination all levels	Strong
32	NLE	Numbers up to 100, without anchor points	Strong
E-nonsymbolic game			
1	NMC	Numbers up to 10	No
2	NLE	Numbers up to 10, with anchor points on units	No
3	NMC	Numbers up to 10	Average
4	NLE	Numbers up to 10, with anchor points on units	Average
5	NMC	Numbers up to 10	Strong
6	NLE	Numbers up to 10, with anchor points on units	Strong
7	NMC	One number up to 10, other up to 100	No

(continued)

Table 2 (continued)

E-symbolic game			
Level	Task	Numbers presented	Time pressure
8	NLE	Numbers up to 10, without anchor points	No
9	NMC	One number up to 10, other up to 100	Average
10	NLE	Numbers up to 10, without anchor points	Average
11	NMC	One number up to 10, other up to 100	Strong
12	NLE	Numbers up to 10, without anchor points	Strong
13	NMC	Numbers from 10 to 100, different decade, large ratio	No
14	NLE	Numbers up to 100, anchor points on decades	No
15	NMC	Numbers from 10 to 100, different decade, large ratio	Average
16	NLE	Numbers up to 100, anchor points on decades	Average
17	NMC	Numbers from 10 to 100, different decade, large ratio	Strong
18	NLE	Numbers up to 100, anchor points on decades	Strong
19	NMC	Numbers from 10 to 100, different decade, small ratio	No
20	NLE	Numbers up to 100, anchor point on 50	No
21	NMC	Numbers from 10 to 100, different decade, small ratio	Average
22	NLE	Numbers up to 100, anchor point on 50	Average
23	NMC	Numbers from 10 to 100, different decade, small ratio	Strong
24	NLE	Numbers up to 100, anchor point on 50	Strong
25	NMC	Combination of all levels	No
26	NLE	Numbers up to 100, without anchor points	No
27	NMC	Combination of all levels	Average
28	NLE	Numbers up to 100, without anchor points	Average
29	NMC	Combination of all levels	Strong
30	NLE	Numbers up to 100, without anchor points	Strong
31	NMC	Combination of all levels	Strong
32	NLE	Numbers up to 100, without anchor points	Strong

Note. NMC = numerical magnitude comparison, *NLE* = number line estimation

For each game, there are specific criteria to move to the next level, which will be outlined below. All these criteria were tested in a pilot study, which showed that these criteria were set appropriately for the children of this age. If the children do not reach the criterion, they have to replay the level until the criterion score is reached.

E-symbolic game. In this version of the game-based learning environment, children have to perform at an accuracy of 90 % on the numerical magnitude comparison task to succeed that level. Again, this criterion score is based on previous empirical studies (e.g., Linsen, Verschaffel, Reynvoet, & De Smedt, 2014; Vanbinst et al., 2012), which included symbolic comparison tasks in children of a similar age. In the levels that comprise a number line estimation task, children need to answer 70 % of the trials correctly to pass the level, taking into account the allowable error range of 12.5 % around the to-be-positioned magnitude. This criterion is based on a study by Linsen et al. (2014).

Children first play two levels without time pressure (one with a numerical magnitude comparison task and one with a number line estimation task), followed by two similar levels with strong time pressure. They are given 500 ms to respond and the residual time of each trial is added to the next trial cumulatively, within the level.

E-nonsymbolic game. In the numerical magnitude comparison task levels, children are required to achieve an accuracy of at least 75 %. In the number line estimation task, their accuracy needs to be above 60 %, again taking into account the error range of 12.5 %. These criteria are based on a study by Linsen et al. (2014).

Furthermore, children first play a numerical magnitude comparison task and a number line estimation task with average time pressure (1500 ms) followed by these tasks with strong time pressure (500 ms). Within each level, the residual time of each trial is again added to the next trial cumulatively.

Motivational aspects. Motivation is an important aspect in game-based learning and, therefore, several motivational aspects are added to the game-based learning environments. By situating the different levels into an attractive story, we want to keep the game interesting for the children. All game-based learning environments comprise three different polluted worlds and the player needs to clean these. The first levels (five levels for the K-comparison game, six levels for the K-number line game, and 12 for the E-games) are situated under water. Next, the player moves on to the land (five levels for the K-comparison game, six levels for the K-number line game, and ten for the E-games) and finally into the air (four levels for the K-comparison game, six levels for the K-number line game, and ten for the E-games). While progressing through each zone, the world becomes increasingly clean and the music changes accordingly, which provides an extra audiovisual reward for good performance. Additionally, each level is populated by a different kind of animal, adding a second visual incentive to continue playing.

Feedback. Motivating feedback appears visually and auditory when the player gives an answer. Nielsen (1995) formulated principles for user interface design, one of which stated that the game should always keep the player informed about what is going on through appropriate feedback. Visual feedback is provided by a blue bar in the middle of the screen indicating the progress of the child in this level (Fig. 4). By adding this bar, children can see how many trials they already completed and how many trials they still need to do. Auditory feedback is given by a voice-over, following the theory of multimedia learning that states that it is better to present words as auditory narration than as visual on-screen text (Moreno & Mayer, 2002), especially for children in kindergarten, which are not yet able to read feedback presented in words. This feedback encourages the children to perform well, independent of their performance. If the child waits too long to answer a trial, the voice-over encourages the child to hurry up.

Different kinds of feedback on accuracy are integrated in the game-based learning environment. Firstly, children are given feedback on the accuracy of each trial they play. More specifically, the vehicle in the comparison game collects the animal(s) when they correctly tap on the numerically larger item and a positive "ping" sound is played. If they do not respond correctly, the vehicle does not collect the animal(s) and a negative error sound is played. In the number line estimation

Fig. 4 The *round bar* at the top of the screen shows the progress in the level by the *blue color* that fills up the *round bar*. In the E-games, the *red bar* indicates the time pressure element, i.e., how close is the animal that can catch them. This *red bar* also fills up the *round bar*. If the *red bar* catches up with the *blue bar*, the player was not fast enough and has to replay the level again

task, the animal appears and the vehicle collects the animal when the child's answer is within the allowable range of the correct answer, but the animal is not collected by the vehicle when an answer outside the allowed range is given. In this case, the animal still appears at the position of the correct answer and hereby provides the player with feedback on the correct answer. Again, a corresponding sound is played to indicate whether the child answered correctly or not.

Secondly, children are given feedback on the overall accuracy of a level. After finishing a level, children receive general feedback on their performance in that level, that is, whether they can go to the next level or not. Specifically, if they solve the required percentage of correct trials, the world becomes more beautiful and they can start the next level. If they do not reach the required percentage of correct trials, Dudeman points out to Sidegirl that she did not collect a sufficient amount of animals and she has to restart the level until the required percentage of correct trials is reached.

Logging

The game-based learning environment is developed to register a great amount of data while children played the game. These data are stored locally during the session and are uploaded to an online central database at any chosen time. This allows the user to play in any environment, without the requirement of a wireless Internet connection, as for example is the case in many schools. First, all speed and timing measures are saved. This includes children's response time per trial, their total training time per session, and the total time that the game is played. Second, children's answer and its accuracy are saved for each trial.

Technical Specifications

The game is developed for pc as well as iOS and Android tablets. To avoid that the data collection would be influenced by the different native aspect ratios of different tablets (4:3 for iOS tablets, and 16:10 for Android tablets), all critical user interface elements are fixed to a 4:3 aspect ratio. In other words, when running on a wider screen, the extra horizontal space is occupied only by background art, and not by interactive elements.

The Unity engine was used for development of the game, due to its expansive community, affordable price, and ease of publishing code to multiple platforms. Data are stored locally on the tablets using a SQLite database, and subsequently synchronized to a server-side MySQL database.

Conclusion

The four game-based learning environments described in this contribution were specifically developed for two concrete studies, one in which we investigated whether numerical magnitude processing interventions should focus on training with numerical magnitude comparison or number line estimation, and one in which we determined whether there is a different impact of training symbolic versus non-symbolic numerical magnitude processing skills. However, despite these specific research questions, the content of our game-based learning environments can be adapted to fit other research questions. Currently, only these four versions are available, but it would, for example, be possible to use these game-based learning environments with older elementary school children simply by adapting the numerosities that are presented. One could also separate the four different basic components in the games, that is, symbolic numerical magnitude comparison, nonsymbolic numerical magnitude comparison, symbolic number line estimation, and nonsymbolic number line estimation, and only use one of these tasks, several of these tasks, or all of them. At this time, the four game-based learning environments are completely fixed, so the player itself cannot change the content of the game. For future research, it would be interesting and useful to make the game modular. In a school context, for example, this adaptation to the game would allow teachers to decide on the characteristics of the game.

Besides that, as a great amount of data is logged while children play the game, these games are also appropriated to be used for microgenetic research concerning the development of the skills trained in the games. Additionally, our game-based learning environment was developed to be played on tablets and computers, which provides the opportunities for a widespread use of the game.

Acknowledgment This research was supported by grant GOA 2012/010 of the Research Fund KU Leuven, Belgium. We would like to thank all participating children and teachers.

References

Ashcraft, M. H., & Moore, A. M. (2012). Cognitive processes of numerical estimation in children. *Journal of Experimental Child Psychology, 111,* 246–267. doi:10.1016/j.jecp.2011.08.005.

Bailey, D. H., Siegler, R. S., & Geary, D. C. (2014). Early predictors of middle school fraction knowledge. *Developmental Science, 17*(5), 775–785.

Barth, H., & Paladino, A. M. (2011). The development of numerical estimation: Evidence against a representational shift. *Developmental Science, 14,* 125–135.

Berteletti, I., Lucangeli, D., Piazza, M., Dehaene, S., & Zorzi, M. (2010). Numerical estimation in preschoolers. *Developmental Psychology, 46,* 545–551.

Booth, J. L., & Siegler, R. S. (2006). Developmental and individual differences in pure numerical estimation. *Developmental Psychology, 41,* 189–201.

Booth, J. L., & Siegler, R. S. (2008). Numerical magnitude representations influence arithmetic learning. *Child Development, 79,* 1016–1031.

Bugden, S., & Ansari, D. (2011). Individual differences in children's mathematical competence are related to the intentional but not automatic processing of Arabic numerals. *Cognition, 118,* 32–44. doi:10.1016/j.cognition.2010.09.005.

Connolly, T. M., Boyle, E. A., MacArthur, E., Hainey, T., & Boyle, J. M. (2012). A systematic literature review of empirical evidence on computer games and serious games. *Computers & Education, 59,* 661–686.

De Smedt, B., & Gilmore, C. (2011). Defective number module or impaired access? Numerical magnitude processing in first graders with mathematical difficulties. *Journal of Experimental Child Psychology, 108,* 278–292.

De Smedt, B., Noël, M. P., Gilmore, C., & Ansari, D. (2013). The relationship between symbolic and non-symbolic numerical magnitude processing and the typical and atypical development of mathematics. A review of evidence from brain and behaviour. *Trends in Neuroscience and Education, 2,* 48–55.

De Smedt, B., Verschaffel, L., & Ghesquière, P. (2009). The predictive value of numerical magnitude comparison for individual differences in mathematics achievement. *Journal of Experimental Child Psychology, 103,* 469–479.

Dehaene, S. (1992). Varieties of numerical abilities. *Cognition, 44,* 1–42.

Dehaene, S. (1997). *The number sense: How the mind creates mathematics.* London, England: The Penguin Press.

Gallistel, C. R., & Gelman, R. (1992). Preverbal and verbal counting and computation. *Cognition, 44,* 43–74.

Garris, R., Ahlers, R., & Driskell, J. E. (2002). Games, motivation and learning: A research and practice model. *Simulation & Gaming, 33,* 441–467.

Griffin, S. (2004). Building number sense with Number Worlds: A mathematics program for young children. *Early Childhood Research Quarterly, 19,* 173–180.

Halberda, J., Mazzocco, M. M. M., & Feigenson, L. (2008). Individual differences in non-verbal number acuity correlate with maths achievement. *Nature, 455,* 665–668.

Holloway, I. D., & Ansari, D. (2009). Mapping numerical magnitudes onto symbols: The numerical distance effect and individual differences in children's mathematics achievement. *Journal of Experimental Child Psychology, 103,* 17–29.

Jordan, N. C., Glutting, J., Dyson, N., Hassinger-Das, B., & Irwin, C. (2012). Building kindergartners' number sense: A randomized controlled study. *Journal of Educational Psychology, 104,* 647–660.

Kucian, K., Grond, U., Rotzer, S., Henzi, B., Schönmann, C., Plangger, F., ... von Aster, M. (2011). Mental number line training in children with developmental dyscalculia. *Neuroimage, 57,* 782–795.

Landerl, K., & Kölle, C. (2009). Typical and atypical development of basic numerical skills in elementary school. *Journal of Experimental Child Psychology, 103,* 546–565. doi:10.1016/j.jecp.2008.12.006.

Laski, E. V., & Siegler, R. S. (2007). Is 27 a big number? Correlational and causal connections among numerical categorization, number line estimation, and numerical magnitude comparison. *Child Development, 78,* 1723–1743.

Lee, S. S., & Lee, Y. H. K. (1991). Effects of learner-control versus program-control strategies on computer-aided learning of chemistry problems: For acquisition or review? *Journal of Educational Psychology, 83*(4), 491–498.

Libertus, M. E., Feigenson, L., & Halberda, J. (2011). Preschool acuity of the approximate number system correlates with school math ability. *Developmental Science, 14,* 1292–1300. doi:10.1111/j.1467-7687.2011.01080.x.

Linsen, S., Verschaffel, L., Reynvoet, B., & De Smedt, B. (2014). The association between children's numerical magnitude processing and mental multi-digit subtraction. *Acta Psychologica, 145,* 75–83.

Lonnemann, J., Linkersdörfer, J., Hasselhorn, M., & Lindberg, S. (2011). Symbolic and nonsymbolic distance effects in children and their connection with arithmetic skills. *Journal of Neurolinguistics, 24,* 583–591. doi:10.1016/j.jneuroling.2011.02.004.

Mazzocco, M. M. M., Feigenson, L., & Halberda, J. (2011). Preschoolers' precision of the approximate number system predicts later school mathematics performance. *PLoS One, 6,* 1–8.

Moreno, R., & Mayer, E. R. (2002). Verbal redundancy in multimedia learning: When reading helps listening. *Journal of Educational Psychology, 94,* 156–163.

Mundy, E., & Gilmore, C. K. (2009). Children's mapping between symbolic and nonsymbolic representations of number. *Journal of Experimental Child Psychology, 103,* 490–502.

Mussolin, C., Mejias, S., & Noël, M. P. (2010). Symbolic and nonsymbolic number comparison in children with and without dyscalculia. *Cognition, 115,* 10–25. doi:10.1016/j.cognition.2009.10.006.

Nielsen, J. (1995, January 1). 10 Usability heuristics for user interface design. Retrieved from http://www.nngroup.com/articles/ten-usability-heuristics/

Obersteiner, A., Reiss, K., & Ufer, S. (2013). How training on exact or approximate mental representations of number can enhance first-grade students' basic number processing and arithmetic skills. *Learning and Instruction, 23,* 125–135.

Ramani, G. B., & Siegler, R. S. (2008). Promoting broad and stable improvements in low-income children's numerical knowledge through playing number board games. *Child Development, 79,* 375–394.

Ramani, G. B., & Siegler, R. S. (2011). Reducing the gap in numerical knowledge between low- and middle-income preschoolers. *Journal of Applied Developmental Psychology, 32,* 146–159.

Ramani, G. B., Siegler, R. S., & Hitti, A. (2012). Taking it to the classroom: Number board games as a small group learning activity. *Journal of Educational Psychology, 104,* 661–672.

Räsänen, P., Salminen, J., Wilson, A. J., Aunio, P., & Dehaene, S. (2009). Computer-assisted intervention for children with low numeracy skills. *Cognitive Development, 24,* 450–472.

Rousselle, L., & Noël, M. P. (2007). Basic numerical skills in children with mathematics learning disabilities: A comparison of symbolic vs non-symbolic number magnitude processing. *Cognition, 102,* 361–395. doi:10.1016/j.cognition.2006.01.005.

Sasanguie, D., De Smedt, B., Defever, E., & Reynvoet, B. (2012). Association between basic numerical abilities and mathematics achievement. *British Journal of Developmental Psychology, 30,* 344–357.

Sasanguie, D., & Reynvoet, B. (2013). Number comparison and number line estimation rely on different mechanisms. *Psychologica Belgica, 53*(4), 17–35.

Sasanguie, D., Van den Bussche, E., & Reynvoet, B. (2012). Predictors for mathematics achievement? Evidence from a longitudinal study. *Mind, Brain and Education, 6,* 119–128.

Scheiter, K., & Gerjets, P. (2007). Learner control in hypermedia environments. *Educational Psychology Review, 19,* 285–307.

Sekuler, R., & Mierkiewicz, D. (1977). Children's judgements of numerical inequality. *Child Development, 48,* 630–633.

Siegler, R. S., & Booth, J. L. (2004). Development of numerical estimation in young children. *Child Development, 75,* 428–444.

Siegler, R. S., & Ramani, G. B. (2009). Playing linear number board games—but not circular ones—improves low-income preschoolers' numerical understanding. *Journal of Educational Psychology, 101*, 545–560.

Soltész, F., Szücs, D., & Szücs, L. (2010). Relationships between magnitude representation, counting and memory in 4- to 7-year-old children: A developmental study. *Behavioral and Brain Functions, 6*, 1–14.

Van Merriënboer, J. J. G., Clark, R. E., & de Croock, M. B. M. (2002). Blueprints for complex learning: The 4C/ID-model. *Educational Technology Research and Development, 50*(2), 39–64.

Vanbinst, K., Ghesquière, P., & De Smedt, B. (2012). Numerical magnitude representations and individual differences in children's arithmetic strategy use. *Mind, Brain and Education, 6*, 129–136.

Whyte, J. C., & Bull, R. (2008). Number games, magnitude representation, and basic number skills in pre-schoolers. *Developmental Psychology, 44*, 588–596.

Wilson, K. A., Bedwell, W. L., Lazzara, E. H., Salas, E., Burke, C. S., Estock, J. L., … Conkey, C. (2009). Relationships between game attributes and learning outcomes. Review and research proposals. *Simulation & Gaming, 40*, 217–266. doi:10.1177/1046878108321866

Wilson, A. J., Dehaene, S., Dubois, O., & Fayol, M. (2009). Effects of an adaptive game intervention on accessing number sense in low-socioeconomic-status kindergarten children. *Mind, Brain, and Education, 3*, 224–234.

Wilson, A. J., Dehaene, S., Pinel, P., Revkin, S. K., Cohen, L., & Cohen, D. (2006). Principles underlying the design of "The Number Race," an adaptive computer game for remediation of dyscalculia. *Behavioral and Brain Functions, 2*(19), 1–14.

Wilson, A. J., Revkin, S. K., Cohen, D., Cohen, L., & Dehaene, S. (2006). An open trial assessment of "The Number Race," an adaptive computer game for remediation of dyscalculia. *Behavioral and Brain Functions, 2*, 20. doi:10.1186/1744-9081-2-20.

Description of the Educational Math Game "Monkey Tales: The Museum of Anything"

Sylke Vandercruysse, Marie Maertens, and Jan Elen

Abstract In this contribution, we present the game-based learning environment Monkey Tales in which pupils and students can practice mathematics. The learning content and goals, as well as the story line and game design are discussed. The environment can be used for several research purposes, such as studies which focus on the effects of the use of educational games in the classroom (e.g., effect on performance, motivation) as well as studies which focus on learners' behavior in the game and their mathematical performances during game play.

Keywords Mathematics • Math game • Game design • Educational game

The Monkey Tales series is a set of commercial 3D game-based learning environments (GBLE), designed for mathematics practice in elementary school.[1] The series is designed and developed by the game-developer Larian Studios and the educational publisher Die Keure. The GBLEs are based on the national curriculum for math instruction as developed by the Flemish ministry of education. The GBLE is available in Belgium, the Netherlands, the United Kingdom, and the United States. In all versions, the mathematical content is identical and based on the Flemish math curriculum. The story line and content are, however, translated so they can be used in the different countries. Especially for the version in the United States, the original GBLE has been redesigned to follow the Common Core Standards as well as the DoDEA (Department of Defense Education Activity) standards.

---

[1] A demo-version can be found on http://www.monkeytalesgames.com/UKen/games/2.

S. Vandercruysse (✉)
Center for Instructional Psychology and Technology, KU Leuven,
Etienne Sabbelaan 53, Kortrijk 8500, Belgium
e-mail: sylke.vandercruysse@kuleuven-kulak.be

M. Maertens
ITEC—iMinds—KU Leuven—Kulak, Interactive Technologies, KU Leuven Kulak,
Kortrijk, Belgium
e-mail: Marie.Maertens@kuleuven-kulak.be

J. Elen
Center for Instructional Psychology and Technology, KU Leuven, Leuven, Belgium
e-mail: jan.elen@ppw.kuleuven.be

© Springer International Publishing Switzerland 2015
J. Torbeyns et al. (eds.), *Describing and Studying Domain-Specific Serious Games*,
Advances in Game-Based Learning, DOI 10.1007/978-3-319-20276-1_3

27

Table 1 Different GBLEs of
the monkey tales series with
the recommended age of
players

Name of the game	Recommended age of the players
The princess of Sundara	7 years and up
The museum of anything	8 years and up
The abbey of Aviath	9 years and up
The castle of Draconian	10 years and up
The valley of the Jackal	11 years and up

The Monkey Tales series consists of different GBLEs (see Table 1), according to the different elementary school grades. As the GBLE is developed for different countries (i.e., Belgium, the Netherlands, the United Kingdom, and the United States), the recommended age for each GBLE is presented in Table 1 instead of the intended grade.

Each GBLE has its own story line. In the first part of this contribution, we will describe the story line and game-environment in more detail (see section "Story Line and Game-Environment"). Secondly, the learning content, which is presented in a fun and challenging manner, is outlined (see section "Learning Content"). As the Monkey Tales series contains mainly rehearsal exercises, the GBLE is not meant to instruct but to reinforce lessons learned in school covered in the previous grades. Third, the specific game-elements of the Monkey Tales games will be discussed as they reveal specific choices of the game-developers according to the game design (see section "Game-Elements"). In the fourth part of this chapter, we focus on the customization of the commercial GBLE for research purposes (see section "Use in Research").

Typology

The Monkey Tales series can best be described as an adventure game (Rollings & Adams, 2003). Elements of an adventure game that appear in the Monkey Tales series are an interactive story line in which the player has to solve puzzles, the aim of collecting items during gameplay and the lack of physical activities such as shooting or combatting. In addition, some characteristics of action games (e.g., the use of levels and an enemy at the end of a level/game) and role playing games (i.e., players have to explore the world, driven by quests) can be linked to the Monkey Tales series (Rollings & Adams, 2003). In addition, when considering the way math is offered to players, we can describe it as drill and practice because players learn through rehearsal, repetition, and practice of tasks (Burkolter, Kluge, Sauer, & Ritzmann, 2010).

Use

The Monkey Tales series is a pc-game; some technical requirements are essential to be able to install the game on your pc (with the CD-ROM) and play it. The requirements are determined for the platform (i.e., Windows XP SP2 or higher, Windows Vista or Windows 7), processor (1.6 Ghz or higher), RAM memory (512 MB or more), graphic card (Intel GMA950 or higher, ATi 9600 or higher, or GeForce 5 or higher), sound card (DirectX 9.0c), and video memory (128 MB).

In practice, the Monkey Tales series is suitable for double use. On the one hand, Monkey Tales can be used at school during class hours (e.g., to differentiate between high and low performing players) or as homework (e.g., to rehearse the learning content which was taught at school). Second, as the Monkey Tales series is seen as stand-alone, it is possible for children to play the GBLE outside the school context. Parents can buy the commercial GBLE so children can play Monkey Tales at home, again irrespective whether the associated textbooks are used in class.

Story Line and Game-Environment

In the Monkey Tales series, learners have to prevent that Huros Stultos conquers parts of the world. In order to master the universe, he has accomplices who steal knowledge and make all other people stupid. Huros trained an army of super intelligent monkeys who are experts in math. Luckily, Huros Stultos' plan was discovered by the old gray professor Moudrost and his assistant Emótje. During the game, players help Moudrost and Emótje to stop Huros and his assistant-monkeys. As the monkeys are very good at math, players can only ruin Huros Stultos' plans by defeating all the monkeys, i.e., being smarter than them in the math games. For example, in "The museum of Anything," the huge dinosaur Carmen Pranquill (also an accomplice of Huros Stultos) has taken over the museum whereby no one dares to enter anymore. Hence, the museum is closed for public. To assist Moudrost and Emótje, players have to search every room, defeat all accomplices and find Carmen Pranquill to conquer her. When the game is finished and the player wins, the museum is cleared, so people can again enter and gain knowledge. In what follows, we will exemplary focus on "The Museum of Anything" as all GBLEs have an analogue story line and game-environment.

Each GBLE contains several stages which represent different parts of the museum (e.g., the entrance hall, the sealife center, hallways, storages) and each stage consists of seven rooms (see section "Rooms") and within each room a mini-game (see section "Mini-Games"). After each stage, the Bridge of Death (as depicted with a bridge-icon) is presented to the player to close a stage (see section "Bridge of Death"). At the end of the entire GBLE, players play the Boss Level (see section "Boss Level"). So in the entire GBLE, players play 48 rooms, five Bridges of Death, and one Boss Level. The overview of a part of the GBLE with the different stages and rooms is presented in Fig. 1.

Fig. 1 Overview of the museum of anything

The first time players enter the GBLE, they can choose to visit the learning levels. By doing this, they learn all the tips and tricks to move from one room to another and solve the puzzles. They get to know most common puzzle elements (see Fig. 2) and learn how to operate them (e.g., use the Ctrl-key to get an overview, activating magnets which attract metal boxes). This is done by Emótje who explains and illustrates what players have to do by using an interactive tutorial. For example, when she tells players to use the Ctrl-key to get an overview, a keyboard is displayed and the Ctrl-keys are highlighted. During the learning levels, the players can test tips and tricks to experience the different functionalities in the GBLE in order to be able to solve the puzzles.

Rooms

Every room has two major components: first, a console with a mathematical mini-game and second, a 3D-puzzle in which the console is integrated.

There is a console in each room and each console contains a monkey. When players activate a console, they can play a mini-game. As part of the overall gameplay and in order to be able to advance in the GBLE, players have to play the mini-games to beat Huros Stultos' monkeys. If a player wins a mini-game, he liberates the imprisoned monkey which is added to his personal zoo (see Fig. 3) and advances to the next room. All the liberated monkeys are brought together in the player's

Fig. 2 Room with several puzzle-elements (e.g., lasers and magnets) and bananas

Fig. 3 Personal zoo with two liberated monkeys

personal zoo. At the end of the GBLE, the zoo is full with monkeys as players liberate one monkey in every room. Players can visit their zoo at any moment during gameplay. When players lose a mini-game, a new mini-game with an easier math rule is offered. It is compulsory for players to win a mini-game in each room. Otherwise, they cannot move onto the next room.

In each room, players have to (1) reach the console in order to activate it and (2) gain as much bananas as possible for their monkeys. In the rooms, the console is part of a larger 3D-puzzle and players have to think logically to solve those puzzles to be able to reach and activate the console. While solving these puzzles, bananas (see Fig. 2) can be collected. Players need enough bananas to feed all their monkeys (see Fig. 3). The more bananas the monkeys eat, the happier they will be. So the bananas are the first scoring mechanism.

Mini-Games

The GBLE contains six different types of mini-games: Number Cruncher, Math Cards, Pebble Rebel, Cannon Battle, Rocket Science, and Cypher shooter (see Table 2 for more details about the tasks players have to perform in the different mini-games). Information about the actions and tasks in the different mini-games is offered just-in-time when players activate a mini-game for the first time. For example, when a player for the first time enters in the mini-game *Number Cruncher*, Emótje tells how the *Number Cruncher* works and explains the different actions and tasks: Move left or right by using the arrow-buttons, shoot at a number by using the spacebar and finally how to get liberated from the green toxic slime by fast pressing on the arrow-buttons.

Each mini-game features math exercises in accordance to one specific math rule (e.g., item "$8 \times 6 = \ldots$" for the math rule "Table of 6"). Research about the Monkey Tales series revealed that mini-games differ with respect to difficulty (Maertens, Vandewaetere, Cornillie, & Desmet, 2014). As Maertens et al. (2014) stated, the number of elements and element interactivity that is present in the mini-games, influences the complexity and difficulty of the mini-games and is likely to affect the in-game performance for learners with low and high math ability. The mini-games Number Cruncher and Pebble Rebel are the most difficult mini-games because the number of mental and motor actions that should be performed simultaneously is rather high, leading to higher element interactivity and thus higher added difficulty (Maertens et al., 2014). In contrast, Cannon Battle and Rocket Science are the easiest mini-games. In these latter mini-games, the number of motor actions is less than in the more difficult mini-games. Hence, the element interactivity is much lower. Combining difficult, mediocre, and easy mini-games together results in sufficient fun and challenge without arousing frustration.

Bridge of Death

At the end of each stage, players have to cross the Bridge of Death (see Fig. 4). The Bridge consists of tiles. When on a tile, a multiple choice assignment is presented to the players (see Fig. 5) and after answering the question correct, the next safe tile will light up green. When the player makes an error, the bridge will lie and the player has to guess which tile is safe and take the risk of falling through the Bridge of Death. When players fall through the bridge, they have to start all over again. So, players have to reach the other side of the bridge by giving multiple correct answers in a row and hence choosing the correct tiles.

Table 2 Description of the six types of mini-game in the game-environment

Number Cruncher	Players are controlling the blue rocket and the monkey controls the red rocket. By using the left and right arrow, players can navigate left or right. An assignment is presented at the bottom of the screen and three different answers can be chosen (of which only one is correct). Players have to shoot the correct answer by pressing the spacebar. While doing this, they have to avoid the green toxic drops falling from the roof because this makes them immobile for a few seconds. By making combo's they can get higher scores. Combo's can be upgraded by giving as many correct answers in a row

Math Cards	During the mini-game "Math Cards" players are playing at the poker table. Cards with numbers are running on the table. At the bottom of the table, an assignment is given. This assignment can be completed by dragging the right card into the blank. There are also yellow bonus cards which improve players' score. But players have to watch out for the monkey who is very smart and tries to solve the puzzle before they will do

Pebble Rebel	During the mini-game, "Pebble Rebel" players are in control of the blue spaceship and the monkey controls the red one by using the arrow keys. At the bottom of the screen, an assignment is presented (i.e., complete the series). Several rocks fly into the space containing different numbers. Players can catch a rock by flying against it. Then, they have to shoot it in the blue basket by pressing the spacebar. By combining several rocks players have to try to compose the right answer. When the right answer is collected, they can press enter. While playing, players have to watch out for tornados that make them immobile for a few seconds

Cannon Battle	During the mini-game, "Cannon Battle" players are controlling the blue cannon at the left side of the screen. They can move the cannon up or down by using the arrow keys. At the bottom of the screen, an assignment is presented (i.e., shoot on everything that equals 100). Several chips with correct and incorrect answers are falling down
	Players must try to hit the correct answer as fast as possible. From time to time, purple chips are falling down. When players hit the purple chip, the monkey is paralyzed for a few seconds. When the monkey shoots the purple chip, the player is immobile

(continued)

Table 2 (continued)

Rocket Science	In the Rocket Science mini-game, the player and the monkey fly with respect to the blue and red rocket. Both fly independent. They have to avoid the rocks by solving assignments. After completing the right exercise, they fly to the right. If they complete the one on the left side, they fly to the left (i.e., 16–7 to move to the left and 13–8 to move to the right). When a wrong answer is giving, the position remains. When a rock hits them, their rocket is damaged and time is lost. Green arrows are accelerators which make the rocket go faster. Hostile ships can kill the player so they have to calculate fast to avoid them or shoot them first by using the spacebar

Cypher Shooter	The mini-game Cypher Shooter is a shooting gallery. The math-assignment appears at the bottom of the screen (i.e., "Shoot on the numbers smaller than 7") and on the treadmill, cards with the possible answers pop-up on the screen (i.e., 2, 4, and 8). By using the mouse to aim and throw a ball towards the cards (left click) with the correct answer, they gain points (blue/left score). By choosing—as fast as they can—the right answers, they can beat the monkey (red/right score). Special bonus cards can be collected to improve the score

Fig. 4 Endgame bridge of death

Fig. 5 Multiple choice
assignment in the bridge of
death

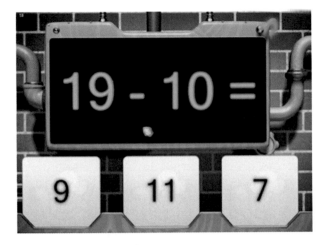

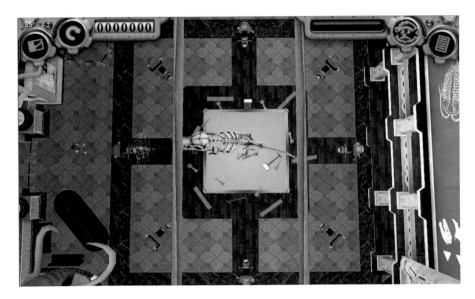

Fig. 6 Boss level with eight consoles

Boss Level

The Boss Level can be compared with a room, but with eight consoles instead of
one. So in order to win the Boss Level, eight mini-games with math content have to
be played (see Fig. 6). The mini-games are the same as those in the regular rooms
(see section "Rooms").

Learning Content

The learning content of each game from the Monkey Tales series consists of a sequence of math rules (e.g., "Table of 6," "Addition to 100," "Odd and even"). The sequence is defined by the math curricula as developed by the Flanders' ministry of education. In Table 3, the sequence of the math rules in the game "The Museum of Anything" is displayed. The math rule "tens and units" is the most easy math rule and "Subtraction to 100 with bridge Ten Unit – Ten Unit" the most difficult one.

Each math rule is operationalized by a predefined number of items that can be offered to Monkey Tales players. Items in a mini-game do not differ with respect to the underlying math rule, they only differ in the numbers that are used (e.g., items "40 + 20" and "30 + 40" for the math rule "Addition to 100 with tens"). It is assumed that items having the same rule as origin will also have the same difficulty level.

Game-Elements

To discuss the Monkey Tales game, we follow the recommendation from Aldrich (2005) to think about distinct game-elements instead of thinking about games as such. In the following sections, specific game-elements will be discussed as they reveal specific choices of the game-developers. In general, it is presupposed that

Table 3 Math rules in the game "the museum of anything"

Math rules	
Tens and units	Table of 4
Number of times	Division table of 4
Split	Table of 3
Table of 2	Division table of 3
Division table of 2	Table of 6
Understanding numbers to 100	Division table of 6
Addition with 3 tens	Table of 8
Subtraction with 3 tens	Division table of 8
Addition with 1 ten	Table of 9
Subtraction with 1 ten	Division table of 9
Table of 10	Table of 7
Addition and subtraction to 100 without bridge	Division table of 7
Division table of 10	Structure of tens
Structure of 100	Addition to 100 with bridge Ten Unit + Unit
Odd and even	Subtraction to 100 with bridge Ten Unit – Unit
Table of 5	Addition to 100 with bridge Ten Unit + Ten Unit
Division table of 5	Subtraction to 100 with bridge Ten Unit – Ten Unit

players and their learning process would benefit from these game-elements (Garris, Ahlers, & Driskell, 2002; O'Neil, Wainess, & Baker, 2005; Prensky, 2001; Vogel et al., 2006; Wilson et al., 2009).

Goal

The goal of the game is clearly presented to the player at the beginning of the game and this is supposed to be beneficial for players' motivation and engagement (Akilli, 2007; Bergeron, 2006; Garris et al., 2002; Hays, 2005; Malone, 1980; Prensky, 2001). The players get an introduction of Moudrost and Emótje before the GBLE starts. This is done by showing the players a short introduction movie in which Moudrost and Emótje explain the story line and goal. During this intro-duction, they hear about the occupation of The museum of Anything by the huge dinosaur Carmen Pranquill. Then, the player gets the quest to defeat the dinosaur and his accomplice monkeys. For feeding the monkeys, the player must also gather bananas. So the goal is twofold (1) liberate the museum by defeating monkeys in every room of the museum and (2) catch bananas for them. After finishing a level, Moudrost repeats the importance of beating as much monkeys as possible and to go on with the liberation of the museum. During the puzzle-solving, the players are shown directly how much bananas they already gathered and how happy the monkeys are.

Content Integration

The Monkey Tales series can be categorized as an extrinsically integrated GBLE because the learning content is not integrated with the core game-mechanics which embody the rule-systems and player interactions, but separates the learning and the playing component in the game. After completing a part of the learning content, students are provided with a reward by having the chance to advance in the game without dealing with learning content (e.g., solving the 3D-puzzle). This differs from intrinsically integrated games which

> (1) deliver learning material through the parts of the game that are the most fun to play, riding on the back of the flow experience produced by the game, and not interrupting or diminishing its impact and; (2) embody the learning material within the structure of the gaming world and the players' interactions with it, providing an external representation for the learning content that is explored through the core mechanics of the game play. (Habgood, Ainsworth, & Benford, 2005, p. 494).

It is argued that intrinsically integrated games motivate and engage players more than extrinsically integrated games because they maintain the flow experience (e.g., Garris et al., 2002).

Competition

Competition is often inevitably implemented in GBLEs in the shape of a score, bonus, or high-ranking. In this GBLE, competition can be defined as the activity of players comparing their own performances with the performance of a virtual opponent (i.e., the monkeys), as described by Alessi and Trollip (2001). This is in line with Fisher's (1976) interpersonal competition and with Yu's (2003) anonymity competition. According to Cheng, Wu, Liao, and Chan (2009) competition is motivating because it creates an extra challenge, and the learning activity provides more structure by prefacing a clearly defined goal. The extra challenge is created through the desire to win that is generated by competition and the opportunity to improve their own performance (Franken & Brown, 1995). The proposition of these researchers that competition is an important motivator within games is supported by a large number of studies (e.g., Charsky, 2010; Ebner & Holzinger, 2005; Tjosvold, Johnson, Johnson, & Sun, 2006; Worm & Buch, 2014).

Scoring Mechanism

The GBLE contains a double scoring-mechanism. On the one hand, players have to answer items correctly to beat the monkey. The number of items players have to answer correctly before the monkey is defeated, differs from mini-game to mini-game (see Table 4). By solving the assignments correctly, players raise their score. Secondly, bonuses and obstacles are implemented in the games which also influence players score. Three mini-games have implemented bonuses: yellow bonus cards in Math Cards, blue bonus cards in Cypher Shooter, and purple chips in Cannon Battle. Although these points have no specific purpose in the entire game, they offer extra points. Opposite to the bonuses, obstacles are implemented in the other mini-games

Table 4 Gameplay mechanics of the six types of mini-games in the game-environment

Mini-game	Gameplay mechanics
Number Cruncher	The mini-game contains 12 items and the winner is the player/monkey with the most correct answers
Math Cards	The mini-game stops when the player/monkey has four correct answers. The yellow bonus cards have no influence on winning/losing the mini-game, they only provide extra points
Pebble Rebel	The mini-game stops when the player/monkey has three correct answers
Cannon Battle	The mini-game stops when the player/monkey has seven correct answers. A wrong answer gives an extra correct answer for the opponent
Rocket Science	Player and monkey play independently in this mini-game. The winner is the player/monkey who first reaches the finish
Cypher Shooter	The mini-game stops when the player/monkey has ten correct answers. Hitting the blue bonus cards has no influence on winning/losing the mini-game, they only provide extra points

to make it more difficult to answer items correctly, for example, tornados in Pebble Rebel, green slime in Number Cruncher and rocks in Rocket Science. Unfortunately, this second mechanism is not transparent for players so it is not clear how much extra points players can earn with certain actions. Additionally, while solving the 3D-puzzle games (i.e., collecting as much bananas as possible), players can raise their score.

This game-element (scoring mechanism) is related to the competition element in the game. When searching for the effects of competition, the scoring mechanism plays a distinctive role. On the one hand, competition is stated to have positive consequences because it is related to challenge, and challenge in turn has been related to intrinsic motivation (Malone & Lepper, 1987). On the other hand, according to Aldrich (2005), overemphasizing a score can make students rely too much on the scores and will make them less engaged in the learning materials. Consequently, adding a score can subvert motivation and learning instead of supporting it.

Adaptivity

The commercial version of the game features adaptivity on the level of the math rules: When players lose a mini-game against the monkey, a—presupposed but not empirically verified—easier math rule is offered. This type of adaptivity is a basic example of adaptive item sequencing: If a learner fails to complete a task, the subsequent task is easier and when a learner successfully completes a task, the subsequent task is more difficult, hence increasing the challenge. With the implementation of this adaptivity mechanism, the learning content is adapted to the skills of the player (i.e., the learner; Wauters, Desmet, & Van Den Noortgate, 2010).

Feedback

Different kinds of feedback are integrated in the GBLE. Players get feedback about their accuracy (whether their solution is right or wrong), their efficiency (how many assignments did they solve correctly), and their progress (how many rooms they still have to conquer).

A first kind of feedback is the immediate corrective feedback in the mini-games. When players answer an assignment, they get immediate feedback about the accuracy of their answer. This—more simple but immediate—feedback (FT, correct/wrong) might suffice for the players because they already master the learning content from earlier grades, whereas learners who still need to learn the content or the problem take more advantage of more detailed/elaborated feedback (Vandewaetere, Cornillie, Clarebout, & Desmet, 2013). However, no textual or content-related feedback is given to the players. This was a conscious decision of the game-developers, who were concerned that this kind of feedback would disturb the game-flow.

Fig. 7 Feedback: Scoreboard after mini-game

Additionally, when a mini-game is finished, regardless who won, players get feedback about their accuracy. This visually presented feedback informs the player about how well they performed in the mini-game; they can see how many assignments they solved correctly and how many wrong. They also see how many points they earned during this mini-game and the difficulty of the math rule that was incorporated in the mini-game. They also get this overview of the monkeys' scores, so players can be compared (see Fig. 7). In this case, the player outperformed the monkey and won the mini-game.

Finally, players also get visual feedback about their overall progress in the GBLE. Before players enter a new room, they get an overview of the museum and see their progression: How many rooms are already passed, how many rooms still needs to be done (see Fig. 1). By giving the players this overview, they get a reminder of the game goal (reach the end-game to beat the dinosaur) but also stimulated by seeing the approaching end-game.

Use in Research

The game-based learning environment "The Museum of Anything" is used in various studies as, for example, in the studies "Performance in educational math games: Is it a question of math skills?" (this volume) and "The integration of competition as game-element in vocational math course" (this volume). Because the Monkey Tales series are already existing commercial game environments, no thorough adjustments of the environment can be carried through. More concrete, the story line and the game-environment cannot be adjusted and remain the same for research purposes as in the commercially released version of the games. However, some customization is possible to conduct studies. For instance, the adaptivity mechanism can be deactivated, the learning content can be changed and all player actions can be logged in log files.

First, the existing adaptivity mechanism (i.e., easier math rule after losing a mini-game) can be disabled. Consequently, if a player loses a mini-game against the monkey, the same math rule in the same mini-game format is offered. The removal of the original adaptivity model entails that the math content and hence the mini-games were offered in a fixed order: Each console contained one specific mini-game with all items following the same fixed math rule.

Second, the content of the GBLE can be adapted. The math rules that are used in the GBLE can be adapted to the age or curriculum of the target group and consequently the environment can be applied for different target groups. However, these changes are only possible after consultation with the game-developers. Access to the math rules is necessary which can only be given by the game-developers. After receiving this access, the math rules can easily be adapted, but have to be in line with the format of the mini-games (i.e., not all math-rules can be applied in all the mini-games because of the specificity of the mini-games).

Another advantage of using the Monkey Tales Series for research purposes is the possibility of logging all the actions of the players. The logging can happen online (on a server) but also local (on the pc the player is using). During playtime, all actions are logged (e.g., number of bananas picked up while solving the 3D-puzzle, number of correct answers during the mini-games on the math exercises, timestamps). These extensive log-data create extra research opportunities, for instance, to investigate players' game behavior, learning, and performance during game-play.

To conclude, Monkey Tales can be used for a variety of research purposes. First, it can be used for studies which focus on the effects of the use of educational games in the classroom (e.g., effect on performance, motivation, …). Although the Monkey Tales series were developed for learners from 7 till 11 years, the content can be adapted and the environment can be applied for different target groups. Secondly, the availability of accurate log files allows researchers to look at learners' behavior in the game in a very objective way as well as their mathematical performances during game play. However, contact with the developers is essential to receive these log files, as well as for several manipulations in the environment itself. This constrains the widespread use of the environment for research purposes.

Acknowledgment The environment described in this manuscript is used for studies based on a research project funded by iMinds Flanders (ICON, Games@School (G@S), 2012–2013) and on a research project funded by the Fund of Scientific Research (FWO—G.O.516.11.N.10). Additionally, the authors would like to express their great appreciation to Martin Vanbrabant, for the technical support concerning the customization options.

References

Akilli, G. K. (2007). Games and simulations: A new approach in education? In D. G. Gibson, C. A. Aldrich, & M. Prensky (Eds.), *Games and simulations in online learning: Research and development frameworks* (pp. 1–20). Hershey, PA: Information Science Publishing.

Aldrich, C. (2005). *Learning by doing: The comprehensive guide to simulations, computer games, and pedagogy in e-learning and other educational experiences*. San Francisco, CA: Pfeiffer.

Alessi, S. M., & Trollip, S. R. (2001). *Multimedia for learning. Methods and development* (3rd ed.). Needham Heights, MA: Allyn & Bacon.

Bergeron, B. (2006). *Developing serious games*. Hingham, MA: Charles River Media.

Burkolter, D., Kluge, A., Sauer, J., & Ritzmann, S. (2010). Comparative study of three training methods for enhancing process control performance: Emphasis shift training, situation awareness training, and drill and practice. *Computers in Human Behavior, 26*, 976–986. doi:10.1016/j.chb.2010.02.011.

Charsky, D. (2010). From edutainment to serious games: A change in the use of game characteristics. *Games and Culture, 5*, 177–198. doi:10.1177/1555412009354727.

Cheng, H. N. H., Wu, W. M. C., Liao, C. C. Y., & Chan, T.-W. (2009). Equal opportunities tactic: Redesigning and applying competition games in classrooms. *Computers & Education, 53*, 866–876. doi:10.1016/j.compedu.2009.05.006.

Ebner, M., & Holzinger, A. (2005). Successful implementation of user-centered game-based learning in higher education: An example from civil engineering. *Computers & Education, 49*, 873–890. doi:10.1016/j.compedu.2005.11.026.

Fisher, J. E. (1976). Competition and gaming. An experimental study. *Simulation & Games, 7*, 321–328.

Franken, R. E., & Brown, D. J. (1995). Why do people like competition? The motivation for winning, putting forth effort, improving one's performance, performing well, being instrumental, and expressing forceful/aggressive behavior. *Personality and Individual Differences, 19*, 175–184. doi:10.1016/0191-8869(95)00035-5.

Garris, R., Ahlers, R., & Driskell, J. E. (2002). Games, motivation, and learning: A research and practice model. *Simulation & Gaming, 33*, 441–467. doi:10.1177/1046878102238607.

Habgood, M. P. J., Ainsworth, S., & Benford, S. (2005). Endogenous fantasy and learning in digital games. *Simulation & Gaming, 36*, 483–498. doi:10.1177/1046878105282276.

Hays, R. T. (2005). *The effectiveness of instructional games: A literature review and discussion* (Report No. 2005-004). Orlando, FL: Naval Air Warfare Center Training Systems Division.

Maertens, M., Vandewaetere, M., Cornillie, F., & Desmet, P. (2014). From pen-and-paper content to educational math game content for children: A transfer with added difficulty. *International Journal of Child-Computer Interaction, 2*, 85–92. doi:10.1016/j.ijcci.2014.04.001.

Malone, T. (1980). What makes things fun to learn? Heuristics for designing instructional computer games. *Proceedings of the 3rd ACM SIGSMALL Symposium and the first SIGPC Symposium* (pp. 162–169). Palo Alto, CA: ACM.

Malone, T. W., & Lepper, M. R. (1987). Making learning fun: A taxonomy of intrinsic motivation for learning. In R. E. Snow & M. J. Farr (Eds.), *Aptitude, learning, and instruction* (Conative and affective process analysis, Vol. 3, pp. 223–253). Hillsdale, NJ: Erlbaum.

O'Neil, H. F., Wainess, R., & Baker, E. L. (2005). Classification of learning outcomes: Evidence from the computer games literature. *The Curriculum Journal, 16*, 455–474. doi:10.1080/09585170500384529.

Prensky, M. (2001). *Digital game-based learning*. New York, NY: McGraw-Hill.

Rollings, A., & Adams, E. (2003). *On game design*. Berkeley, CA: New Riders.

Tjosvold, D., Johnson, D. W., Johnson, R. T., & Sun, H. F. (2006). Competitive motives and strategies: Understanding constructive competition. *Group Dynamics: Theory, Research and Practice, 10*, 87–99. doi:10.1037/1089-2699.10.2.87.

Vandewaetere, M., Cornillie, F., Clarebout, G., & Desmet, P. (2013). Adaptivity in educational games: Including player and gameplay characteristics. *International Journal of Higher Education, 2*, 106–114. doi:10.5430/ijhe.v2n2p106.

Vogel, J. J., Vogel, D. S., Cannon-Bowers, J., Bowers, C. A., Muse, K., & Wright, M. (2006). Computer games and interactive simulations for learning: A meta-analysis. *Journal of Educational Computing Research, 34*, 229–243. doi:10.2190/FLHV-K4WA-WPVQ-H0YM.

Wauters, K., Desmet, P., & Van Den Noortgate, W. (2010). Adaptive item-based learning environments based on the item response theory: Possibilities and challenges. *Journal of Computer Assisted Learning, 26*, 549–562. doi:10.1111/j.1365-2729.2010.00368.x.

Wilson, K. A., Bedwell, W. L., Lazzara, E. H., Salas, E., Burke, C. S., Estock, J. L., … Conkey, C. (2009). Relationships between game attributes and learning outcomes. Review and research proposals. *Simulation & Gaming, 40*, 217–266. doi:10.1177/1046878108321866

Worm, B. S., & Buch, S. V. (2014). Does competition work as a motivating factor in e-learning? A randomized controlled trial. *PLoS One, 9*(1), 1–6. doi:10.1371/journal.pone.0085434.

Yu, F.-Y. (2003). The mediating effects of anonymity and proximity in an online synchronized competitive learning environment. *Journal of Educational Computing Research, 29*(2), 153–167. doi:10.2190/59CX-3M7L-KKB4-UYDD.

Number Navigation Game (NNG): Design Principles and Game Description

Erno Lehtinen, Boglárka Brezovszky, Gabriela Rodríguez-Aflecht,
Henrik Lehtinen, Minna M. Hannula-Sormunen, Jake McMullen,
Nonmanut Pongsakdi, Koen Veermans, and Tomi Jaakkola

Abstract This chapter describes the Number Navigation Game (NNG), a game-based learning environment aimed at the promotion of flexibility and adaptivity with arithmetical problem solving in 10- to 13-year-old students. The game design is based on an integrated approach in which the different elements of the game are directly related to the mathematical content, i.e., the use of rich networks of numerical connections in solving arithmetic problems. The interface of the game is a hundred square superimposed on various maps of land and sea, where players have to strategically navigate a ship by using different combinations of numbers and arithmetic operations. The game has two different modes encouraging the use of different arithmetic operations and number combinations. The openness of the gameplay allows players the opportunities to explore different numerical connections in an environment where there are no right or wrong answers. Future directions of the game development include additional game features and extensions to larger numbers and rational numbers.

Keywords Adaptive number knowledge • Arithmetic problem solving • Game design • Hundred square

E. Lehtinen (✉) • B. Brezovszky • G. Rodríguez-Aflecht • H. Lehtinen • J. McMullen
N. Pongsakdi • K. Veermans • T. Jaakkola
Department of Teacher Education, Centre for Learning Research,
University of Turku, Turku 20014, Finland
e-mail: erno.lehtinen@utu.fi; bogbre@utu.fi; gabriela.rodriguez@utu.fi; erno.lehtinen@utu.fi; jake.mcmullen@utu.fi; nopong@utu.fi; koen.veermans@utu.fi; tomi.jaakkola@utu.fi

M.M. Hannula-Sormunen
Department of Teacher Education, Turku Institute for Advanced Studies,
University of Turku, Turku 20014, Finland
e-mail: mimarha@utu.fi

There has been an increasing interest in possibilities to enrich classroom teaching and improve students' motivation through the use of game-based learning environments. In public discussion in recent years, game-based learning environments have often been seen as a solution for the commonly recognized problem of decreased learning outcomes and motivation in mathematics education. Most of the existing commercial or free-ware mathematics games are based on standard school tasks which have been enriched with gaming elements. However, there have been also attempts to use game-based learning environments for enhancing new types of learning, which are not easily supported by conventional classroom practices of textbook exercises. In this article, we describe one game-based learning environment, which is aimed at enhancing arithmetic skills which go beyond mere remembering of arithmetic facts and mechanical solving of tasks.

The Number Navigation Game (NNG) is a game-based learning environment which aims to promote the development of flexibility and adaptivity with arithmetic problem solving of upper elementary school students aged 10–13 years old. NNG was designed based on the theoretical premise that the use of flexible and adaptive arithmetic strategies is largely dependent on the development of the mental representations of numbers as rich networks of numerical connections (McMullen, Brezovszky, Rodríguez Padilla, Pongsakdi, & Lehtinen, 2015; Threlfall, 2002, 2009; Verschaffel, Luwel, Torbeyns, & Van Dooren, 2009). The game design is based on an integrated approach (Devlin, 2011; Habgood & Ainsworth, 2011), which means that different elements of the game are directly related to the mathematical content. In the NNG, this means that (a) the external representation provided by the game, (b) the game mechanism, and (c) the feedback given to the player are all directly related to strengthening the network connections within the system of natural numbers.

The Hundred Square as the External Representation of Number System

Extensive research shows that external representations of natural numbers such as the number line or the number square can be successfully used for supporting the development of number sense (Beishuizen, 1993; Klein, Beishuizen, & Treffers, 1998; Laski & Siegler, 2014; Siegler & Booth, 2004). Using these external representations in a playful manner can be beneficial in many ways. For example, playing linear board games with numbers may benefit the numerical understanding of children (Siegler & Ramani, 2009). However, NNG was not designed on the basis of the one-dimensional number line but on the two-dimensional hundred square. The use of number line representations in training arithmetic with larger numbers is based on the assumption that all numbers including multi-digit numbers are processed holistically (Dehaene, Dupoux, & Mehler, 1990). However, the holistic processing hypothesis has been questioned by increasing evidence indicating that multi-digit processing is substantially different from single-digit processing, as it is based on the use of place value (Nuerk, Moeller, Klein, Willmes, & Fisher, 2011). In the case of multi-digit processing, recent evidence emphasizes decomposed processing or hybrid processing, combining decomposed and holistic processing (Nuerk, Willmes, & Fias, 2005; Thomas, 2004). There is some evidence suggesting that the tens-unit, clearly presented in the hundred square, has a specific mediating role between single-digit numbers and larger multi-digit numbers (Nuerk et al., 2011). Many studies (see Laski, Ermakova, & Vasilyeva, 2014 for a recent summary) have emphasized the importance of well-developed base-10 knowledge for further development of arithmetic strategies.

From a game design point of view, a two-dimensional plane offers more opportunities for the game mechanism than the one-dimensional number line. However, the main reason for using hundred square in NNG is that a two-dimensional plane is more powerful in representing the base-10 system and in facilitating decomposed processing. There are cultural and inter-individual differences in young students' understanding of base-10 system but the assumption when developing NNG was that the target group of the game, students in the age of 10–13 years, already have a basic understanding of the natural number system, including at least some emerging ideas of the base-10 system (Fuchs, Geary, Fuchs, Compton, & Hamlett, 2014; Geary, Bow-Thomas, Lin, & Siegler, 1996). In Finland, the hundred square is widely used in teaching place value and base-10 system during the first elementary school years, and instructions and methods on how to use it are available for teachers (e.g., http://www.lukimat.fi). Thus, it was possible to build the game on the basis of the hundred square, even though it is a more abstract and demanding representation of numbers than the number line, as there is only a partial analogy between the numerical distance and the physical distance of numbers. Although, for younger students it could be confusing that in a hundred square, the physical distance between 1 and 2 is as big as between 2 and 12, for the target age group of NNG, it was expected that this would not cause too many problems (see Laski & Siegler, 2014).

Additional support for the use of the hundred square as the basic representation in the game can be found from general cognitive flexibility theory, which emphasizes the use and integration of multiple representations and particularly representations that make different ways to approach learning tasks and solutions visible (Jacobson & Spiro, 1995). The hundred square simultaneously offers two different representations: (a) horizontal rows can be seen as analogical number lines and (b) vertical columns as a representations of the base-10 system. The integration of these representations provides students with flexible opportunities to mentally move in the system horizontally, vertically, or diagonally (see Aebli, 1980). Within this representational system, players can imagine and explore many trajectories between any two numbers by using different combinations of arithmetic operations.

Accordingly, in NNG the main interface of the game is a hundred square superimposed on various maps of land and sea (Fig. 1), where players have to strategically navigate a ship by using different combinations of numbers and operations.

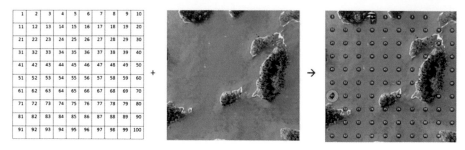

Fig. 1 Number navigation game basic layout

Game Mechanics Supporting the Development of Adaptive Number Knowledge

The aim of NNG is to provide an engaging game-based learning environment where strategic work with different combinations of numbers and operations constitutes the core game mechanism. It is expected that extended playful practice with these number-operation combinations will lead to a more advanced representation of the system of natural numbers and consequently to more flexibility and adaptivity with arithmetic problem solving. Becoming flexible and adaptive in arithmetic problem solving requires the conceptual understanding of relationships between numbers and operations, which develops as a result of discovering number patterns and working with different number-operation combinations (Baroody, 2003; Schneider, Rittle-Johnson, & Star, 2011; Threlfall, 2009). One example of using the conceptual understanding of relationships between numbers and operations is the estimation strategy based on known "nice numbers" presented by Dowker (1992) in her analysis of strategies used by professional mathematicians in solving complex mental arithmetic tasks. In NNG this means, for example, that players have to find numbers between the starting point and target number which have a multiplicative relationship to the starting and target numbers or some other numbers close to them (in terms of numerical value).

The metaphor used in the game design is partly based on Aebli's (1980) analysis of mobility in knowledge networks. Aebli's mobility theory is based on the observation that mere associative activation of elements of knowledge (such as remembered arithmetic facts $4 + 5 = 9$) is not enough for explaining the knowledge underlying flexible activities in complex situations. Instead, flexible activity requires intentional activation of knowledge networks, including alternative ways to move from premises to targets (for example from 12 to 146 there are several routes: $12 + 134$; $12 \times 12 + 2$; $12 \times 10 + 26$, etc.).

The game mechanism of NNG is based on the metaphor of moving in the system of numbers by conducting different sequences of arithmetic operations. In the game, the player has certain starting points (harbors) and targets (different construction materials located at different numbers). The player's task is to find the most optimal route to the target and back to the starting point. In order to trigger thinking about alternative routes and what an optimal route is, the game has two different playing modes, which encourage the use of certain combinations of arithmetic operations (see later in the description of scoring modes). Based on earlier studies on educational games (e.g., Malone & Lepper, 1987), it is assumed that because of the integrated nature of the game, students' engagement in finding different solutions and optimizing their routes through the increasingly demanding tasks is one of the main motivating features of the game.

Feedback That Strengthens the Understanding of Numerical Relations

Many authors have highlighted the role of feedback in game-based learning environments (Moreno & Mayer, 2005; Tobias, Fletcher, Dai, & Wind, 2011). However, the feedback can be organized in many different ways. The feedback provided by the system can merely indicate that a player's answer was correct or incorrect without any additional hints, or the feedback can be deliberately aimed at triggering explanations and reflection (Moreno & Mayer, 2005). It is typical for most of game-based learning environments that the system gives feedback about the correctness of a player's answers without any further explanations.

In NNG there are no right or wrong answers, but the player has many alternative ways to carry out operations (except for the situations when the ship hits an island or leaves the map). Thus, the game is not based on correctness (right/wrong) feedback but the player gets immediate visual feedback of the outcome of an arithmetic operation. It is then the player's task to evaluate if the outcome was expected or desired. As a consequence of the operation, the ship moves to a certain number and the user can observe the movement within the hundred square. This makes it possible for players to try novel operations even if they are not sure that these lead to desired results. The aim of the visual feedback is that players can understand reasons for undesired results and learn new network connections within the number system. In addition to the animated feedback that the game provides after each move, there is an additional feedback system which informs players about their overall success in the game. After each move, the system presents points which can be compared to the requirements of different achievement levels and the player is able to monitor his/her progress.

Game Description

Overall Structure of the Game

The current game version runs from a USB stick, and can be played in a Windows operating system (future versions will be platform independent and have possibilities to collect the log-data through the internet). Technical requirements are minimal, as there is no need for an internet connection, advanced graphic cards, or

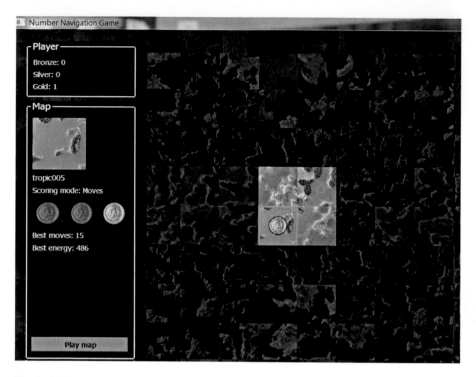

Fig. 2 Main screen of the number navigation game

speakers. There is a separate online video available for teachers and students which describes the aims and game rules (i.e., different scoring modes). In later versions, the video will be integrated into the help function of the game.

Upon double clicking on the NNG icon in the USB stick, the player is taken to a main screen (see Fig. 2). The opening screen consists of a grid of 64 squares arranged eight by eight. Each of these squares represents a unique map. At first, most of the maps are shaded out, which signals they are inaccessible to the player. The central four maps, which constitute Level 1, can be immediately accessed. When the maps in Level 1 are completed, the player will gain access to maps at higher difficulty levels. Level 2 is made up of the 12 maps on the outer edge of Level 1, Level 3 consists of the subsequent 20 maps, and Level 4 consists of the 24 maps located in the grid's outermost frame. Within a level, maps can be played in any order. All maps can be replayed as many times as a player likes.

On the left side of the main screen, there is a sidebar in which a player can keep track of the bronze, silver, and gold coins collected. Coins represent students' performance on a particular map. Clicking on a map will show a thumbnail, the name of the map, and that map's particular scoring mode (Fig. 2). If the map has been played before, it will show an icon of the coin collected as well as information on the player's performance in that map (left sidebar, Fig. 2). More information on scoring modes and rewards will be presented in the next section.

To access a map, players need to click on the "Play map" button at the bottom of the left sidebar. When a player clicks "Play map," the screen will switch to that map. Maps represent different archipelago landscapes. Maps differ from each other in many ways, but all are images superimposed on a hundred square. Due to a particular map's unique geographical layout only part of the numbers from the hundred square are available for the players. For example, in the map in Fig. 3, the numbers 9, 10, 27, 28, 37, 39, etc. are covered by land and thus not available in this map.

There is a fixed position as the starting point of each map called the harbor. In the map presented in Fig. 3, the harbor is located at number 4. Players control a ship which sets out from the harbor seeking construction materials for settlements. In the current game version, there are four materials in every map, appearing always in the same order: wood, brick, stone, and iron. A player must retrieve a material in order for the next one to appear. In the example shown in Fig. 3, wood can be found at number 61. The player's task is to retrieve the wood, taking into consideration that map's particular scoring mode, which is signalled in the left sidebar below the number pad. For each scoring mode, there is a specific achievable score that will determine if a player earns a gold, silver, or bronze coin.

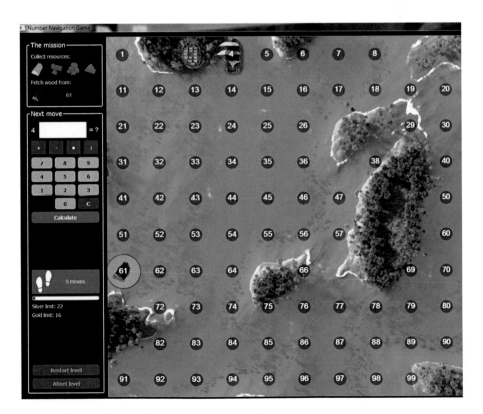

Fig. 3 Example of a map in the moves scoring mode

In the example shown in Fig. 3, the blue color and footprint icon indicates that this is a map in the moves scoring mode and that so far zero moves have been made. The text indicates that completing a map with 16 or less moves will lead to a gold coin, whereas completing it with 17–22 moves will earn a silver coin. A progress bar fills up with each move, so if the bar is completely full, it means a player did not reach the required score and will get a bronze coin when he/she completes the map. In order to enter to upper levels, a player needs to complete each level having completed 75 % of the maps with silver or gold coins. Players are able to quit or restart maps using the "Abort level" button at the bottom of the sidebar.

Game Mechanics

The objective of NNG is to navigate around the maps, retrieving four different items in each map. For this, a player must take control of the ship and sail it by inputting mathematical equations which will take the ship from one number to another. This is done through the number pad and the command box above it. The first number in an equation will always be the player's location, which at the start of the map shown in Fig. 3 is the number 4. Players need to click on the operation they want to use, and type or click the numbers in the number pad. Only one operation can be entered into the response box at a time. For example, if a player clicked on "+" and then typed "1" into the command box (see Fig. 3), the ship would move to number 5 ($4 + 1 = 5$). If instead the player clicked on "×" and then typed in "11" into the command box, the ship would move to number 44 ($4 \times 11 = 44$). On the other hand, if a player clicked on "−"and then typed in "1," this move would not be allowed, as $4 - 1$ equals 3 and there is land at 3 and the ship cannot sail over land. This blocked move would be indicated by a red cross. The player would remain at his/her location without penalization. This is also the case when a player exceeds the dimensions of the map, for example by subtracting 5 ($4 - 5 = -1$).

Since the objective is to collect the wood at number 61, a player is faced with moving from 4 to 61. There are a great number of ways a player can reach number 61. For example, $4 + 57 = 61$ or $4 + 10 = 14$, $14 + 10 = 24$, $24 + 10 = 34$, $34 + 10 = 44$, $44 + 10 = 54$, $54 + 10 = 64$, $64 - 3 = 61$ or $4 \times 11 = 44$, $44 + 17 = 61$.

Upon reaching the material, a pop-up window will appear informing the player they need to return it to harbor. A player could go back by reversing operations (i.e., $61 - 57$ or $61 + 3$, $64 - 10$, $54 - 10$, etc.) but it is also possible to go back in a different way (i.e., $61 - 6 = 55$, $55/11 = 5$, $5 - 1 = 4$). It is entirely up to the player. However, there are two different scoring modes. The player must pay attention to which of the modes, the moves mode or the energy mode, is used in the map he/she is playing. In the current game version, from the total of 64 maps, 25 maps are in the moves scoring mode and 39 maps are in the energy scoring mode. Maps are placed in the game so that the number of maps in the energy scoring grows as the player progresses in the game.

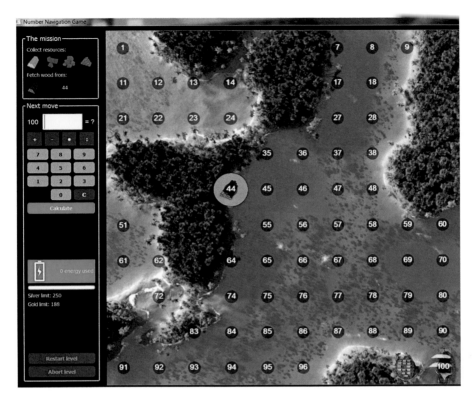

Fig. 4 Example of a map in energy scoring mode

Figure 3 shows a map in the moves scoring mode, which is indicated on the left sidebar by the blue icon with the white footsteps. The premise of the first scoring mode, the *moves* scoring mode, is simple: a player must collect all materials using the least number of moves possible. A move corresponds to an operation. In Fig. 3 for example, if the player moved from the harbor (number 1) to the target (number 61) by adding 10s (until 64) and then subtracted 3, there were a total of 7 operations needed to reach the material. Supposing the player returned to the harbor by inverting operations, a total of 14 moves would have been used. However this map indicates that in order to get a gold coin, one can use a maximum of 16 moves. A strategic player would realize they are close to exceeding the gold limit already at the first material, and might consider restarting the map. The best possible route to 61 would require only one move, $4+57=61$, and $61-57=4$ for returning to the harbor. This means it is possible to retrieve the wood material with a maximum of two moves. Under this scoring mode, players need to be aware of what would be the most direct route, taking into account the harbor, the different positions of the materials, and the map's geographical layout.

The second scoring mode is the *energy* scoring mode, as indicated by the green color and battery icon (Fig. 4). In this map, the harbor is located at 100 and the wood is at 44. In a moves scoring mode map, the best route would be "$100-56=44$." This would be one move. However, in an energy map, this equation would take 56 energy points, which is a lot when we consider that the gold limit for this map is 188 and that there are three additional materials to collect. Energy is measured by adding up all the numbers entered into the operation box. The smaller the number is, the more energy-efficient the move. The aim of the energy scoring mode is to encourage the use of all four arithmetic operations as well as the use of a larger variety of numbers. So, instead of trying to reach materials in the quickest way, a player must consider the most energy-efficient way. For example, a player could do the following to save energy: (a) $100 - 10 = 90$ (this move costs 10 energy points); (b) $90/2 = 45$ (this move costs 2 energy points); and (c) $45 - 1 = 44$ (this move costs 1 energy point). This route would have a total energy cost of 13 ($10 + 2 + 1$). The player could return by using inverse operations or via an altogether new route (i.e., $44 \times 2 = 88, 88 + 12 = 100$).

In order to trigger the use of alternative routes, apart from the minimum moves and energy scoring modes, the current game version has two additional features which can be activated in any map. First, after reaching a material, a *pirate* ship may appear somewhere along the route players took to reach the material. A player would then have to come up with an alternate route back to the harbor. Only the exact number where a pirate ship appears must be avoided, and players are still able to go through or around that number. In the current game version, pirates appear in 18 % of the maps. Within a map, the pirate ship appears randomly. Next, the *hidden operations* feature appears only in some Level 4 maps to make them even more challenging. In maps with hidden operations, some operations—for example, addition and subtraction—are not usable. This reduces the player's options, which adds complexity to the task of finding the best route. The layout of maps using the hidden operations feature is usually more open (more available numbers), ensuring that even if the amount of solutions is limited, maps can always be completed.

Customization Options

An important consideration when designing NNG was that different features of the game could be easily customized and adapted for different age groups and skill levels. Although the main target group is elementary school students aged 10–13, the game can be easily adapted to serve younger children (e.g., using move mode maps only) or even adults (e.g., using energy mode maps with hidden operations). All of the main features of NNG are customizable. On the general level, each map can be relocated. This feature is useful if maps prove to be too easy or difficult for a certain level or to create "gaming areas" using geographically more similar maps. Furthermore, within each map, harbors and all items can easily be relocated and the scoring mode of the map can be changed from moves to energy or vice versa. By manipulating these options, the difficulty level of each map can be carefully adjusted so that there is a gradually increasing difficulty.

Finding the most optimal location for targets and harbors depends a lot on the geographical layout of a given map. For example, locating target materials in a moves map at places which are surrounded by islands can make the task more challenging.

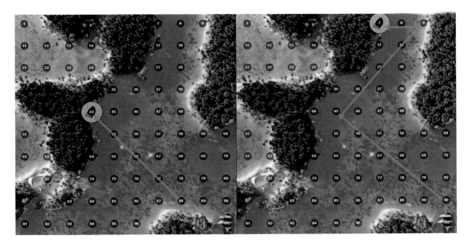

Fig. 5 Example of relocating the target material (*wood*) within the same map

In energy maps, good harbor-target locations require finding the balance between the amount of obstacles (areas covered by land) and possible alternative solutions. This is usually a result of experimenting with many different alternative locations. Hence, the possibility to easily change these locations is crucial in terms of game design. Additional challenges within each map can be added by activating the pirate or hidden operations options.

Defining limits for silver and gold coins is a further customizable feature. As mentioned before, the game shows the amount of minimum moves or energy that players need to use in order to get silver or gold coins when completing a map. These limits are defined based on the position of the materials and harbors and are calculated according to the moves/energy needed in order to complete a map in the most optimal way. Naturally, as the location of targets changes, optimal routes will be different and the amount of minimum moves/energy needs to be recalibrated.

Many different alternatives need to be considered and compared when selecting the location of harbor-targets and defining the limits for silver and gold coins within a map. Figure 5 shows a map where the location of islands is ideal for using the energy mode. The image shows two alternative locations for the first target material (wood). If the wood is placed at number 44, one of the most optimal routes could be $100 - 12$ and $88/2$ using 14 energy points in total $(12 + 2)$. However, if wood is located at number 7, the player would need to consume more energy using, for instance, the route $100 - 10$, $90/2$, $45/5$, and $9 - 2$, using 19 energy points. Gold and silver limits are defined per map, so all four target materials need to be collected in an optimal way in order to achieve gold or silver coins. When deciding on the location of items within a map it is ideal that the optimal route for reaching them becomes increasingly challenging (i.e., from wood to brick to stone up to iron), as the player gains a better understanding of the most useful numbers for navigating in that map.

All of the above-mentioned options can be activated or deactivated and modified using a simple text file. For the current game version, locations and limits were calibrated based on the results of several pilot studies and by comparing many alternative location options and solutions within each map. In the future, it would be possible for teachers and parents to access these settings and adjust the game according to the needs of their students/children.

In addition to these options, different language versions of the game are also available. At the moment there are versions in Finnish, English, Spanish, Swedish, and Greek, and many other language versions are under development.

Use of the Log-data as a Measure of Game Progress and Performance

The progress and performance of each player is continuously saved in time-stamped event logs. In the current version, the log files are saved on the memory stick, in a folder that is inaccessible for the player. The data is saved in text files which can be copy-pasted independently of the game and imported to Excel. The raw data can then be summarized by using Excel Macros or by more complex data mining methods.

The main variables saved in the log-data are:

- Time: frequency and duration of playing sessions, time of completing a map, time for retrieving materials
- Overall game performance: number of maps completed, number of maps recompleted, number of maps just accessed but not completed
- Map-specific game performance: number of moves/energy used, number of blocked moves, type of medal received when completing a map (gold, silver, bronze)

In addition to the above-described variables, all of a player's routes (all numbers and operations used in their calculations) are saved in the log-data.

With regards to learning outcomes, the total amount of gold, silver, or bronze coins collected is an important indicator of a player's performance. However, the log-data is more detailed and can provide a much finer picture of a player's performance and progress throughout the game. As mentioned, all maps can be replayed as many times as needed and a player needs to have in at least 75 % of the maps silver or gold coins in order to access the next difficulty level. Therefore, changes in a player's performance within recompleted maps can provide further information on their progress. Reducing the amount of moves/energy needed, as well as reducing the amount of time or blocked moves in each completed and recompleted map can be considered as an indicator of progress.

As all of the numbers and operations used by players are saved in the logs, it is also possible to compare the change in a player's routes when recompleting maps. It is possible to track how solution strategies become more and more refined as a player recomplete the same map. Additionally, it is possible to compare different solution strategies across different players within the same map. Thus, it is possible to distinguish the most general type of solutions and identify more or less skilled solutions.

In addition to player's game performance, a wide variety of player experiences can be collected during the gaming process. Upon completing a map, a pop-up window appears which can ask players to answer different questions. The questions can be related to game-experience (e.g., how much do you agree with the statement "I like this game," using a 5 point Likert scale where 1 is "completely disagree" and 5 is "completely agree?") or the questions can be related to more general motivational experiences such as "This type of learning makes mathematics more interesting."

Developmental Design and Future Ideas

NNG is constantly under development based on the results of empirical studies, observational data, and feedback from users. For the large scale experimental study carried out in spring 2014 across schools in Finland (Rodriguez Padilla et al., 2015, this volume), two different versions of the game were used. So far, the changes have largely focused on the usability and clarity of the interface. Changes between versions are detailed in the Appendix.

Based on these empirical findings, a third version of the game is under development. There are two major challenges future development has to take into account. In the current version, there is no built-in support for the development of the most advanced strategies and there are very little motivating elements. First, with respect to the support for developing the most advanced strategies, in the current version the use of more advanced strategies (particularly needed in energy maps) depends on students' own discoveries or teacher guidance. NNG has been planned for use in mathematics classrooms and thus the teacher's role will be important for providing relevant support for students. The future version of the game will be accompanied by a teacher manual and training package which will help teachers when organizing game situations and scaffolding students' development during gameplay. In addition, future versions will have a built-in dynamic help function, which is activated by the player whenever needed or when the player repeats unsuccessful strategies. For example, in the energy mode maps the system can give a hint that students should think about strategic numbers between the harbor and targets.

Second, regarding the motivational mechanisms in the game, it is a big challenge for future studies to make the NNG more motivating without reducing the mathematical demands of the gameplay. The third version of the NNG will restructure the maps into more levels in order to better scaffold difficulty and provide users with a clearer sense of progress and development. It will also introduce scoring modes and features in a more gradual way as part of the gameplay and not as a separate tutorial video, as in the current version. A "shop" will be added in order to give meaning to the coins gained by completing maps. Players will be able to exchange their coins for in-game rewards, such as a faster ship, a ship with a different design, or other bonuses and perks such as tips. More customization of the visual aspects of the game may also be introduced. The new version will also include more possibilities for variation within the gameplay. In addition to pirates, there will be other obstacles such as sea monsters, and instead of collecting materials one-by-one, there will be maps in which the players have to plan an optimal route to collect several materials during one tour.

In the current version, players can use as much time as they need for planning each step and NNG has no "action elements." This is a limitation particularly for students who have different expectations of games. In the future versions, we will experiment with time constrained maps and with some quickly executed mathematical operations players could do to, for example, arrest pirates or catch sea monsters.

Plans are also underway for different mathematical extensions of the game. This requires rethinking the two-dimensional plane. There are many possibilities for altering the hundred square grid currently under use—for example, numbering it 101–200 instead of 1–100, or having a mirror image of the map so that the current location of 1 and 100 are inversed. The number domain could be extended to larger numbers (e.g., 1–1000 or 10,000) and negative numbers could also be introduced. In order to trigger more variety in the type of number patterns available in the game, future versions may also see a change in the number base used. For example, apart from using the base-10 system, more challenging game levels could use alternative systems such as base-9 or base-12 systems. Particularly for the rational number version of NNG, there are plans to replace the hundred square with a Cartesian coordinate system. In this rational number version, it is important to have zooming opportunities to demonstrate the density of rational numbers.

Acknowledgment The present study was funded by grant 274,163 awarded to the first author by the Academy of Finland.

Appendix

Examples of Game Development in Two Consecutive Versions of the Number Navigation Game

Version 1 →	Observation →	Version 2
Coin display on main screen	Players had a hard time distinguishing between bronze and gold coins	Improved coin display
On the sidebar, below a map's thumbnail, the coin earned on that particular map would appear		Below a map's thumbnails, the shadowed outlines of the 3 coins were displayed, with only the coin earned on that map highlighted

(continued)

(continued)

Version 1 →	Observation →	Version 2
No number pad	Players disliked having to constantly switch between mouse and keyboard to input operations	Number pad
Players needed to click on the operation and then type numbers into the command box		The number pad allows players to use only keyboard, only mouse, or a combination of both
No scoring mode icon	Players had difficulties noticing if a map's scoring mode was moves or energy based	Scoring mode icons
Small text above the gold/silver score limits indicated whether a map was moves or energy based		Visual cues were introduced, such as blue and footprints for moves-based maps and green and battery for energy-based maps
No material icons	Players said they would forget which materials had been collected and how many were still left	Material icons
The sidebar did not have icons of the 4 materials		The sidebar shows an icon for each material, and the material a player is currently working on is highlighted
1 saving point	A large deal of progress could be lost due to external factors such as the length of class period or one mistake	4 saving points
When restarting a map, a player would need to retrieve all 4 items		Maps are automatically saved after each item is retrieved and players may restart from that point
Village icon	Players expressed a wish for villages to be displayed more prominently	Village pop-up window
There was a small icon of the village on the sidebar above the command box		Upon retrieving all 4 materials, a pop-up window displays a large picture of the village
Moves and energy	Players thought the game could get monotonous and repetitive at times	Moves, energy, pirates, and hidden operations
Players only needed to focus on the scoring mode		Pirates and hidden operations were introduced to add an extra angle to gaming
Log-data	Researchers saw the need for real-time feedback from users to complement pre and post questionnaires	Query pop-up function
		Researchers can include a pop-up scale question to appear after a map is completed, and have answers logged

References

Aebli, H. (1980). *Denken: das Ordnen des Tuns. Bd. 1: Kognitive Aspekte der Handlungstheorie.* Stuttgart, Germany: Klett-Cotta [Thinking: putting actions in order].

Baroody, A. J. (2003). The development of adaptive expertise and flexibility: The integration of conceptual and procedural knowledge. In A. J. Baroody & A. Dowker (Eds.), *The development of arithmetic concepts and skills: Constructing adaptive expertise* (pp. 1–33). London, England: Lawrence Erlbaum.

Beishuizen, M. (1993). Mental strategies and materials or models for addition and subtraction up to 100 in Dutch second grades. *Journal for Research in Mathematics Education, 24,* 294–323. doi:10.2307/749464.

Dehaene, S., Dupoux, E., & Mehler, J. (1990). Is numerical comparison digital? Analogical and symbolic effects in two-digit number comparison. *Journal of Experimental Psychology, 6,* 626–641.

Devlin, K. (2011). *Mathematics education for a new era: Video games as a medium for learning.* Natick MA: AK Peters.

Dowker, A. (1992). Computational estimation strategies of professional mathematicians. *Journal for Research in Mathematics Education, 23,* 45–55.

Fuchs, L. S., Geary, D. C., Fuchs, G., Compton, D. L., & Hamlett, C. L. (2014). Sources of individual differences in emerging competence with numeration understanding versus multidigit calculation skill. *Journal of Educational Psychology, 106,* 482–498. doi:10.1037/a0034444.

Geary, D. C., Bow-Thomas, C. C., Lin, F., & Siegler, R. S. (1996). Development of arithmetical competencies in Chinese and americal children: Influence of age, language, and schooling. *Child Development, 67,* 2022–2044.

Habgood, M. P. J., & Ainsworth, S. E. (2011). Motivating children to learn effectively: Exploring the value of intrinsic integration in educational games. *The Journal of the Learning Sciences, 20,* 169–206. doi:10.1080/10508406.2010.508029.

Jacobson, M. J., & Spiro, R. J. (1995). Hypertext learning environments, cognitive flexibility, and the transfer of complex knowledge: An empirical investigation. *Journal of Educational Computing Research, 12,* 301–333. doi:10.2190/4T1B-HBP0-3F7E-J4PN.

Klein, A. S., Beishuizen, M., & Treffers, A. (1998). The empty number line in Dutch second grades: Realistic versus gradual program design. *Journal for Research in Mathematics Education, 29,* 443–464. doi:10.2307/749861.

Laski, E. V., Ermakova, A., & Vasilyeva, M. (2014). Early use of decomposition for addition and its relation to base-10 knowledge. *Journal of Applied Developmental Psychology, 35,* 444–454. doi:10.1016/j.appdev.2014.07.002.

Laski, E. V., & Siegler, R. S. (2014). Learning from number board games: You learn what you encode. *Developmental Psychology, 50,* 853–864. doi:10.1037/a0034321.

Malone, T. W., & Lepper, M. R. (1987). Making learning fun: A taxonomy of intrinsic motivations for learning. In R. E. Snow & M. J. Farr (Eds.), *Aptitude, learning and instruction: III. Conative and affective process analyses* (pp. 223–253). Hilsdale, NJ: Erlbaum.

McMullen, J., Brezovszky, B., Rodríguez Padilla, G., Pongsakdi, N., & Lehtinen, E. (2015). *Adaptive number knowledge: exploring the foundations of adaptivity with whole-number arithmetic.* Manuscript submitted for publication.

Moreno, R., & Mayer, R. E. (2005). Role of guidance, reflection, and interactivity in an agent-based multimedia game. *Journal of Educational Psychology, 97,* 117–128. doi:10.1037/0022-0663.97.1.117.

Nuerk, H.-C., Moeller, K., Klein, E., Willmes, K., & Fisher, M. H. (2011). Extending the mental number line: A review of multi-digit number processing. *Zeitschrift für Psychologie/Journal of Psychology, 219,* 3–22. doi:10.1027/2151-2604/a000041.

Nuerk, H. C., Willmes, K., & Fias, W. (2005). Perspectives on number processing: Editorial. *Psychology Science, 47,* 4–9.

Rodríguez Padilla, G., Brezovszky, B., Pongsakdi, N., Jaakkola, T., Hannula-Sormunen, M., McMullen, J., & Lehtinen, E. (2015). Number Navigation Game-based learning environment: Experience and motivational effects. In J. Torbeyns, E. Lehtinen & J. Elen (Eds.), *Developing competencies in learners: From ascertaining to intervening* (pp. xx–xx). New York, NY: Springer.

Schneider, M., Rittle-Johnson, B., & Star, J. R. (2011). Relations among conceptual knowledge, procedural knowledge, and procedural flexibility in two samples differing in prior knowledge. *Developmental Psychology, 47,* 1525–1538. doi:10.1037/a0024997.

Siegler, R. S., & Booth, J. L. (2004). Development of numerical estimation in young children. *Child Development, 75,* 428–444. doi:10.1111/j.1467-8624.2004.00684.x.

Siegler, R. S., & Ramani, G. B. (2009). Playing linear number board games-but not circular ones-improves low-income preschoolers' numerical understanding. *Journal of Educational Psychology, 101*, 545–560. doi:10.1037/a0014239.

Thomas, N. (2004). The development of structure in the number system. In M. J. Hoines & A. B. Fuglestad (Eds.), *Proceedings of the 28th annual conference of the international group for the psychology of mathematics education* (Vol. 4, pp. 305–312). Bergen, Norway: Bergen University Collage.

Threlfall, J. (2002). Flexible mental calculation. *Educational Studies in Mathematics, 50*, 29–47. doi:10.1023/A:1020572803437.

Threlfall, J. (2009). Strategies and flexibility in mental calculation. *ZDM—The International Journal on Mathematics Education, 41*, 541–555. doi:10.1007/s11858-009-0195-3.

Tobias, S., Fletcher, J. D., Dai, D. Y., & Wind, A. P. (2011). Review of research on computer games. In S. Tobias & J. D. Fletcher (Eds.), *Computer games and instruction* (pp. 127–222). Charlotte, NC: Information Age.

Verschaffel, L., Luwel, K., Torbeyns, J., & Van Dooren, W. (2009). Conceptualizing, investigating, and enhancing adaptive expertise in elementary mathematics education. *European Journal of Psychology of Education, 24*, 335–359. doi:10.1007/BF03174765.

"Zeldenrust": A Mathematical Game-Based Learning Environment for Prevocational Students

Sylke Vandercruysse, Judith ter Vrugte, Ton de Jong, Pieter Wouters, Herre van Oostendorp, Lieven Verschaffel, Wim Van Dooren, and Jan Elen

Abstract In this contribution, we present a game-based learning environment for 12–16-year-old vocational students in which they can practice proportional reasoning problems. The learning content and goals, as well as the specific game features are discussed. We can conclude that developing a serious game implies many choices and decisions led by theoretical foundations, as well as by practical limitations and pragmatic considerations.

Keywords Number sense • Game development • Educational game

Serious games have become a hot issue in educational technology and are considered as a potential instruction tool for effective and efficient delivery of complex subject matter (Ke, 2008). Despite the flourishing popularity of implementing games in education and the promising claims that arose, empirical research and evidence to support these claims remains scarce (Papastergiou, 2009). The absence

S. Vandercruysse (✉)
Center for Instructional Psychology and Technology, KU Leuven,
Etienne Sabbelaan 53, Kortrijk 8500, Belgium

KU Leuven, Kortrijk, Belgium
e-mail: Sylke.Vandercruysse@kuleuven-kulak.be

J. ter Vrugte • T. de Jong
Department of Instructional Technology, Faculty of Behavioral Sciences, University of Twente, Enschede, The Netherlands
e-mail: j.tervrugte@utwente.nl; A.J.M.deJong@utwente.nl

P. Wouters • H. van Oostendorp
Department of Information and Computing Sciences, Utrecht University,
Utrecht, The Netherlands
e-mail: jan.wouters@med.kuleuven.be; H.vanoostendorp@uu.nl

L. Verschaffel • W. Van Dooren • J. Elen
KU Leuven, Leuven, Belgium
e-mail: lieven.verschaffel@ppw.kuleuven.be; Wim.VanDooren@ppw.kuleuven.be;
jan.elen@ppw.kuleuven.be

© Springer International Publishing Switzerland 2015
J. Torbeyns et al. (eds.), *Describing and Studying Domain-Specific Serious Games*,
Advances in Game-Based Learning, DOI 10.1007/978-3-319-20276-1_5

of an univocal and generic definition of educational games, a shared framework to talk about educational games and clear methodological guidelines to evaluate their effectiveness, results in a gap between what is theoretically claimed and what has been empirically demonstrated as well as in insufficient guidance for game designers on how to develop effective serious games. In order to make a step forward with respect to this guidance, there is a need for rigorous scientific studies that pinpoint instructional design features that improve instructional effectiveness (Aldrich, 2005; DeLeeuw & Mayer, 2011). Also, to make sure scientific results are more generalizable and comparable, scientific research would benefit from more detailed and clear descriptions of the games that are implemented in scientific studies. Therefore, we provide a detailed description of the development of a game-based learning environment (GBLE) in which we focus on the learning content, the story line, game design, and other specific game features. The environment is developed for prevocational students (second grade) and aims at stimulating their proportional reasoning abilities.

Learning Content: Proportional Reasoning

When developing a game for educational purposes, two points considering learning content draw the attention. First, the learning content has to fit educational goals to make the game attractive for use in educational settings and second, the learning content has to be suitable for integration in a game context. The game we describe focuses on the content domain of mathematics, since math is particularly suited for game-based learning (Hays, 2005). More specifically, we focus on "number sense" because number sense is a central component in the curriculum of our target group. Number sense is defined in different ways in the mathematics education literature. We use the definition of McIntosh, Reys, and Reys (1992): "Number sense refers to a person's general understanding of number and operations along with the ability and inclination to use this understanding in flexible ways to make mathematical judgments and to develop useful strategies for handling numbers and operations." (p. 3).

In the game, number sense was operationalized by exercises on proportional reasoning, or "reasoning in a system of two variables between which there exists a linear functional relationship" (Karplus, Pulos, & Stage, 1983a, p. 219). This operationalization is in line with the abovementioned definition of number sense by McIntosh et al. (1992), since students, in order to advance in the game, need to understand proportional reasoning problems, be able to conduct operations with them and apply the provided strategies in a flexible way to handle the proportional reasoning problems and operations correctly and efficiently. As Berk, Taber, Gorowara, and Poetzl (2009) stated "proportional reasoning readily lends itself to the development of flexibility in that multiple methods are available for solving proportion problems, and for particular problems, particular methods are more efficient than others" (p. 116). According to Lamon (1999), there are six mathematical content areas that contribute to the development of proportional reasoning: relative thinking, partitioning, unitizing, attending to quantities and changes, ratio sense, and rational number interpretations. Consequently, playing the game might also strengthen these content areas that proportional reasoning encompasses.

Besides its relation to number sense, proportional reasoning was chosen because it is a well-defined domain with concrete applications (not too abstract). These characteristics make proportional reasoning suitable for implementation in an educational game and scientific evaluation. Additionally, proportional reasoning is seen as a crucial topic in school mathematics, and considering the tight connections of proportional reasoning with ratios, rational numbers, and other multiplicative concepts, it spans the entire curriculum—from elementary school through university level mathematics (Lamon, 2007). Also, in both the Flemish and Dutch prevocational curriculum, the math domain of proportional reasoning is relevant and the prevocational students are expected to understand the proportional reasoning language and be able to solve simple proportional reasoning problems. However, proportional reasoning is also considered as a frequent source of difficulty for students (Lamon, 2007) and teachers in (prevocational) math education mention that their students often experience difficulties with it because of its mathematical complexity and its cognitive challenge. For the target group of this GBLE, this is confirmed by the Flemish national assessment results (Vlaamse Overheid, 2009). The relevance of proportional reasoning in the curriculum, the shortage of proportional reasoning skills, and the search for alternative instructional approaches creates a setting where research on the topic is desirable.

Types of Problems

Three types of proportional problems were selected based on the literature: (1) missing value problems, (2) transformation problems, and (3) comparison problems (e.g., Harel & Behr, 1989; Kaput & West, 1994; Vergnaud, 1983). For the first type of problems, missing value problems, a missing value in one of two ratios needs to be found. These problems can be schematically presented as $a/b = ?/d$ or as $a/b = c/?$ (e.g., $3/4 = 12/?$). The second type of problems, transformation problems, are problems in which two ratios are given but one (or two) values need to be adapted to create two equivalent ratios. For instance, the ratios $3/6$ and $4/12$. In the second ratio, 2 needs to be added to 4 to make this ratio equivalent to the first ratio ($3/6 = 6/12$). This latter type of problems is assumed to be more difficult than missing value problems because the student has to figure out independently how much has to be added and to what amount it has to be added. This in contrast to the missing value problems where it is clear what number is missing where. Next to this, the strategies that are used to solve transformation problems require more steps than the strategies involved when solving missing value problems. The third type of problems, comparison problems, are problems where the relationship between two ratios needs to be determined. One ratio can be "equal to," "less than," or "more than" the other ratio (e.g., is $1/2$ equal to $11/20$?). This third type of problems is different from the other two types of problems because in the former case no values are missing (type 1) or need to be adapted (type 2). The two ratios are given and the student has to compare them with each other (or with a simple reference point, e.g., 1/2) in order to solve the problems.

Difficulty Levels

Several task-related and subject-related factors influence performance of students on proportional reasoning problems (Tourniaire & Pulos, 1985) and thus influence the difficulty of these problems. For the missing value problems, two factors were used to divide the type of problems in different difficulty levels, namely (1) the presence or absence of integer or non-integer (internal or external) ratios and (2) numerical complexity (i.e., the value of the numbers and thus the value of the ratios). To explain the first factor (integer or non-integer internal or external ratio), an example is given: $1/2 = 3/6$. The internal ratio is the "between ratio" or in this case the values 1 and 3 or the values 2 and 6. The external ratio is the "within ratio" or in this example value 1 and 2 and value 3 and 6. In ratios, the multiplicative relationship can be integer or non-integer. In our example, the problem has integer multiples for the internal ratio ($1 \times 3 = 3$ and $2 \times 3 = 6$) as well as for the external ratio ($1 \times 2 = 2$ and $3 \times 2 = 6$) because we can multiply the values of the ratios with a natural number (in this case respectively 3 and 2). In the following example: $2/6 = 3/9$, the external ratio is non-integer because we need to multiply 2 and 6 with 1.5 to have 3 and 9. Taking this together, four combinations can be made. A rational task analysis (e.g., Kaput & West, 1994; Karplus et al., 1983a; Tourniaire & Pulos, 1985; Vergnaud, 1983), but also empirical validation (e.g., Van Dooren, De Bock, Evers, & Verschaffel, 2009), suggest the following difficulty hierarchy in the combinations (with increasing degree of difficulty): (1) two integer ratios, (2) integer internal ratio and non-integer external ratio, (3) non-integer internal ratio and integer external ratio, and (4) two non-integer ratios. For this game, this classification was combined with a second factor of difficulty: the numerical complexity of the ratios or the value of the number, that is, ratios bigger than 1 or not. It is assumed that a ratio bigger than 1 (in the example 39/3 and 13/1 both the internal (39/13) and the external (39/3) ratio are bigger than 1) leads more to deficiencies of reasoning than a ratio smaller than 1 (in the example 1/2 and 4/8 both the internal (1/4) and the external (1/2) ratio are smaller than 1) (Steinhorsdottir, 2006; Tourniaire & Pulos, 1985).

Also for the transformation problems two factors were used to divide this type of problems in different difficulty levels, namely (1) the presence or absence of integer or non-integer (internal or external) ratios and (2) the number of values (i.e., one or two) that must be adapted to become the correct answer. In the first difficulty level, both values can be adapted, but it is not compulsory. So if the two ratios that are given are 3/6 and 4/12, the player can add 2 to value 6 to make this ratio equivalent with the first ratio (3/6 = 6/12), but the player can also add 5 to 4 and 6 to 12 (3/6 = 9/18). All the equivalent answers (e.g., 10/20, 12/24) are also correct. In the second difficulty level, only one value must be adapted. For these exercises, it is not allowed to adapt both and multiply both numbers in the first ratio to obtain an equivalent ratio. Only one correct answer is possible. In the last difficulty level, both numbers must be adapted in the sense that the player cannot solve the problems by changing only one number. Take for example 3/6 and 4/13. Both numbers need to be adapted to be able to solve this task. In this example 5 needs to be added to 4 and 6 to 13 to obtain the correct sollution: 3/6=9/18. All other equivalent answers are also correct. Table 1 gives an overview of these difficulty levels for the missing value and transformation problems.

Because the third type of problems, the comparison problems, is—as abovementioned—different from the other two types of problems, the difficulty

Table 1 Overview of difficulty levels for missing value and transformation problems

Difficulty level	Sub-level	Internal ratio (IR)	IR<or>1	External ratio (ER)	ER<or>1	Amount of values that can/must be adapted
Missing value problems						
1	a	Integer	<1	Integer	<1	
	b	Integer	<1	Integer	>1	
	c	Integer	>1	Integer	<1	
	d	Integer	>1	Integer	>1	
2	a	Integer	<1	Non-integer	<1	
	b	Integer	<1	Non-integer	>1	
	c	Integer	>1	Non-integer	<1	
	d	Integer	>1	Non-integer	>1	
3	a	Non-integer	<1	Integer	<1	
	b	Non-integer	<1	Integer	>1	
	c	Non-integer	>1	Integer	<1	
	d	Non-integer	>1	Integer	>1	
4	a	Non-integer	<1	Non-integer	<1	
	b	Non-integer	<1	Non integer	>1	
	c	Non-integer	>1	Non-integer	<1	
	d	Non-integer	>1	Non-integer	>1	
Transformation problems						
1	a	Integer		Integer		2 values can
	b	Integer		Integer		1 value must
	c	Integer		Integer		2 values must
2	a	Integer		Non-integer		2 values can
	b	Integer		Non-integer		1 value must
	c	Integer		Non-integer		2 values must
3	a	Non-integer		Integer		2 values can
	b	Non-integer		Integer		1 value must
	c	Non-integer		Integer		2 values must
4	a	Non-integer		Non-integer		2 values can
	b	Non-integer		Non-integer		1 value must
	c	Non-integer		Non-integer		2 values must

Table 2 Overview of difficulty levels for comparison problems

Difficulty level	Specification		Example
Comparison problems			
1	Quantitative reasoning	Equal values for ingredient 1	81/43 and 81/39
		Equal values for ingredient 2	80/43 and 83/43
		Extreme large and small ratios	1/36 and 42/4
2	Solved by estimation	Internal ratio easy multiplication	11/20 and 22/36
		External ratio easy multiplication	30/60 and 42/80
		External ratio matches simple reference point (1/2, 1/3, 1/4, 1/10)	17/36 and 21/41
3	Complete calculation		16/41 and 33/85

levels are based on another type of task analysis (e.g., Cramer, Post, & Currier, 1993; Karplus, Pulos, & Stage, 1983b; Spinillo & Bryant, 1999) and empirical validation (Hendrickx, 2013). Comparison problems are divided into three levels of difficulty, based on the procedure(s) that can be used to solve the problems (e.g., comparing both ratios with each other). The first level includes problems that can be solved directly by quantitative reasoning. These problems can be solved by reasoning because either the values for two dimensions are equal (e.g., 81/43 vs. 81/39) or the comparison involves ratios that are inversed (e.g., 1/36 vs. 42/4). In the second difficulty level, the problems can be solved by estimation because the internal or external ratio show an easy multiplication, and hence is integer (e.g., 11/20 vs. 22/36) or the external ratio matches a simple reference point (e.g., 1/2 in the example 17/36 and 21/41). In the third and final level, the answer cannot be determined directly by qualitative reasoning or estimation, but by using full calculation (e.g., 16/41 vs. 33/85). This level contains only non-integer multiplicative relationships. Table 2 gives an overview of the difficulty levels for the comparison problems. With the game we strive for practice and knowledge gains on all three types of problems by integrating the proportional reasoning problems into the story line of the game.

The Game

The development of the game involved an iteration process including: (1) a prototype showing how students could act in the game, (2) a base version, and (3) a revised base version. Each milestone was followed by an evaluation through small focus groups of teachers/students (prototype) and pilot studies (base/revised version). The iteration approach was chosen to allow modifications in the concept and specifications of the game.

The self-developed game we describe is designed for 12–16-year-old Flemish and Dutch prevocational students. The game is available in an online and standalone version. The online version requires an Internet connection and Adobe's FlashPlayer. The game can be started from a central Internet address and all player actions are logged (e.g., number of attempts for every exercise, number of correct answers on the tasks, the use of the calculator and handbook (tutorial), how many bottles are put in the refrigerator, timestamps). These extensive loggings create extra research opportunities, that is, to investigate players' game behavior, performance, and learning during game-play. The standalone version has to be installed on PCs, does not require a separate FlashPlayer, and does not support logging of player actions. Both the online and stand-alone version consist of a 2D cartoon-like environment. The choice in graphics (2D, 3D) and the level of detail were a compromise between the advice to make games as realistic as possible and the practical constraints with respect to development time and cost and capacity of school networks and available hardware.

Game Design

To foster immersive and engaged gameplay and create context for the educational content, a story line was created. The theme of the story line was tailored to fit the teenage students' interests and world. In the game the students take on a role as hotel employee, more specifically in the hotel of their uncle and aunt. They work there and complete several tasks to earn money for a summer journey. The destination of the holiday depends on the amount of money they can gather through playing the game. During this virtual career they encounter problems and fulfill tasks that help them to understand, practice and master the math domain of proportional reasoning.

Lead Game

The game consists of a lead game and different subgames. When players enter the (lead) game, they can activate an avatar with a choice for gender and origins (see Fig. 1). Choosing one's own avatar is assumed to increase players' arousal (Lim & Reeves, 2009) and intrinsic motivation (e.g., Cordova & Lepper, 1996). After having picked an avatar, the lead game continues and players are introduced (see Fig. 2) to the main story line and game goal (i.e., the wish to go on holiday, the need for money, the job in the hotel). This is done by an automatic tutorial in which text and images are combined with each other (see Fig. 2). After this short introduction, players are accompanied by the two non-playable characters (NPGs), being their

Fig. 1 Overview of the four avatars the players can choose based on gender and origin

Fig. 2 Short introduction in which the story line and game goal are explained

Fig. 3 The central room in the game. From this room, subgames can be activated by clicking on the paintings. The paintings that are highlighted and can be played. Because this is the start of the game, only the first refrigerator subgame is accessible. The map gives the player an overview of his score and the countries he can already visit

uncle and aunt, to their room where they can sleep during the stay. There, the NPGs give additional information about the importance of the room. The room is the central place of the game because from this point the players have to choose the tasks they want to execute (see Fig. 3) and they can consult their game score, that is, the money they already earned, and keep track of the destinations they can already visit with that amount of money (see further). Hence, from the lead game the players can navigate to each of the three different subgames. Each subgame represents a specific environment in which the player can complete a number of specific tasks, that is, (1) fill refrigerators, (2) mix/blender cocktails, and (3) serve drinks (see further). Successful completion of the tasks will lead to an increase in money (score). The amount of money earned depends on how well jobs are done. The more accurate and efficient the job is done, the higher the amount of money earned.

In total, the game consists of four levels. Every level equals one day of work in the hotel (i.e., day 1 = level 1, day 2 = level 2, day 3 = level 3, and day 4 = level 4) and all three subgames are available in every level. Only the first subgame in the first level (the refrigerator) is fixed. The player cannot choose to start with another subgame because this first subgame contains a tutorial which provides the player with useful information concerning the game mechanics. After all tasks in the first subgame are finished (four tasks in every subgame; see further), the players return to their room where they can activate a new subgame by clicking on the two remaining paintings: the serving subgame or the blender subgame.

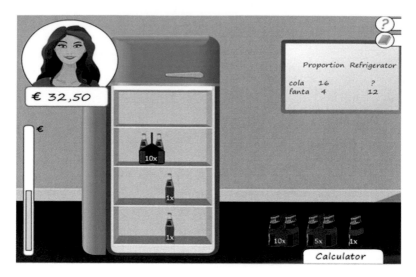

Fig. 4 The refrigerator subgame. The task is presented on the board on the right side of the screen (i.e., 16/4 = ? /12). The player has to click or drag the correct amount of bottles in the refrigerator. When the player thinks he solved the task, he has to close the refrigerator by clicking on the door

When the players complete all three subgames of one level, the players finished the level and will automatically proceed to the consecutive level, which means that all the subgames will be available again. When players finish the complete game (four levels with 12 tasks each), 48 tasks are completed.

Subgames

As mentioned above, the first subgame is the refrigerator subgame. In this subgame, the players encounter missing value problems. Here, players need to fill the refrigerator in accordance with a given proportion (e.g., for every x bottles of lemonade, there need to be y bottles of cola in the refrigerator. If there are z bottles of lemonade in the refrigerator, how many bottles of cola do you need?). The task appears on the board which is located on the upper right corner of the screen (see Fig. 4). When players have decided how many bottles are missing, they can place the correct number of bottles in the refrigerator (by clicking on the correct bottles, or dragging and dropping the bottles in the correct place). To confirm their answer they have to close the door. After this, the players receive feedback on their answer and proceed to another attempt (when the answer was incorrect) or a new task (when the answer was correct).

In the blender subgame, the players encounter transformation problems. Here, the players need to complete a cocktail in accordance with a provided recipe. Again, the task is visualized on the board by offering the recipe to the players (see Fig. 5).

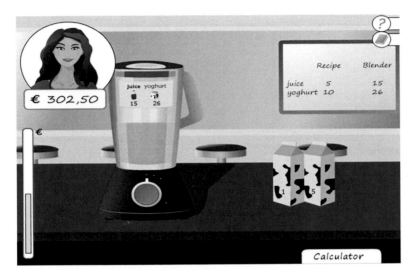

Fig. 5 The blender game. The player has to adapt one or two ingredients according to the recipe presented on the board. When they player thinks he/she is ready, he can confirm his answer by clicking on the blender button

The players are presented with a blender that already contains a mixture of yoghurt and strawberry juice, but the quantity of the ingredients does not fit the recipe. The players are asked to add yoghurt and/or strawberry juice to "fix" the mixture so that it is in accordance with the ratio that the recipe prescribes. The players can add the ingredients by dragging the bottles over the blender.

In the serving subgame, the players encounter comparison problems. Here, the players need to serve the drink that matches the order (e.g., serve the least sweet mix). Again, the task appears on the board at the upper right corner of the screen. To complete the order, players need to compare the mixtures that are presented in two pitchers and choose the mixture that fits the order. After selecting the correct pitcher players need to place it on a serving tray using a drag-and-drop motion (see Fig. 6).

In every subgame, four tasks (or items) are presented in which the learning content is integrated. Depending on the subgame, the players have either one or three attempts to solve the task. For the refrigerator and blender subgame, three attempts for each task are offered to the players. The incorporation of multiple attempts was done to lessen frustration (raise the chance for a correct answer), to stimulate the players to rethink their calculations (in-game reflection), and to discourage guessing (a wrong guess will not immediately lead to a new task). Due to the nature of the tasks in the serving subgame, only one attempt per task is possible. Either they serve the correct pitcher or they serve the wrong one. A second attempt would possibly bias the results because it would always be correct. If the players do not find the correct answer during the provided attempts, they automatically continue to the following task. The decision to continue the game even when a task was not solved was made to avoid players getting stuck in the game and becoming frustrated.

Fig. 6 The serving subgame. The task is presented on the board, i.e., put the sweetest cocktail on the serving tray. By placing a pitcher on the tray, the player immediately gets feedback about the correctness of his answer

The tasks in the subgames are implemented based on their difficulty level of the proportional reasoning types of problems (see above) and the difficulty increases as players progress through the levels. The first level is the easiest level and contains items of the first difficulty level of the missing value problems, transformational problems, and comparison problems. The second level is a bit more difficult and contains items of the second and third difficulty level of the missing value and transformation problems and the second difficulty level of the comparison problems. When players enter the third level, they get items of the highest difficulty level of all three types of problems. For the last level, we opted to combine items of the previous levels as a kind of rehearsal exercise but also to prevent feelings of failure and to provide all students with an experience of success at the end of the game. An overview of the types of problems and difficulty level of these problems per subgame are presented in Table 3.

Game Characteristics

In the following sections, specific game characteristics will be discussed based on literature and on the (pragmatic) choices we had to make when developing the game.

Goal. Because it is a relatively simple game, the goal was kept relatively simple and clear: make as much money as possible to travel as far as possible. Clear goals stimulate engagement and engage players' self-esteem (Malone, 1980). Therefore, the current game's goal is clearly presented to the player at the beginning of the

Table 3 Overview of the difficulty levels implemented in the game per level and type of problems (see Tables 1 and 2 for the specification of the difficulty levels)

Game level	Difficulty level
Missing value problems	
1	1abcd
2	2ab 3cd
3	4abcd
4	4d3c2b1a
Comparison problems	
1	1aa1bb
2	2aa2bb
3	3aaaa
4	3a2b2a1a
Transformation problems	
1	1abcc
2	2ab3ab
3	4abcc
4	4c3b2a1a

game (i.e., earn money for the journey; the more money the players earn, the further they can travel) and in every subgame (i.e., execute the tasks as good as possible to gain money). The importance of the goal is repeated throughout the game in both implicit (showing players the money they made) and explicit (showing players how well they perform in contrast to others) ways. As advised by Malone (1980), the goal is tailored so that students could identify with it (making money is something teenagers are interested in, as well as travelling), is given meaning by making it part of an intrinsic fantasy as sketched by the story line (the money was necessary to fund a holiday trip) and is different from, but related to, the educational content (the educational content plays a role in successfully achieving the goal).

Content integration. Games where the learning content and game content are fully—or intrinsically—integrated are expected to be superior with respect to learning outcomes (Habgood & Ainsworth, 2011). Therefore, the story line and contexts that are addressed in the current game environment are designed to create natural settings that foster seamless integration of the learning content. The learning content is not an extra layer to the game or completely separated from it, but is an integral part of the game experience. Solving proportional reasoning problems is not an isolated activity, but is intrinsically integrated in the story line (e.g., filling the refrigerator in order to earn money). Also, the controls required to solve the problems are in line with all other game controls (point-and-click, drag-and-drop). In addition, the content is integrated in such a manner that the "fantasy-world" of the game actually shows the players indications of how their newly learnt skill (i.e., proportional reasoning) can be used to accomplish real world goals (e.g., adjusting recipes).

Tools. Within the game several tools to aid gameplay are implemented. They help players to understand the game mechanics to understand how to tackle the tasks and assist players during their problem-solving. Two kinds of tutorials are implemented.

Fig. 7 Tutorial in which player gets an overview of the game mechanics, tools, and tasks. This tutorial is interactive. Only after executing the operations that are described in the tutorial, the game continues. In this example, the player has to activate the extra aid (column), put the correct amount of milk in the blender, and confirm his answer by clicking on the blender button

A first tutorial focuses on game mechanics. When activating the subgames the first time, the tutorial starts automatically. Players get information about the tasks they have to perform, and what they have to do in the different subgames. Additionally, they get the chance to practice different functionalities like drag-and-drop (see Fig. 7). With this tutorial, we want to prevent uncertainties with students' gaming abilities, and give them the information they need to progress through the game. This tutorial is integrated in an interactive manner. By integrating an interactive tutorial, students might find the game easier to play, experience less frustration and understand the instructions better (Goodman, Bradley, Paras, Williamson, & Bizzochi, 2006). Next to these advantages, students who are confronted with a tutorial can perform better in the game-play (Goodman et al., 2006).

Secondly, a content-related tutorial is implemented. This tutorial is permanently accessible for the players during the game (see Fig. 8). This tutorial gives players information about the different types of proportional reasoning problems and the strategies they can use to solve these problems. This information is supportive to the learning of solving different proportional reasoning problems and provides a bridge between students' prior knowledge and the learning tasks (van Merriënboer, Clark, & de Croock, 2002). With this information, players should be able to handle the

HANDBOOK TO SOLVE PROBLEMS IN THE GAME

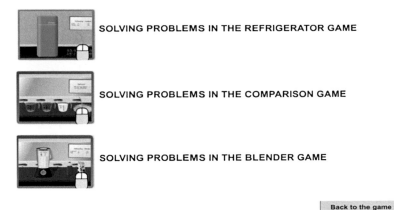

SOLVING PROBLEMS IN THE REFRIGERATOR GAME

SOLVING PROBLEMS IN THE COMPARISON GAME

SOLVING PROBLEMS IN THE BLENDER GAME

Back to the game

Fig. 8 Content-related tutorial. This tutorial can be activated by clicking on the book-icon which is visible during every subgame in the right upper corner of the screen. After clicking on it, players access the tutorial. They can choose for which subgame they want the additional information

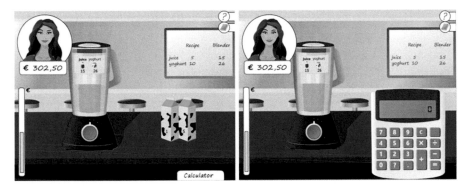

Fig. 9 The calculator can be used by players during the game by clicking on the "calculator" button. A calculator pops up and can be closed by clicking on the "off" button

problems presented in the subgames. This tutorial is not automatically activated but can be activated by the players whenever they need it. Although previous research indicated that using tools in accordance with the learning needs presupposes some self-regulation skills that not every student masters (Azevedo, 2005), this was preferred over an automatic (fixed) tutorial because a forced presentation of this tutorial might lead to loss of game-flow.

In addition to the tutorials, students can use several other tools that also facilitate their problem-solving. Students can add a column to the representation of the problems (see Fig. 9) to help them to simplify the first ratio. In this column, they can fill out their interim solution so they do not have to calculate too many steps in their head. Also, students can use their resources to "buy" help from a calculator (see Fig. 10).

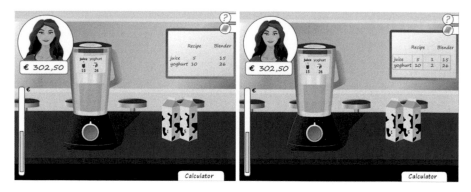

Fig. 10 An extra aid can be activated on the board by clicking on it. An extra column appears and can help solving the task

Feedback. During the game, players receive different kinds of feedback to their actions. This feedback is focused on the proportional reasoning skills of the players, as well as on their gaming skills. More concrete, the feedback is either related to their accuracy of solving proportional reasoning problems (after each item the player is told whether their solution is right or wrong), the efficiency of their gaming skills (whether they are not spoiling materials as dropping bottles, or whether they start off with a right move), or their performance of the overall game (after a sub-game players are told how their score, i.e., amount of money, relates to that of other players). The feedback is provided by one of the two NPGs, an increase or decrease in score, or a visual representation of ranking (Fig. 11).

Feedback on accuracy of solving the proportional reasoning problems is immediately provided after solving an item by an increase (correct answer) or decrease (incorrect answer) in score and by a visual component (point bar becomes green if the players answers correctly and red if the player's answer is wrong). This immediate corrective feedback about the accuracy of their answers coupled with the opportunity to answer-until-correct (with a limitation of three attempts) promotes greater retention and a greater correction of initially inaccurate strategies (Dihoff, Brosvic, & Epstein, 2003).

Additionally, feedback on accuracy of solving the proportional reasoning problems is also textually provided by an NPG. After the first attempt in a task, their feedback states whether the given solution is right or wrong (e.g., "Perfect!" or "Well done!"). After a second attempt, the feedback states either that the answer is correct or that the answer is less or more than the expected answer (e.g., "This number is not correct. You have used too many bottles of cola"). After a third attempt, the feedback states whether the answer is right or wrong and the game proceeds to the next task. During this feedback on accuracy, also textual feedback on efficiency is given (e.g., "Watch out! You are spoiling bottles of cola. They are not for free and go off your salary!").

Fig. 11 The map on which player can see which countries he/she can already visit (orange countries) and which countries the other virtual players can already visit (the red drawing-pins)

When a subgame is completed, players are automatically referred to the room from which they can access the map on which they get feedback about their performance of the overall game. On the map, they can see how many countries they can visit (the orange countries). Next to this, they see how their score relates to that of others. The players are informed that the other scores (visualized with red drawing-pins; see Fig. 11) represent scores from other players when these had played a similar time. However, these scores are a calculated adaptive representation that changes depending on the current score of the player. This was done because of technical limitations: Live updates of ranking were technically difficult to realize.

Scoring mechanism. Students earn money by solving the tasks in the subgames. They can increase the money by performing positive actions such as starting the task in a correct way (e.g., putting the first bottle in the refrigerator), but the money will decrease when performing undesired actions (e.g., using the calculator will cost money). On the map, players can see to which destinations they can travel with the money they have earned.

Conclusion

The development of "Zeldenrust" was time intensive and susceptible to opposite expectations between math educators and game developers. It implied many choices and decisions led by theoretical foundations, as well as by practical limitations and pragmatic considerations. The environment can now be used for several research purposes with our target group: research that focuses on the use of educational games in the classroom (e.g., effect on performance, motivation), research that focuses on learners' behavior in an educational game (based on the logfiles), and research that focuses on the design of educational games (e.g., which tools are stimulating, which kind of feedback is advisable). For the research purposes, customization options in the environment are available. For instance, the number of exercises or levels can be changed, the subgames can be deactivated (so only one or two types of problems are offered to the players). Additionally, more fundamental changes are also possible. A variety of versions of "Zeldenrust"—in which these changes are carried through, has already been employed in several studies (ter Vrugte et al., 2015; Vandercruysse et al., submitted) and proved its user- and research-friendliness. However, it is not possible for teachers and parents to carry through personal customizations since this has to be applied in the xml-files and they do not have access to it.

Acknowledgment The environment described in this manuscript is developed and used for studies based on a research project funded by NWO/PROO (project number 411-00-003) and the Fund of Scientific Research (FWO—project number G.O.516.11.N.10).

References

Aldrich, C. (2005). *Learning by doing: The comprehensive guide to simulations, computer games, and pedagogy in e-learning and other educational experiences.* San Francisco, CA: Pfeiffer.

Azevedo, R. (2005). Using hypermedia as a metacognitive tool for enhancing student learning? The role of self-regulated learning. *Educational Psychologist, 40,* 199–209. doi:10.1207/s15326985ep4004_2.

Berk, D., Taber, S. B., Gorowara, C. C., & Poetzl, C. (2009). Developing prospective elementary teachers' flexibility in the domain of proportional reasoning. *Mathematical Thinking and Learning, 11,* 113–135. doi:10.1080/10986060903022714.

Cordova, D. I., & Lepper, M. R. (1996). Intrinsic motivation and the process of learning: Beneficial effects of contextualization, personalization, and choice. *Journal of Educational Psychology, 88,* 715–730. doi:10.1037/0022-0663.88.4.715.

Cramer, K., Post, T., & Currier, S. (1993). Learning and teaching ratio and proportions: Research implications. In D. Owens (Ed.), *Research ideas for the classroom: Middle grades mathematics* (pp. 159–178). New York, NY: Macmillan.

DeLeeuw, K. E., & Mayer, R. E. (2011). Cognitive consequences of making computer-based learning activities more game-like. *Computers in Human Behaviour, 27,* 2011–2016. doi:10.1016/j.chb.2011.05.008.

Dihoff, R. E., Brosvic, G. M., & Epstein, M. L. (2003). The role of feedback during academic testing: The delay retention effect revisited. *The Psychological Record, 53,* 533–548.

Goodman, D., Bradley, N. L., Paras, B., Williamson, I. J., & Bizzochi, J. (2006). Video gaming promotes concussion knowledge acquisition in youth hockey players. *Journal of Adolescence, 29,* 351–360. doi:10.1016/j.adolescence.2005.07.004.

Habgood, M. P. J., & Ainsworth, S. E. (2011). Motivating children to learn effectively: Exploring the value of intrinsic integration in educational games. *Journal of Learning Sciences, 20,* 169–206. doi:10.1080/10508406.2010.508029.

Harel, G., & Behr, M. (1989). Structure and hierarchy of missing-value proportion problems and their representations. *Journal of Mathematical Behavior, 8,* 77–119.

Hays, R. T. (2005). *The effectiveness of instructional games: A literature review and discussion* (Report No. 2005-004). Orlando, FL: Naval Air Warfare Center Training Systems Division.

Hendrickx, M. (2013). *De invloed van getalstructuren op het proportioneel redeneren. Een empirisch onderzoek naar de hypothetische rangordening gebruikt in 'serious games'* (Unpublished master's thesis). KU Leuven, Belgium.

Kaput, J., & West, M. M. (1994). Missing-value proportional reasoning problems: Factors affecting informal reasoning patterns. In G. Harel & J. Confrey (Eds.), *The development of multiplicative reasoning in the learning of mathematics* (pp. 237–292). New York, NY: SUNY Press.

Karplus, R., Pulos, S., & Stage, E. K. (1983a). Early adolescents' proportional reasoning on 'rate'. *Educational Studies on Mathematics, 14*, 219–233. doi:10.1007/BF00410539.

Karplus, R., Pulos, S., & Stage, E. K. (1983b). Proportional reasoning of early adolescents. In R. Lesh & M. Landau (Eds.), *Acquisition of mathematics concepts and processes* (pp. 45–90). New York, NY: Academic.

Ke, F. (2008). A case study of computer gaming for math: Engaged learning from gameplay? *Computers & Education, 51*, 1609–1620. doi:10.1016/j.compedu.2008.03.003.

Lamon, S. J. (1999). *Teaching fractions and ratios for understanding: Essential content knowledge and instructional strategies for teachers.* Mahwah, NJ: Erlbaum.

Lamon, S. J. (2007). Rational numbers and proportional reasoning. In F. K. Lester (Ed.), *Second handbook of research on mathematics teaching and learning. A project of the national council of teachers of mathematics* (pp. 629–667). Reston, VA: NCTM.

Lim, S., & Reeves, B. (2009). Being in the game: Effects of avatar choice and point of view on psychophysiological responses during play. *Media Psychology, 12*, 348–370. doi:10.1080/15213260903287242.

Malone, T. (1980). What makes things fun to learn? Heuristics for designing instructional computer games. *Proceedings of the 3rd ACM SIGSMALL Symposium and the 1st SIGPC Symposium, Palo Alto (USA)*, 162–169.

McIntosh, A., Reys, B. J., & Reys, R. E. (1992). A proposed framework for examining basic number sense. *For the Learning of Mathematics, 12*(3), 2–8.

Overheid, V. (2009). *Peiling wiskunde in de eerste graad secundair onderwijs (B-stroom).* Brussels, Belgium: Vlaams Ministerie van Onderwijs en Vorming.

Papastergiou, M. (2009). Digital game-based learning in high school computer science education: Impact on educational effectiveness and school motivation. *Computers & Education, 52*(1), 1–12. doi:10.1016/j.compedu.2008.06.004.

Spinillo, A. G., & Bryant, P. (1999). Proportional reasoning in young children: Part-part comparisons about continuous and discontinuous quantity. *Mathematical Cognition, 5*, 181–197. doi:10.1080/135467999387298.

Steinhorsdottir, O. B. (2006). Proportional reasoning: Variable influencing the problems difficulty level and one's use of problem solving strategies. In J. Novota, H. Maraova, M. Kratka, & N. Stehlikova (Eds.), *Proceedings 30th Conference of the International Group for the Psychology of Mathematics Education 5* (pp. 169–176). Prague, Czechia: PME.

ter Vrugte, J., de Jong, T., Wouters, P., Vandercruysse, S., Elen, J. & van Oostendorp, H. (2015). When a game supports prevocational math education but integrated reflection does not. *Journal of Computer Assisted Learning.* doi: 10.1111/jcal.12104.

Tourniaire, F., & Pulos, S. (1985). Proportional reasoning: A review of the literature. *Educational Studies in Mathematics, 16*, 181–204. doi:10.1007/BF02400937.

Vandercruysse, S., ter Vrugte, J., de Jong, T., Wouters, P., van Oostendorp, H., Verschaffel, L., Van Dooren, W., & Elen, J. (Submitted). Content integration as a factor in math game effectiveness. *Educational Technology Research & Development.*

Van Dooren, W., De Bock, D., Evers, M., & Verschaffel, L. (2009). Students' overuse of proportionality on missing-value problems: How numbers may change solutions. *Journal for Research in Mathematics Education, 40*, 187–211.

van Merriënboer, J. J. G., Clark, R. E., & de Croock, M. B. M. (2002). Blueprints for complex learning: The 4C/ID-model. *Educational Technology Research and Development, 50*(2), 39–64. doi:10.1007/BF02504993.

Vergnaud, G. (1983). Multiplicative structures. In R. Lesh & M. Landau (Eds.), *Acquisition of mathematics concepts and processes* (pp. 127–174). New York, NY: Academic.

Applying Motivation Theory to the Design of Game-Based Learning Environments

Jon R. Star, Jason Chen, and Chris Dede

Abstract Although there has been a wealth of research exploring motivation within game-based learning environments, few of these studies employ frameworks that are grounded in well-established theories of motivation. This chapter brings a rigorous theoretical framework for motivation to the study and design of a game-based learning environment. First, we outline a key motivation construct that has potential value for the design of game-based learning environments—Eccles and Wigfield's expectancy-value theory. We then provide a description of a game whose design was informed by this motivational theory, where the game was intended to promote students' interest in and motivation to pursue science, technology, engineering, and mathematics (STEM) careers.

Keywords Expectancy-value theory • Motivation • Game-based learning environment • STEM

Though much effort has been put toward integrating game elements in educational spaces to improve learning, results have been disappointing (Hogle, 1996; Kerawalla & Crook, 2005). One reason for this unsuccessful hybrid is that designers have taken a "chocolate-covered broccoli" (Bruckman, 1999) approach in which the gaming element is a reward for completing the educational component. Game-based learning environments need to be designed in a way that allows for the learning material to be delivered through the parts of the game that are most motivating (Habgood, Ainsworth, & Benford, 2005). The purpose of this chapter is to bring rigorous theoretical frameworks of motivation to the study and design of game-based learning environments. Although there has been a wealth of research exploring motivation within game-based learning environments, few of these studies employ frameworks that are grounded in well-established theories of motivation (Moos & Marroquin,

J.R. Star (✉) • C. Dede
Graduate School of Education, Harvard University, 442 Gutman Library,
6 Appian Way, Cambridge, MA 02138, USA
e-mail: jon_star@harvard.edu; chris_dede@gse.harvard.edu

J. Chen
The College of William and Mary, Williamsburg, VA, USA
e-mail: jachen@email.wm.edu

© Springer International Publishing Switzerland 2015
J. Torbeyns et al. (eds.), *Describing and Studying Domain-Specific Serious Games*,
Advances in Game-Based Learning, DOI 10.1007/978-3-319-20276-1_6

2010). In this chapter, we first introduce a prominent theory of motivation that can be applied to the design of game-based learning environments—expectancy-value theory. Second, we illustrate how this motivational theory was drawn upon in the design of a game designed to promote students' interest in and motivation to pursue science, technology, engineering, and mathematics (STEM) careers.

Theories of motivation can offer researchers, educators, and designers useful and theoretically grounded constructs that can be empirically applied and studied in educational contexts. By motivation, we are referring to the "the process whereby goal-directed activity is instigated and sustained" (Pintrich & Schunk, 2002, p. 5). Increasing student motivation is a prime target for improving education because what people believe is quite often a better predictor of actual performance than is previous achievement or even actual capability (Bandura, 1997). In this light, it is quite disheartening for teachers, for example, to see a student who exhibits great potential, but because of self-doubt or lack of interest in a subject, does not perform on par with what that student should be able to do. Some scholars argue that motivational factors play a larger role than academic performance in predicting continued learning. For instance, in an introductory undergraduate psychology course during freshman year, motivation was more predictive of subsequent course taking and majoring in psychology over a 7-year span than were grades from that introductory course (Harackiewicz, Barron, Pintrich, Elliot, & Thrash, 2002). Similar patterns have been found for middle school and high school students (Harackiewicz et al., 2002; Hidi, 1990; Hidi & Harackiewicz, 2000; Hidi & Renninger, 2006). Though research on motivational theories and their applications to education has generated thousands of journal articles, there is relatively little empirical evidence about whether these theories also hold up in game-based learning environments.

Expectancy-Value Theory

One widely used theory of motivation in education research is Eccles and Wigfield's expectancy-value theory (e.g., Eccles, 1987, 1993; Eccles et al., 1983, 1989; Wigfield, 1994; Wigfield & Eccles, 1992, 2000). As its name implies, expectancy-value theory proposes that students' motivation to engage in an activity is influenced by two factors—the degree that students believe that they expect to succeed in the activity, and the degree that students value participation in the task. This theory provides a useful framework for understanding students' beliefs about how competent they are and what they value within the context of their academic studies.

With regard to expectancy, students are motivated toward or away from particular activities by answering the question, "Can I do this?" This question refers to students' belief in their own competence, also known as self-efficacy. Decades of research have shown that students' self-efficacy, defined by Bandura (1997) as "the belief in one's capabilities to organize and execute courses of action required to produce given attainments" (p. 3), is a powerful influence on motivation and achievement. Bandura (1997) hypothesized several sources of self-efficacy, including *mastery experience* (the interpreted results of one's past performance), *vicarious experience* (observations of others' activities, particularly individuals perceived as similar to oneself), and *physiological and affective states* (anxiety, stress, and fatigue)—each of which has been linked to performance in math and science, including students' persistence in STEM fields and choice of STEM majors (e.g., Britner & Pajares, 2001; Gwilliam & Betz, 2001; Lau & Roeser, 2002; Lent, Brown, & Larkin, 1984). Furthermore, teachers with higher self-efficacy plan lessons better demonstrate higher levels of organizational skills, and put in more effort in helping struggling learners than do their peers who have lower self-efficacy (Allinder, 1994; Ashton & Webb, 1986; Gibson & Dembo, 1984).

The second component of expectancy-value theory is value. To be motivated to do something, students must not only believe that they have the competence to do it, but they also need to see the value of doing it. For instance, students can easily decide that they are highly capable at succeeding in math; but, if they do not see the point of becoming proficient, there is no reason for them to exert the necessary effort to succeed. The construct of value is considered to have four components: The perceived importance of the task based on it being enjoyable and fun to engage in (interest), influential to the individual's identity (attainment), useful in the individual's life (utility), and having perceived negative aspects of engaging in the activity, such as negative emotional states (cost). Studies have indicated that task values (particularly interest and utility) are associated with course enrollment decisions, free-time activities, and intentions (Jacobs, Lanza, Osgood, Eccles, & Wigfield, 2002).

In sum, the expectancy-value framework of motivation posits that individuals will be motivated to engage in a task to the extent that they feel they can be successful at it and to the extent they perceive the task as being important to them.

Application of Expectancy-Value Theory to the Design of a Game-Based Learning Environment

A project at Harvard's Graduate School of Education, entitled Transforming the Engagement of Students in Learning Algebra (TESLA), illustrates how a theory of motivation (in particular, expectancy-value theory) can be incorporated into game-based learning environments. For this project, the researchers created a 4-day mathematics intervention, 2 days of which involve one of several game-based learning environments for students in Grades 5–8 before classroom instruction. In this chapter, we describe one of the game-based learning environments that was specifically designed to increase students' motivation for STEM by aligning with expectancy-value theory. This game was an Immersive Virtual Environment (IVE) that was designed to introduce students to the mathematical concepts that were to follow in a subsequent lesson. The IVE was professionally produced such that it was similar in look and feel to video games that students may have had experience playing.

Fig. 1 Opening screen, space rescue mission

Game description. Prior to beginning the IVE, each student viewed a short (5-min) video clip of a young STEM professional who talked about the nature of the work they do (e.g., designing astronaut space suits), the difficulties they had encountered in their K-12 math and science classes, and how they were able to overcome these difficulties. Students were provided with a selection of several of these videos, which varied according to the demographic attributes of the STEM professionals (e.g., gender, ethnicity); students were allowed to select whichever single video they wanted to view before beginning the IVE.

For the story line of the IVE, students were provided with the opportunity to explore an outer space environment in the context of a space rescue mission (see Fig. 1). A total of five mathematical puzzles were encountered as students moved around the planet; all puzzles related to the generation of and identification of mathematical patterns, similar to what would subsequently be discussed in a mathematics lesson. The first puzzle allows students to become accustomed to how to function and interact in the virtual world and is similar to a combination-lock problem in that students must identify all possible ways that three numbers can be combined to produce a unique 3-digit number (see Fig. 2). When students finish, they proceed to a more complex and difficult second puzzle.

In the second puzzle, students encounter a door that is locked (see Fig. 3). Next to the door is a box with complex circuitry. Parts of this circuit board are complete, but the great majority of it is broken. Students must "fix" each section of the circuit board by building circuits with 1- and 2-unit length fuses. The circuits that must be constructed differ in size—at first, students build a 1-unit long circuit (only one

Fig. 2 First puzzle, combination-lock problem

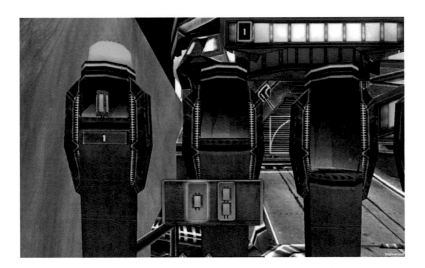

Fig. 3 Second puzzle, Fibonacci circuit problem

possible combination if presented with only 1- and 2-unit long fuses). Then, they build circuits that are 2-unit long (2 possibilities: 1 + 1 and 2), 3-unit long (3 possibilities: 1 + 1 + 1; 2 + 1; and 1 + 2), and so forth, until they reach a circuit that is 9-unit in length (55 possible combinations) (see Fig. 3). What emerges from this activity is the fact that a Fibonacci series, in which each subsequent number of possible combinations is the sum of the previous two, underlies the pattern (1, 2, 3, 5, 8, 13, 21, 34, 55). Because students are not explicitly taught the Fibonacci series in school, most students are likely to enter this activity unaware of this pattern. However, due to its simplicity, the activity is well within students' cognitive abilities.

Beyond the second puzzle, the game included three more puzzles that were increasingly difficult but mathematically related to the first two puzzles—in that these later puzzles also focused on mathematical patterns and the Fibonacci series. Upon completion of the final puzzle, the game concludes as a final door opens and the player is able to rescue the ship's captain.

Design elements focusing on expectancy. In creating a game that is motivationally sound and that draws upon expectancy-value theory, we made a number of purposeful design choices. To begin, consider the following design elements intended to foster the growth of expectancy for success (self-efficacy). First, we removed common elements of many commercial games that the motivational literature suggests may undermine or distract students from the learning and motivational goals, including competition, time-sensitive pressures, and overt performance goals. As a result, the IVE did not include a timer or clock, did not focus on the accumulation of points or levels, and did not place players in competition with one another. Second, the IVE began with a relatively easy first puzzle so that students could familiarize themselves with the controls as well as experience early success. This type of initial success in the game was intended to build students' self-efficacy for solving these types of problems as they began playing the game.

Third, the later puzzles in the game are designed with a complex progression of scaffolds and hints, which are included and removed purposely to promote the growth of self-efficacy. In particular, consider the scaffolds that are in place in the second puzzle, which is considerably more complex than the first puzzle and is designed to be quite challenging for students. If students were given the entire second puzzle all at once, many could be overwhelmed and quickly become discouraged. Instead, we designed this activity with supports and hints that are progressively removed so that students can develop a belief that they are able to solve this type of problem, which is directly related to expectancy. For example, students start out by building actual circuits that are 1-unit, 2-unit, and 3-unit in length using only 1-unit and 2-unit long fuses before tackling longer circuits that require pattern recognition. Through these mastery experiences, students' perceived past successes lead them to become more confident in being able to accomplish similar tasks. According to Bandura (1997), mastery experiences are the most powerful source of self-efficacy, which makes it an attractive way to build expectancy for success in this virtual environment.

Furthermore, when students reach circuits that are 4- and 5-unit long, the number of circuits that can be built at each height increases dramatically. Building each individual circuit becomes not only more difficult, but also more tedious. Therefore, students are shown all the different combinations that can be built at 3-unit high (e.g., $1 + 1 + 1$; $2 + 1$; and $1 + 2$ for a total of three circuits) and 4-unit high. From this information, they must make an educated guess as to how many circuits can be made, using 1- and 2-unit length fuses, when the circuit is 5-unit in length. Students are no longer building this circuit from scratch (removing a scaffold) but are instead deducing patterns. If they guess incorrectly, feedback is provided to students so that they can begin to build the individual circuits in a systematic and orderly fashion.

As students progress through this step to more complicated circuits (6-, 7-, 8-, and 9-unit high), more scaffolds are removed so that students are progressively given more autonomy and responsibility for providing the correct response. Again, appropriate feedback is provided every time a student does not generate the correct response. At the end (for the 9-unit long circuit that requires 55 unique combinations), the environment is constructed so that students are not given the opportunity to build the circuits if their initial estimate is incorrect. Rather, students are given a visual cue showing the entire series of circuits that has been constructed, highlighting how many circuits were built at each length (1, 2, 3, 5, 8, etc.); students are then asked if they can identify a pattern from these numbers.

Together, this rather complex series of scaffolds (which we describe for the second puzzle but which are also present in the third, fourth, and fifth puzzles) are designed to help students come to the realization that they can in fact solve what appears to be complex problems—to provide them with mastery experiences to bolster their expectancy for success.

Design elements focusing on value. In addition to fostering expectancy, the game also includes elements designed to bolster value. In particular, students are introduced to eight real-life STEM professionals before attempting to solve the five puzzles. Students choose one of these STEM professionals to be the "team lead" for the puzzle-solving mission. They then watch a short video that introduces them to the STEM professional. In this video, students are able to find out answers to questions such as, "Why is your job so awesome?" and "What obstacles have you faced in your path to becoming a STEM professional and how did you overcome them?" Because the models in the interview are young, are in careers that students are apt to view as attractive (e.g., space suit designer for NASA), and are ethnically diverse, we hope that students can readily identify with the role model to whom they are matched and can reap the motivational benefits more easily than if the models were perceived as completely dissimilar to the students. These videos address the value component of the expectancy-value theory by illustrating the relevance of algebra knowledge (utility construct) and presenting careers that may be appealing to some students to increase motivation to pursue STEM careers (interest construct).

Conclusion

It is clear that, for learning to be optimal, students must be motivated. The theoretical framework addressed here provides rigorously studied and theoretically grounded constructs with which researchers and designers can study and create game-based learning environments that enhance the experience of learning. We have provided one example of how a theory of motivation can be applied to the design of a game-based learning environment, but there are a great many other ways that these theories can be applied. Even more exciting is the fact that game-based learning environments can be designed in ways that can allow researchers to test many different experimental variations, providing researchers and designers with empirical evidence for which design decisions may be appropriate for whom under what conditions. We encourage researchers to conduct these types of micro-level analyses, which can provide useful information on designing motivationally optimal game-based learning environments.

Acknowledgments Parts of this chapter appeared in: Tran, C., Chen, J., Warschauer, M., Conley, A., and Dede, C. (2012). Applying motivation theories to the design of educational technology. In C. Martin, A. Ochsner, and K. Squire (Eds.), *Proceedings of the Games, Learning, and Society Conference: Vol. 2* (pp. 291–297). Pittsburgh, PA: ETC Press.

The research was supported by a grant from the National Science Foundation (DRL #0929575) to Chris Dede and Jon R. Star. The ideas in this chapter are those of the authors and do not represent official positions of the National Science Foundation.

References

Allinder, R. M. (1994). The relationship between efficacy and the instructional practices of special education teachers and consultants. *Teacher Education and Special Education, 17*(2), 86–95.

Ashton, P. T., & Webb, R. B. (1986). *Making a difference: Teachers' sense of efficacy and student achievement.* New York, NY: Longman.

Bandura, A. (1997). *Self-efficacy: The exercise of control.* New York, NY: W.H. Freeman.

Britner, S. L., & Pajares, F. (2001). Self-efficacy beliefs, race, and gender in middle school science. *Journal of Women and Minorities in Science and Engineering, 7,* 271–285.

Bruckman, A. (1999). *Can educational be fun?* Paper presented at the Game Developers Conference '99, San Jose, CA.

Eccles, J. S. (1987). Gender roles and women's achievement-related decisions. *Psychology of Women Quarterly, 11,* 135–172.

Eccles, J. S. (1993). School and family effects on the ontogeny of children's interests, self-perceptions, and activity choice. In J. Jacobs (Ed.), *Nebraska symposium on motivation, 1992: Developmental perspectives on motivation* (pp. 145–208). Lincoln, NE: University of Nebraska Press.

Eccles (Parsons), J. S., Adler, T. F., Futterman, R., Goff, S. B., Kaczala, C. M., Meece, J. L., & Midgley, C. (1983). Expectancies, values, and academic behaviors. In J. T. Spence (Ed.), *Achievement and achievement motivation* (pp. 75–146). San Francisco, CA: W. H. Freeman.

Eccles, J., Wigfield, A., Flanagan, C., Miller, C., Reuman, D., & Yee, D. (1989). Self-concepts, domain values, and self-esteem: Relations and changes at early adolescence. *Journal of Personality, 57,* 283–310.

Gibson, S., & Dembo, M. (1984). Teacher efficacy: A construct validation. *Journal of Educational Psychology, 76,* 569–582.

Gwilliam, L. R., & Betz, N. E. (2001). Validity of measures of math- and science-related self-efficacy for African Americans and European Americans. *Journal of Career Assessment, 9,* 261–281.

Habgood, M. P. J., Ainsworth, S., & Benford, S. (2005). Endogenous fantasy and learning in digital games. *Simulation and Gaming, 36*(4), 483–498.

Harackiewicz, J., Barron, K., Pintrich, P. R., Elliot, A., & Thrash, T. (2002). Revision of goal theory: Necessary and illuminating. *Journal of Educational Psychology, 94,* 638–645.

Hidi, S. (1990). Interest and its contribution as a mental resource for learning. *Review of Educational Research, 60,* 549–571.

Hidi, S., & Harackiewicz, J. (2000). Motivating the academically unmotivated: A critical issue for the 21st century. *Review of Educational Research, 70,* 151–179.

Hidi, S., & Renninger, K. A. (2006). The four-phase model of interest development. *Educational Psychologist, 41*(2), 111–127.

Hogle, J. G. (1996). *Considering games as cognitive tools: In search of effective "edutainment".* Retrieved from http://www.twinpinefarm.com/pdfs/games.pdf.

Jacobs, J. E., Lanza, S., Osgood, D. W., Eccles, J. S., & Wigfield, A. (2002). Changes in children's self-competence and values: Gender and domain differences across grades one through twelve. *Child Development, 73*, 509–527.

Kerawalla, L., & Crook, C. (2005). From promises to practices: The fate of educational software in the home. *Technology, Pedagogy and Education, 14*(1), 107–125.

Lau, S., & Roeser, R. W. (2002). Cognitive abilities and motivational processes in high school students' situational engagement and achievement in science. *Educational Assessment, 8*, 139–162.

Lent, R. W., Brown, S. D., & Larkin, K. C. (1984). Relation of self-efficacy expectations to academic achievement and persistence. *Journal of Counseling Psychology, 31*, 356–362.

Moos, D. C., & Marroquin, E. (2010). Multimedia, hypermedia, and hypertext: Motivation considered and reconsidered. *Computers in Human Behavior, 26*, 265–276.

Pintrich, P. R., & Schunk, D. H. (2002). *Motivation in education: Theory, research, and application.* Upper Saddle River, NJ: Merrill Prentice Hall.

Wigfield, A. (1994). Expectancy-value theory of achievement motivation: A developmental perspective. *Educational Psychology Review, 6*(1), 49–78.

Wigfield, A., & Eccles, J. (1992). The development of achievement task values: A theoretical analysis. *Developmental Review, 12*, 265–310.

Wigfield, A., & Eccles, J. S. (2000). Expectancy-value theory of motivation. *Contemporary Educational Psychology, 25*(1), 68–81.

DIESEL-X: A Game-Based Tool for Early Risk Detection of Dyslexia in Preschoolers

Luc Geurts, Vero Vanden Abeele, Véronique Celis, Jelle Husson,
Lieven Van den Audenaeren, Leen Loyez, Ann Goeleven, Jan Wouters,
and Pol Ghesquière

Abstract DIESEL-X is a computer game that was developed to detect a high risk for developing dyslexia in preschoolers. The game includes three mini-games that test the player on three skills that are considered to yield outcome measures that predict the onset of dyslexia: the detection threshold of frequency modulated tones, a test on phonological awareness in which the player has to identify words that have the same phonetic ending, and a test on letter knowledge. In order to keep the motivation of the player high during testing, these tests are embedded in a computer game. We discuss the participatory design process that was adopted to design and develop the game, the rationale behind the design decisions, and we describe the resulting games.

Keywords Early detection of dyslexia • Games for dyslexia • Games for preschoolers • Participatory design

L. Geurts (✉) • V. Vanden Abeele • J. Husson • L. Van den Audenaeren
e-Media Lab, KU Leuven, Andreas Vesaliusstraat 13, Leuven 3000, Belgium
e-mail: luc.geurts@kuleuven.be; vero.vandenabeele@kuleuven.be;
jelle.husson@kuleuven.be; lieven.vandenaudenaeren@kuleuven.be

V. Celis • P. Ghesquière
Parenting and Special Education Research Unit, KU Leuven,
L. Vanderkelenstraat 32, Box 3765, Leuven 3000, Belgium
e-mail: veronique.celis@ppw.kuleuven.be; pol.ghesquiere@ppw.kuleuven.be

L. Loyez • A. Goeleven
Department of Speech Language Pathology (MUCLA), University Hospitals
Leuven Belgium, Kapucijnenvoer 33, Leuven 3000, Belgium
e-mail: leen.loyez@uzleuven.be; ann.goeleven@uzleuven.be

J. Wouters
ExpORL, Department of Neurosciences, KU Leuven,
Herestraat 49, Box 721, Leuven 3000, Belgium
e-mail: jan.wouters@med.kuleuven.be

© Springer International Publishing Switzerland 2015
J. Torbeyns et al. (eds.), *Describing and Studying Domain-Specific Serious Games*,
Advances in Game-Based Learning, DOI 10.1007/978-3-319-20276-1_7

Introduction

What Is Dyslexia?

Dyslexia is a neurodevelopmental disorder that is manifested by persistent reading difficulties in children who otherwise possess adequate intelligence and motivation (Gersons-Wolfensberger & Ruijssenaars, 1997; Shaywitz, 1998). With a prevalence of about 5–10 %, dyslexia is perhaps the most common and the most studied of all learning disabilities. Hence, the underlying causes of dyslexia have been the subject of many studies and of fierce debate among researchers. There is now a growing consensus that these insoluble and tenacious reading difficulties reflect a deficiency in phonologic awareness (Snowling, 2000). According to this phonologic-deficit hypothesis, people with dyslexia lack an awareness that words can be broken down into smaller units of sounds. People with dyslexia seem to be less sensitive for the sound structure of language—which is needed to recognize rhyming words, or words starting or ending with the same sound (Bradley & Bryant, 1983). In turn, this phonological deficit is assumed to be caused by difficulties in low-level auditory temporal processing. People with dyslexia tend to have difficulties processing linguistic and nonlinguistic stimuli that are short and enter the nervous system in rapid succession (Bailey & Snowling, 2002; Farmer & Klein, 1995; McArthur & Bishop, 2001). They tend to have difficulties with degraded speech perception or speech-in-noise (Boets, Wouters, van Wieringen, & Ghesquière, 2006a; McBride-Chang, 1995). Additionally, they show an impaired perception of dynamic aspects in the auditory signal itself, like amplitude and frequency modulations (Menell, McAnally, & Stein, 1999; Talcott et al., 2000; Talcott & Witton, 2002; Witton et al., 1998).

How Is Dyslexia Diagnosed?

While the underlying causes of dyslexia have become more and more disclosed, the actual diagnosis of dyslexia is still somewhat obtuse. The diagnosis of dyslexia is simply based on the prevalence of a child's poorly developed reading and writing skills despite normal intelligence, and despite remedial efforts. This implies that an official diagnosis can only be made after the negative consequences of dyslexia have manifested themselves. This poses a paradox, as with many developmental disorders, dyslexia should be detected as soon as possible. The younger the age at the start of remedial treatment, the larger the effect that can be attained (Fawcett & Nicolson, 1995; Hintikka, Mikko, & Lyytinen, 2005; Lefly & Pennington, 1991; Lyytinen & Erskine, 2006). Ideally, early detection of dyslexia enables preventive actions, in order to prepare the child *before* formal reading and writing instruction.

The problem is that no classical reading or writing tests can be taken from preschoolers as obviously children at this age have not learned yet to read and write. However, based on the growing understanding of the phonological deficit and delayed auditory temporal processing underlying dyslexia, other tests can be taken

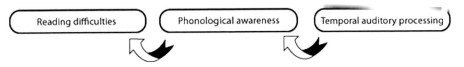

Fig. 1 According to the phonological deficit model, reading difficulties are caused by a lack of phonological awareness which in turn is caused by problems with temporal auditory processing

at this age, that allow for the detection of high risks for dyslexia. These tests do not target reading and writing skills, but include measurements of basal auditory and visual processing skills, speech-in-noise perception tasks, frequency modulation detection, end-phoneme recognition, rapid automatic naming tasks, and measurements of verbal short-term memory. In a series of experiments, Boets and colleagues have demonstrated that such tests can differentiate high risk preschoolers from low risk preschoolers (Boets, Ghesquière, van Wieringen, & Wouters, 2007; Boets, Wouters, van Wieringen, Desmedt, & Ghesquière, 2008; Boets et al., 2006a; Boets, Wouters, van Wieringen, & Ghesquière, 2006b). These studies confirm the theory that more basic processes in the brain are responsible for the observed deficits in learning to read and write (Fig. 1), yet they also show manners of assessing dyslexia before reading and writing difficulties have manifested themselves. The performance on these tests is a good predictor for the development of dyslexia.

However, in the discussions of aforementioned studies, Boets and colleagues also report it was difficult to grab and maintain the children's attention throughout the tests (Boets et al., 2006a; Laneau, Boets, Moonen, van Wieringen, & Wouters, 2005) which often lasted longer than 1 h. Even though the tests contained graphical embellishments (i.e., drawings and sounds), children's interest waned during testing. Consequently, test results showed a lot of variability, certainly when assessing threshold values where the "best performance" of the child is to be measured. This is typical for temporal auditory processing tests where children were tested on their perception of degraded speech, speech-in-noise, frequency modulation (i.e., detecting pitch variations) or amplitude variations. Some of these tests use a staircase procedure. Such a staircase begins with an easy detection task (e.g., which of the tree following sounds is different from the others, with one sound being markedly different) but then the manipulations gradually become more and more subtle, until the child makes a mistake. At this point, the staircase "reverses," and the task becomes easier again. When the child completes the task correct again, this triggers another reversal and the task becomes harder again. Such a staircase procedure is necessary for finding the threshold values of children; however, it is a lengthy procedure, and it is set out to find the level of difficulty where children "fail" to perform correctly. Therefore, not surprisingly, significant differences in Boets et al. experiments' results were found, but only at the group level. The results confirmed that the group of children with a high risk profile for dyslexia performed significantly worse on the tests at preschool age, compared to a group of children with a low risk for dyslexia. However, at an individual level, no reliable predictions could be made. Boets et al. stressed that more accurate measurements are needed to allow for risk detection at the individual level (Boets et al., 2006a).

Game-Based Remediation and Assessment of Dyslexia

More accurate measurements can possibly be achieved by finding better ways to increase the motivation of the child to take part in the test, and to attain a longer attention span. One way to increase a child's motivation and attention is via digital games (Gee, 2003; Kirriemuir & McFarlane, 2004; Malone, 1980; Prensky, 2001). By offering interactive and immersive audio-visual worlds, game designers realize an environment that rouses a child's senses and interests and stimulates exploration. But more importantly, well-designed games tailor to the skills of individual players, by continuously assessing performances and adapting the difficulty level of the task. By offering challenges that match the abilities of the players, game designers create a psychological state known as flow (Csikszentmihalyi, 1990; Sweetser & Wyeth, 2005). During a flow state, a player loses his sense of self and his sense of time and place. Flow is gratifying in and of itself; it is an intrinsic motivation that keeps a player playing. Moreover, this characteristic ensures that players deliver their best performances. As aforementioned, best performance measuring is necessary for temporal auditory processing tests. Finally, games offer reward systems that motivate players (Wang & Sun, 2011). Through scoring systems, experience points, badges that can be unlocked, etc. players are motivated to keep on delivering their best performance (Sailer, Hense, Mandl, & Klevers, 2013). These assumptions with regard to attention, motivation, and games have been confirmed by user evaluation and user testing of games with preschoolers (Barendregt, Bouwhuis, de Ridder, & Bekker, 2006; Hanna, Neapolitan, & Risden, 2004; Markopoulos & Bekker, 2003; Zaman, 2008). These researchers have demonstrated that while traditional user tests with preschoolers should last no longer than 30 min (Hanna et al., 2004), this time can be doubled when testing games (Zaman, 2008). It is therefore a valid assumption that administering "boring" tests via a game will lengthen the attention span of the preschooler. In sum, a well-designed computer game can provide a motivating environment, resulting in preschoolers' increased attention span and hence a higher accuracy and thus a better assessment.

Game-based assessment of dyslexia. The unraveling of the phonological deficit underlying dyslexia is combined with an increasing confidence in neuroplasticity (Merzenich et al., 1996), and the popularity of serious games (Michael & Chen, 2005) has spurred researchers to develop new game-based therapies to train phonological awareness, e.g., FastFoward (Tallal et al., 1996; Temple et al., 2003), Letterprins (Steenbeek-Planting et al., 2013), Nessy (Singleton, Thomas, & Horne, 2000), Dyseggxia (Rello, Bayarri, & Gorriz, 2012). However, we stress that the focus of this research project is not on the remediation of neurological deficits, but rather on the early detection of dyslexia, in preschoolers, before formal reading and writing education has been given. As a consequence, this tool can be considered as a screening tool, but not as a diagnosis instrument.

Game-based *assessment* of dyslexia in preschoolers is less common. To the best of the authors' knowledge, no validated game-based screening test for preschoolers exist today. Perhaps, most closely is the Lucid Rapid Dyslexia Screening tool (Singleton et al., 2000). The tests included in this screening tool are phonological processing (i.e., a rhyming exercise), auditory sequential memory (remembering sequences of animal names), and visual verbal integration memory (remembering sequences of colors). The Lucid Rapid Dyslexia Screening test is standardized for British English speaking children however, which renders it useless for preschoolers outside of Great Britain. Moreover, the screening tool is also very much a test battery and not really a game (Juul, 2011). There is no use of simulations or animations, no rewards, no story line, no character development, etc. Another noteworthy effort is Magno-Fly (Ferwerda & Rehon, 2007) by Gaggi and colleagues, who are also in the process of developing serious games aimed at detecting children with a high risk for the development of dyslexia (Gaggi, Galiazzo, Palazzi, Facoetti, & Franceschini, 2012). However, the games they are developing underscore an alternative model of dyslexia, which attributes dyslexia to the dysfunction of cells involved in processing sensory information in general (Stein & Walsh, 1997). This is a controversial hypothesis as sensory dysfunction is absent in many cases of dyslexia and has no clear causal link to reading problems (Ramus, 2003). Hence, their game-based assessment does not underlie the phonological deficit and is therefore more experimental in nature. However, thus far, no information has been given with respect to validation.

Given the lack of game-based assessment in the area of Flanders, the DIESEL-X project was conceived. However, creating a good serious game is not straightforward. On the one hand, there is always the threat of sugar coating: a superficial embellishment of what is actually a boring task with a couple of fun animations and a little bit of game play. Good serious game design requires a seamless integration of the serious goal and game dynamics. The aim of serious games is "stealth learning" or in this case "stealth testing" (e.g., Shute, 2011): the children should be unaware of the fact that they are tested and the overall game experience should simply be fun. On the other hand, the fun factor should not intrude upon the serious goals. In the following chapters, we present the design process and the result: DIESEL-X, a game-based tool to test whether a five-year-old has a high risk of developing dyslexia.

A Player-Centered, Iterative, Interdisciplinary and Integrated Game Design and Development Process

In order to reconcile the intricacies of a game design process with the serious goals of dyslexia assessment, a player-centered, iterative, interdisciplinary and integrated (P-III) design process was followed (Vanden Abeele et al., 2012).

Player-centered process. In digital game design and development, player involvement is often limited to participation in usability and play tests (Pagulayan, Keeker, Wixon, Romero, & Fuller, 2003). Although such play tests are necessary, they do not offer players to participate in the creative part of the game design itself. This increases the risk of a self-referential design process, where designers or developers fall back on an I-methodology and design games as if they were for themselves (Oudshoorn & Pinch, 2003; Vanden Abeele & Van Rompaey, 2006). Even *if* designers were capable of accurately reliving their own childhood memories and experiences and understanding cognitive, affective, and behavioral characteristics, preschoolers of today have grown up with digital games, and relate to it differently. Preschoolers of today are not the preschoolers of 30 years ago. Therefore, the P-III process specifies methods to involve the player throughout the design process: from ethnographically inspired inquiries at the start of the project, participatory design sessions during the design phase to play tests during the development, to ensure that the result is "meaningful play" (Deterding, Dixon, Khaled, & Nacke, 2011; Salen & Zimmerman, 2003). The specific methods employed during the design process of DIESEL-X will be detailed below.

Interdisciplinary team. Moreover, P-III stresses the importance of including all stakeholders, including, but not limited to, end-users, as co-designers of their technology. In the P-III design process of DIESEL-X, we involved the "creators" of the game (game designer, game developer, and digital artist), two dyslexia experts (a dyslexia researcher and a clinical specialist), several preschoolers, and one preschool teacher to create a truly interdisciplinary game design and development team.

Iterative process. P-III emphasizes the importance of early empirical evaluations with players via concept designs, paper prototypes, and early prototypes. During the design and development process, the application is presented to all stakeholders, to be discussed, tried out and particularly tested and evaluated. These empirical measurements feed the design process in a formative iterative manner. In DIESEL-X, over the course of 18 months, several prototypes were created and tested with preschoolers.

Integrated play and testing. Finally, P-III stresses the importance of integrating the serious goal with the game mechanic in a seamless manner, i.e., games should not be used as a treat in between boring tasks, but rather the task itself should be the game challenge. This requires a careful inspection of the task at hand and which game mechanic maps well to this task. How this was done will be detailed further below.

In addition to the four pillars discussed above, the P-III prescribes three phases: user and tasks analysis, game design, and game development, each with their own steps (Fig. 2). Whereas the illustration of the P-III process might suggest strict delineated boundaries, in reality these boundaries are fluid. During the design and development phase, a further understanding of the users and tasks is inevitable and in fact desirable. And obviously, some design ideas might already linger in the back of a designer's mind during the user and task analysis. Moreover, play tests during development might inspire the team to add some features in the design. Nevertheless, these phases demarcate the broad stages within the design process.

Phase 1: User and Task Analysis

The first phase of the P-III method focuses on a better understanding of the users, tasks (in this case, the tests) and the context in which assessment of dyslexia takes place. The result is not simply a report with a list of requirements, but rather a deep

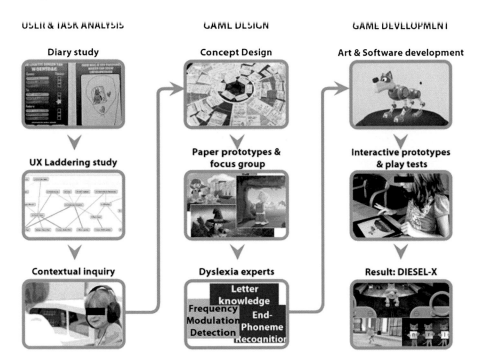

Fig. 2 P-III: A player-centered, iterative, interdisciplinary and integrated method for game design and development of game-based assessment of dyslexia

understanding of the problem domain and the players, and the many implicit rules. In addition, this phase aims to create an implicit bonding between researchers, designers, developers, and the target group, in this case preschoolers.

Diary study. We started our player-centered design process (Vanden Abeele et al., 2012) with a diary study. We wanted to understand better how and what constitutes "fun" for a preschooler, anno 2011 (Zaman & Vanden Abeele, 2007). Therefore, 15 preschoolers (2006) were recruited via two primary schools. These children were asked to keep a diary for 1 week. In this diary, children were asked to list their three favorite activities on three categories: (1) (computer) games, (2) television programs, and (3) activities in a general sense. From these three categories, preschoolers were asked to choose the most preferred item and to describe it via three key words. That way we wanted to get an overview of which characteristics appeal to 5-year-olds. Obviously, parental help was expected when filling out the diary. In addition, a fun daily task was included (e.g., make a drawing or a paper collage). These daily tasks were given as a sensitizing activity to ensure that the preschooler would feel involved (Visser, Stappers, van der Lugt, & Sanders, 2005). This "diary-week" was followed by an interview where the preschooler and researcher went through the diary together. It is important to note that the researchers here were equally game designers, game developers, and digital artists. Hence, this in-depth interview provided the creators of the game with a direct contact to end-users, which is paramount to avoid

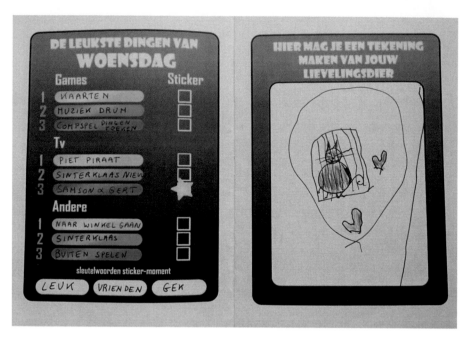

Fig. 3 Excerpt of a boy's diary

a self-referential design. This interview took place at the child's house, so he or she felt at ease and could demonstrate when things were unclear to the researcher ("Show and tell"). A focus was on *deep understanding* of the target audience and their wishes. Figure 3 depicts an excerpt of a page in a boy's diary.

User experience laddering. After the diary study, a User Experience (UX) Laddering study (Zaman & Abeele, 2010) was conducted. UX Laddering is a combination of observations of preschoolers playing games, preference ranking exercises, and depth interviews. Twenty-five preschoolers were asked to play eight selected games, designed specifically for preschoolers, and then asked to rank them from most preferred to least preferred and to explain their preference. The aim of this study was to unveil which game attributes (i.e., game mechanics) link to specific gameplay preferences (game aesthetics). The results of this study is what is called a hierarchical value map (see Fig. 4), a graphical representation of how in-game attributes link to specific game experiences that are valued by preschoolers. Hence, this study provided a set of meaningful and useful design guidelines, directed at this young target group. This study is described in more detail in (Celis et al., 2013); its results will be briefly summarized here. Preschoolers seem to enjoy *collecting different items* through the game as this serves both as a challenge and as a reward system. This gives them a sense of victory and ultimately realizes a challenging gameplay-experience. *Touch input* is also clearly preferred

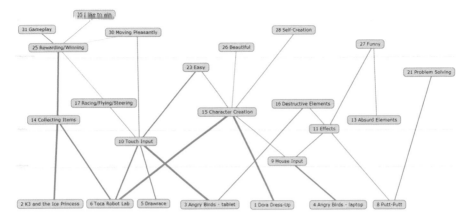

Fig. 4 The hierarchical value map: An overview of meaningful linkages across attributes, consequences, and values

over more classical input (keyboard or mouse), showing that preschoolers like the intuitiveness and physicality of interacting with their hands and fingers. *Character creation* allows for creative expression and is often implemented by providing a standard avatar, which can be outfitted with different clothes and accessories. Finally, implementing *visceral effects and visual gags, destructive elements* (exploding items, breaking walls, etc.) contribute to the aesthetic "Sense-Pleasure." This confirms that preschoolers have a sense of how things should be in reality and find it humorous when things deviate from the norm.

Contextual inquiries with dyslexia experts. Finally, to better understand the problem space of assessment of dyslexia, game designers and game developers followed dyslexia researchers during two days while they were conducting the traditional tests (Laneau et al., 2005) in schools, with preschoolers. This study was done according to the contextual inquiry method (Beyer & Holtzblatt, 1997). This implies that the observations were done in context (i.e., at the schools where the actual assessments would take place) and that the DIESEL-X researchers adhered to a master-apprentice model, where they were to learn from the dyslexia researchers as if they were interns. The open-ended nature of the contextual inquiries and the focus on observations, make it possible to reveal tacit and implicit knowledge of which dyslexia researchers themselves are not consciously aware. Tacit knowledge has traditionally been very hard for researchers to uncover. These observations contributed to a further understanding of the specific tests and measurements that needed to be embedded in the game, but more importantly of the context in which this needs to happen. These contextual inquiries provided insight in the problems of testing children in a school environment, with multiple interrupts by other children and teachers, obsolete ICT-infrastructure, the temporal structure of a school day with many playtime, the lack of reserved space for testing, etc.

Phase 2: Game Design

At the end of this user and task analysis phase, the Diesel-X researchers had established a deep understanding of the problem domain, and established report with their target group of preschoolers. At this point, the design phase can start during which the obtained insights are translated into design concepts.

Co-design sessions. Two brainstorm sessions were organized, taking several constraints into account: (1) the results of the first phase, i.e., the knowledge on how preschoolers experience the classical tests and the representative computer games, (2) the guidelines on motivational factors of a computer game for preschoolers, and (3) the goal of the game, i.e., taking accurate psychophysical measurements within a school environment. Adhering to a player-centered design methodology, all stakeholders were involved: a game designer, game developer, and digital artist, two dyslexia experts (a dyslexia researcher and a clinical specialist), several preschoolers, one preschool teacher, a researcher experienced with the traditional tests, and two kindergarten teachers). At the end of these brainstorm sessions, a list of ideas was created regarding the content and design of the game (see Fig. 5). The most valuable ideas were identified and three game concepts were conceived on the basis of these ideas.

Game concepts and focus groups. These three game ideas where transformed into three game concept (see Fig. 6) documents by the game designer and digital artist. Every concept was a one-page document which contained a splash image with the title, the protagonist(s) in their environment, and an antagonist where applicable. Furthermore, every document contained a brief description of the narrative and the goal of the game.

These concepts were again evaluated by the users (preschoolers) of the game via focus groups. In particular, 20 children (15 girls, 5 boys) of one kindergarten class participated. These children were divided into three focus groups of each six or seven participants. The focus group interviews were adapted to the characteristics and developmental limitations of preschoolers (Fuchs, 2005; Morgan, 1996). Firstly, the evaluation took place in their class room. This natural context increases the reliability and validity of the data (Golafshani, 2003; Patton, 1990) and minimizes the power differential between the researcher and the preschoolers (Eder & Fingerson, 2002) as the preschoolers are in a familiar place whereas the researcher is not. Secondly, at the start of the focus group, the researcher presented the three different prototypes, by means of a story of each approximately five minutes, accompanied by some illustrations (see Fig. 6).

Every story (i.e., game concept) was read aloud, illustrated through the visual image of the game environment and followed by a short discussion. Possible order effects were being counterbalanced by reading the three stories in different sequences. Next, every preschooler was given three small cards, depicting the three game concepts, followed by a voting session. After explaining the three game concepts (i.e., listening to the three stories and looking at their respective artwork), the children were asked to choose the concept card they liked most, but in such a way that the other children and the researcher could not see their preferred game

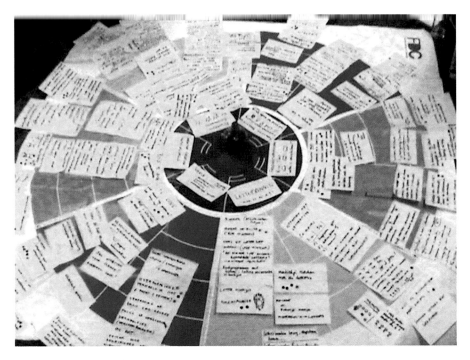

Fig. 5 Result of the first brainstorm session

Fig. 6 Visual example of the three game concepts: (**a**) Diesel-X, (**b**) Liesl de Heks, and (**c**) Lex & Lilly

concept. Upon a signal of the researcher, the preschoolers unveiled their choice (they flipped their chosen card), all at the same time. With the chosen card in front of them, preschoolers were prompted to explain their choice. This process mitigated the risk for group influences and/or social desirability with respect to the researcher. Results showed that, even after this individual voting setup, 18 out of 20 preschoolers preferred DIESEL-X over the two other concepts. The boys liked Diesel ("a smart robot dog with wings"), the girls identified with Alex ("a though girly-girl") and they all liked chasing the mean cats ("I want to throw them in the bath with a lot of dirty mud"). As a result, the theme of "whizz kid Alex, and her robot dog having to save the city from obnoxious cats" was chosen to elaborate further.

Dyslexia experts. Finally, in close consultation with dyslexia experts, several tests were discussed that could possibly be embedded in the game. Three criteria had to be satisfied:

1. *Feasibility* of embedding these tests into a game-based environment. In other words, the test had to be suitable for computerization. Some tests require an administrator to carefully listen to the child's answer, hence requiring a level of automated speech recognition beyond what is currently feasible.
2. *Prediction rate success of the test.* The tests had to be scientifically accepted as a valid means to flag dyslexia. In addition, there was a wish for including tests at the different levels e.g., at the level of reading difficulties itself (e.g., letter recognition), at the level of phonological awareness (e.g., end-phoneme recognition), and at the level of temporal auditory processing (e.g., detecting frequency modulations).
3. *Integrated play and testing.* The test had to allow for an integration of a game mechanic in addition to the test itself. However, the test outcomes should only depend on the player's ability to perform well on the tasks at hand. In other words, the game dynamics should not interfere with the actual test data and yet motivate the player to perform at his or her best.

Upon these criteria, and following several discussions among the interdisciplinary team, three tests were chosen to be embedded in the game. The first test is a *frequency modulation (FM) detection task*, which tests the subject on a very basic sound perception skill (Boets et al., 2006a). The task is to discriminate an unmodulated pure (sinusoidal) tone with a frequency-modulated tone. Typically, an adaptive procedure is used to detect the threshold. Initially, a highly modulated tone is presented that is easy to recognize. As long as the subject's response is correct, the modulation depth is decreased. A three-interval three-alternative-forced-choice procedure was used, meaning that three tones are presented from which one (randomly selected) is frequency modulated. The second task is measuring *phonological awareness*, more specifically the subject has to recognize words that end with the same phoneme (e.g., glass and boss) (Boets et al., 2007). In each trial, four alternatives are presented with one of them ending with the same phoneme as a given reference word. The third task is assessing the subject's *letter knowledge* (Hulme, Bowyer-Crane, Carroll, Duff, & Snowling, 2012). When designing games that test the subject on specific skills, special care should be taken that possible confounding variables such as prior game experience, spatial skills, or problem-solving skills do not interfere with the test outcomes and affect the validity of the tests.

Game Development

Upon these choices, the game development phase started. Over a period of 18 months, the game was gradually developed and tested. The DIESEL-X game consists of three mini-games, each embedding a different test (FM detection, end-phoneme, and letter knowledge), and that were developed and tested in consecutive order. Then, these mini-games were embedded in an overarching story line and a reward system was included.

Art and software development. The game was developed with the Unity engine[1] to run on Android tablets, specifically the Samsung Galaxy Tab 2. We chose the Unity engine due to its expansive community, affordable price, and ease of publishing code to multiple platforms. Art assets were produced using 3D studio Max[2] and Photoshop.[3] Auditory instructions and game dialogue files were recorded with professional actors in a studio. Player data were stored locally on the tablets using an SQLite database, and subsequently synchronized to a server-side MySQL database via a secure web service. Test administrators could inspect the data via this online web platform. More details on the logged data and the web platform are given in Plong, Vanden Abeele, and Geurts (2014).

Prototypes and play tests. Hence over a period of 18 months, 6 play tests with preschoolers were conducted. Intermediate versions of each mini-game were played by preschoolers, which allowed to correct for bugs, to balance the game with the abilities of the young players, and to ensure that the games can be played without the need of supervision. The focus of these play tests was "formative," meaning that the results were fed into the development process again, hence resulting in an iterative development process. As such, many of the play tests were conducted with the designer and developer present. The reason to continue this iterative feedback process is to guarantee that the final product still meets the ultimate goal: a game that is both fun to play and that allows for accurate measurements of the players abilities.

Results

The DIESEL-X game encompasses three mini-games, each of which has four levels. Hence, each mini-game is revisited four times in a linear, predefined sequence, so every preschooler is presented the same challenges. In between mini-games, the story unfolds through cinematic sequences. The game is meant to be completed in one session, which takes approximately 1 h, the exact time depends on how long preschoolers take to complete certain mini-games.

---

[1] http://unity3d.com/

[2] http://www.autodesk.com/products/3ds-max/overview

[3] http://www.photoshop.com/

Tailoring the Game for Preschoolers

First of all, the art style of the game was developed specifically to appeal to young children. The game and its cinematic sequences are rendered in 3D with a cartoony look and feel, with vivid colors and exaggerated proportions (see Figs. 8, 9, and 10). Care has been given to avoid gender stereotypes and to develop content that appeals to boys and girls. The preschoolers are guided with clear auditory instructions, which can be replayed at any time.

Story Line

In DIESEL-X, an evil gang of cat burglars has been creating uproar in the city. The policemen are helpless and the city lies in disarray. Luckily, one brave little girl, Alex, is smart enough to come up with a solution to tackle the cats. Players take on the role of Diesel, the robot-dog that was created by Alex. Together, they will help get rid of the pesky cat burglars once and for all!

Content

At the start of the game, a movie is shown that introduces the situation of the city and its rogue cats. This movie is meant purely to engage the children playing the game. From then on, the player will be prompted to play through the mini-games, by means of a blinking indicator on a map of the city (see Fig. 7). The preschooler has 12 "play tests," as each of the 3 mini-games has 4 levels, hence is to be played 4 times. However, with every level, the mini-game is placed within a new part of the city; although the game mechanic for every mini-game remains the same, the visual styling is different. After completing part of a mini-game, the player either unlocks a new color or gear to customize Diesel, or the player receives a spare part to build a space rocket. This process is repeated until the three mini-games have been played four times and are thus completed. During the course of the game, the player also works towards the end goal of building a complete rocket, necessary for shooting the cats to the moon. When the rocket is complete, the player is rewarded with an ending cinematic seeing the cats transported to the moon.

Mini-Games

As aforementioned, three tests (Letter knowledge, FM detection, end-phoneme recognition) were converted into three mini-games.

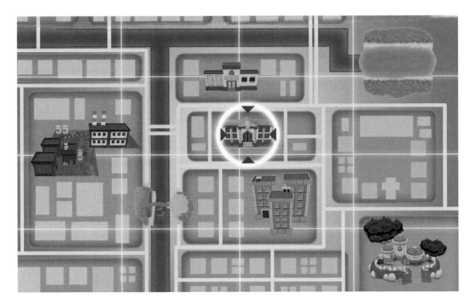

Fig. 7 Map of the city in which the DIESEL-X game takes place. The player has to enter several areas in the city in order to complete a task

Fig. 8 The "Line Up" mini-game showing the main character, the robot dog Diesel, in the middle. Guided by instructions from Alex (girl at the *left*) and a commissioner (at the *right*), the player has to point to the "guilty" cat. The police officer mentions the letter held by that cat

Line Up (letter knowledge). "Line Up" works like a traditional police line up, where the victim of a crime has to identify the suspect (see Fig. 8). The players will have to use their knowledge of the letters of the alphabet to point out the right suspect. The commissioner introduces one of the victims, and the cat burglars are

Fig. 9 The "Chase" mini-game. Diesel chases three cats through the streets of the city. Each cat makes a sound, one of these being frequency modulated (the other two are pure tones). The player has to point to the cat generating this FM tone. As long as the player answers correctly, the modulation depth is decreased

called on stage. They are all holding a certain letter in their hands. The victim then shortly explains what happened and points out which of the cat is the suspect by calling him by the letter he is holding. This letter is repeated by the commissioner. The player now has to indicate the cat with the right letter so Diesel can point at him. Hence, this game tests the player's letter knowledge, which is known as a strong indicator for dyslexia (Hulme et al., 2012).

Chase (FM detection task). In "Chase," cat burglars have to be chased throughout the city, where Diesel tries to retrieve stolen diamonds and money from a bank robbery (see Fig. 9). The player will use auditory cues to detect which cat carries the stolen goods. Every time Diesel barks, the three cats being chased will come to a halt. Every cat is carrying a bag with stolen goods, which is "scanned" by Diesel. While scanning, the player hears either a pure tone (sinusoid) or a frequency modulated tone. Only one of the cats is carrying diamonds (FM tone), the other ones are carrying stones as a decoy (pure tone). The goal for the player is to point the odd one out, with every dilemma increasing in difficulty. It gets harder to detect which sound was the one with frequency modulation, since the modulation depth decreases as long as correct answers are given (according to a staircase procedure) (Boets et al., 2006b).

Lost objects (end-phoneme recognition). "Lost Objects" takes places in several abandoned locations throughout the city, where the cat burglars have hidden their secret stash of stolen goods (see Fig. 10). The player will have to identify which items to retrieve, relying on their recognition of the end-phonemes of said items. The game takes the player from the sewers to the rooftops, to an underwater setting, and finally

Fig. 10 The "Lost Objects" mini-game. Diesel finds several objects, and of them was stolen by the cats. Alex gives indications by mentioning a word that ends with the same phoneme. The player has to point to the "right" object

into a burning factory. Every time Diesel comes to a halt, five items are presented to the player. Alex, via radio, reads the names of the items aloud, and asks the player to indicate the item which has the same end-phoneme as a certain reference item.

Integrated Play and Learning

From the previous paragraphs, it should be clear that special care has been put into the game design of the mini-game, ensuring that the challenge at hand directly maps onto the skill being tested. However, at the same time care needs to be given that the mini-games only assess the player's letter knowledge, end-phoneme recognition and FM threshold, and not their overall gaming skills. Therefore, any game mechanic that would involve complex hand–eye coordination or require timely responses has been avoided. Preschoolers simply needed to tap large objects, and there is no time pressure. Preschoolers can take as long as they please. Play tests confirmed that preschoolers understood the tasks and did not experience difficulty entering their selection.

Motivation

The main hypothesis underlying DIESEL-X is that a game-based assessment increases motivation; hence, it increases the attention span. Therefore, besides the above challenges, several motivational aspects were added to the games.

Rewards. First of all, as mentioned before, preschoolers like to collect things in games, so the game was designed with collectable rewards in mind. However, we focused on intrinsic motivation; hence, rewards should have meaning for the players and be related to their actions. In this case, upon completion the player can unlock new colors for Diesel, playing with a different color Diesel through the rest of the game. Other rewards include unlocking new weapons, unlocking pieces of a rocket to get rid of all those cats, and unlocking new environments to play in. Also, the game rewards the player with auditory comments of both the commissioner and Alex to compliment the player on his actions.

Feedback. Because the game is meant as an assessment tool and not a learning tool, giving feedback about the correctness of the players' actions is tricky. Giving feedback about being right or wrong might indeed start a learning process for the player which might pollute some of the data being collected. Hence, we provided feedback indicating that the game registered the action of the player, but not with respect to the quality of the action itself.

In Line Up, the player needs to select the requested letter. If the game would give the preschooler feedback about the letters he or she selects, he or she might learn new letters while playing the game. Therefore, the choice was made to give the player some neutral feedback, acknowledging the action. We would like to point out that the game does not tell the player whether he or she was correct or not, because it is not the game's purpose of teaching the player any letter knowledge.[4] Visually, the player will see Diesel attacking the selected cat. The auditory feedback is given by Alex who will compliment the player on catching another cat.

In the Chase mini-game, correct response feedback is allowed, as is common in detection threshold measurements. Learning through feedback is considered less of an interfering factor. Also, the player needs to learn this task because identifying a frequency modulated tone from a pure tone is new for preschoolers. As a result, the visual and auditory feedback indicates whether the correct response is selected. The player will receive a bag with money or a diamond when a correct answer is given, and a bag with bricks in the other case. Also, when the player selects the right cat, Alex will compliment him or her on his action and the cat he caught will cry. When the player selects the wrong cat, he or she was tricked and he or she will see the cat being caught laughing.

In the Lost Objects mini-game, learning through feedback is avoided again. So just like in the Letter Knowledge mini-game, the player will receive neutral, acknowledging, and encouraging feedback. Only in the first two trials, he or she will receive feedback about being right or wrong. The game will first show the player what to do to make sure he or she understands his or her task. From the third trial on, the player will no longer receive correct response feedback, but will still be complimented on finding a lost item.

---

[4] In fact, giving feedback that is neutral turned out to be difficult as children tend to interpret feedback signals as positive or negative anyhow. Several iterations were necessary to design this feedback that was perceived as neutral. As a consequence, during play tests children sometimes turned to the test administrator to ask whether their selection was correct.

Discussion and Future Work

As illustrated by the description of the mini-games, the design guidelines mentioned before were taken into account. Touch input ensures that interacting with the game is intuitive. Players can collect different items throughout the game (gear for Diesel, spare parts of the rocket), giving them a sense of mastery. Character creation (unlocking colors and gear for Diesel) is included allowing for creative expression. Finally, showing different funny animations and a variety of environments between and during the tests ensures that playing the game keeps on being engaging in a visceral and humorous manner.

Whatever the performance of the players on the test, encouraging feedback is given throughout the game. This gives both dyslexic and non-dyslexic players a sense of mastery and success, which is needed to keep the motivation at a sufficient level. Prior experience on gaming is made irrelevant by adopting game mechanics that do not rely on typical game skills, such as fast and accurate eye–hand coordination. Although the evaluation of the game is beyond the scope of this chapter, empirical evaluation proofed that preschoolers preferred this game over the traditional tests and had no problem with sustaining attention over an hour.

Further studies are now being conducted in order to find the critical measures that allow for the detection of a high risk for dyslexia.

Conclusion

The DIESEL-X game-based assessment tool is one of the first attempts to incorporate lengthy and boring tests within a game-based application. Further studies are now being conducted to investigate the reliability and validity of the test results. If successful, this project might be an important first step towards a novel way of diagnosing neurological disorders in young children in general.

References

Bailey, P. J., & Snowling, M. J. (2002). Auditory processing and the development of language and literacy. *British Medical Bulletin, 63*(1), 135–146. doi:10.1093/bmb/63.1.135.

Barendregt, W., Bouwhuis, D., de Ridder, H., & Bekker, M. (2006). *Evaluating fun and usability in computer games with children*. Technische Universiteit Eindhoven. Retrieved from http://library.tue.nl/catalog/LinkToVubis.csp?DataBib=6:602065.

Beyer, H., & Holtzblatt, K. (1997). *Contextual design: A customer-centered approach to systems designs* (1st ed.). New York, NY: Morgan Kaufmann.

Boets, B., Ghesquière, P., van Wieringen, A., & Wouters, J. (2007). Speech perception in preschoolers at family risk for dyslexia: Relations with low-level auditory processing and phonological ability. *Brain and Language, 101*(1), 19–30. doi:10.1016/j.bandl.2006.06.009.

Boets, B., Wouters, J., van Wieringen, A., Desmedt, B., & Ghesquière, P. (2008). Modelling relations between sensory processing, speech perception, orthographic and phonological ability, and literacy achievement. *Brain and Language, 106*(1), 29–40. doi:10.1016/j.bandl.2007.12.004.

Boets, B., Wouters, J., van Wieringen, A., & Ghesquière, P. (2006a). Auditory temporal information processing in preschool children at family risk for dyslexia: Relations with phonological abilities and developing literacy skills. *Brain and Language, 97*(1), 64–79. doi:10.1016/j. bandl.2005.07.026.

Boets, B., Wouters, J., van Wieringen, A., & Ghesquière, P. (2006b). Coherent motion detection in preschool children at family risk for dyslexia. *Vision Research, 46*(4), 527–535. doi:10.1016/j. visres.2005.08.023.

Bradley, L., & Bryant, P. E. (1983). Categorizing sounds and learning to read: A causal connection. *Nature, 301*(5899), 419–421. doi:10.1038/301419a0.

Celis, V., Husson, J., Abeele, V. V., Loyez, L., Van den Audenaeren, L., Ghesquière, P., … Geurts, L. (2013). Translating preschoolers' game experiences into design guidelines via a laddering study. In *Proceedings of the 12th International Conference on Interaction Design and Children* (pp. 147–156). New York, NY: ACM. doi:10.1145/2485760.2485772.

Csikszentmihalyi, M. (1990). *Flow: The psychology of optimal experience*. New York, NY: Harper and Row.

Deterding, S., Dixon, D., Khaled, R., & Nacke, L. (2011). From game design elements to gamefulness: defining gamification. In *Proceedings of the 15th International Academic MindTrek Conference: Envisioning Future Media Environments* (pp. 9–15). Retrieved from http://dl.acm. org/citation.cfm?id=2181040.

Eder, D., & Fingerson, L. (2002). Interviewing children and adolescents. In J. F. Gubrium & J. A. Holstein (Eds.), *Handbook of interview research: Context and method* (pp. 181–201). Thousand oaks, CA: Sage.

Farmer, M. E., & Klein, R. M. (1995). The evidence for a temporal processing deficit linked to dyslexia: A review. *Psychonomic Bulletin & Review, 2*(4), 460–493.

Fawcett, A., & Nicolson, R. (1995). *Dyslexia in children: Multidisciplinary perspectives*. London, England: Harvester Wheatsheaf.

Ferwerda, J., & Rehon, B. (2007). MagnoFly: Game-based screening for dyslexia. *Journal of Vision, 7*(9), 520. doi:10.1167/7.9.520.

Fuchs, M. (2005). Children and adolescents as respondents. Experiments on question order, response order, scale effects and the effect of numeric values associated with response options. *Journal of Official Statistics, 21*(4), 701–725.

Gaggi, O., Galiazzo, G., Palazzi, C., Facoetti, A., & Franceschini, S. (2012). A serious game for predicting the risk of developmental dyslexia in pre-readers children. In *2012 21st International Conference on Computer Communications and Networks (ICCCN)* (pp. 1–5). doi:10.1109/ ICCCN.2012.6289249.

Gee, J. P. (2003). *What video games have to teach us about learning and literacy* (1st ed.). Palgrave Macmillan. Retrieved from http://www.amazon.co.uk/dp/1403961697.

Gersons-Wolfensberger, D. C. M., & Ruijssenaars, W. A. J. J. M. (1997). Definition and treatment of dyslexia: A report by the committee on dyslexia of the health council of the Netherlands. *Journal of Learning Disabilities, 30*(2), 209–213.

Golafshani, N. (2003). Understanding reliability and validity in qualitative research. *The Qualitative Report, 8*(4), 597–607.

Hanna, L., Neapolitan, D., & Risden, K. (2004). Evaluating computer game concepts with children. In *Proceedings of the 2004 conference on Interaction design and children: building a community* (pp. 49–56). College Park, MD: ACM. doi:10.1145/1017833.1017840.

Hintikka, S., Mikko, A., & Lyytinen, H. (2005). Computerized training of the correspondences between phonological and orthographic units. *Written Language and Literacy, 8*(2), 79–102.

Hulme, C., Bowyer-Crane, C., Carroll, J. M., Duff, F. J., & Snowling, M. J. (2012). The causal role of phoneme awareness and letter-sound knowledge in learning to read combining intervention studies with mediation analyses. *Psychological Science, 23*(6), 572–577.

Juul, J. (2011). *Half-real: Video games between real rules and fictional worlds*. Cambridge, MA: The MIT Press.

Kirriemuir, J., & McFarlane, A. (2004). *Literature review in games and learning*. Bristol, England: Futurelab.

Laneau, J., Boets, B., Moonen, M., van Wieringen, A., & Wouters, J. (2005). A flexible auditory research platform using acoustic or electric stimuli for adults and young children. *Journal of Neuroscience Methods, 142*(1), 131–136. doi:10.1016/j.jneumeth.2004.08.015.

Lefly, D. L., & Pennington, B. F. (1991). Spelling errors and reading fluency in compensated adult dyslexics. *Annals of Dyslexia, 41*, 143–162.

Lyytinen, H., & Erskine, J. (2006, February 22). Early identification and prevention of reading problems. In *Encyclopedia on Early Childhood Development*. Retrieved from http://www.enfant-encyclopedie.com/Pages/PDF/Lyytinen-ErskineANGxp.pdf.

Malone, T. W. (1980). What makes things fun to learn? Heuristics for designing instructional computer games. In *Proceedings of the 3rd ACM SIGSMALL Symposium and the First SIGPC Symposium on Small Systems* (pp. 162–169). ACM, New York, NY. doi:10.1145/800088.802839.

Markopoulos, P., & Bekker, M. (2003). Interaction design and children. *Interacting with Computers, 15*(2), 141–149. doi:10.1016/S0953-5438(03)00004-3.

McArthur, G. M., & Bishop, D. V. (2001). Auditory perceptual processing in people with reading and oral language impairments: Current issues and recommendations. *Dyslexia, 7*(3), 150–170. doi:10.1002/dys.200.

McBride-Chang, C. (1995). Phonological processing, speech perception, and reading disability: An integrative review. *Educational Psychologist, 30*(3), 109. doi:10.1207/s15326985ep3003_2.

Menell, P., McAnally, K. I., & Stein, J. (1999). Psychophysical sensitivity and physiological response to amplitude modulation in adult dyslexic listeners. *Journal of Speech, Language, and Hearing Research, 42*(4), 797–803.

Merzenich, M., Wright, B., Jenkins, W., Xerri, C., Byl, N., Miller, S., & Tallal, P. (1996). Cortical plasticity underlying perceptual, motor, and cognitive skill development: Implications for neurorehabilitation. *Cold Spring Harbor Symposia on Quantitative Biology, 61*, 1–8. doi:10.1101/SQB.1996.061.01.003.

Michael, D. R., & Chen, S. L. (2005). *Serious games: Games that educate, train, and inform*. New York, NY: Muska & Lipman/Premier-Trade.

Morgan, D. (1996). *Focus groups as qualitative research* (2nd ed.). Thousand Oaks, CA: Sage.

Oudshoorn, N., & Pinch, T. (2003). *How users matter: The Co-construction of users and technology (inside technology)*. Cambridge, MA: The MIT Press.

Pagulayan, R. J., Keeker, K., Wixon, D., Romero, R. L., & Fuller, T. (2003). User-centered design in games. In *The human-computer interaction handbook: fundamentals, evolving technologies and emerging applications* (pp. 883–906). L. Erlbaum Associates. Retrieved from http://portal.acm.org/citation.cfm?id=772072.772128&coll=GUIDE&dl=GUIDE&CFID=11163922&CFTOKEN=41481297.

Patton, M. Q. (1990). *Qualitative evaluation and research methods* (2nd ed.). Newbury Park, CA: Sage.

Plong, M., Vanden Abeele, V., & Geurts, L. (2014). Requirements for an Architecture of a Generic Health Game Data Management System. In B. Schouten, S. Fedtke, M. Schijven, M. Vosmeer, & A. Gekker (Eds.), *Games for health 2014* (pp. 114–124). Springer Fachmedien Wiesbaden. Retrieved from http://link.springer.com/chapter/10.1007/978-3-658-07141-7_16.

Prensky, M. (2001). *Digital game-based learning*. New York, NY: McGraw-Hill.

Ramus, F. (2003). Developmental dyslexia: Specific phonological deficit or general sensorimotor dysfunction? *Current Opinion in Neurobiology, 13*(2), 212–218.

Rello, L., Bayarri, C., & Gorriz, A. (2012). What is wrong with this word? Dyseggxia: A game for children with dyslexia. In *Proceedings of the 14th International ACM SIGACCESS Conference on Computers and Accessibility* (pp. 219–220). ACM, New York, NY. doi:10.1145/2384916.2384962.

Sailer, M., Hense, J., Mandl, H., & Klevers, M. (2013). Psychological perspectives on motivation through gamification. *Interaction Design & Architectures, 19*, 28–37.

Salen, K., & Zimmerman, E. (2003). *Rules of play: Game design fundamentals*. Cambridge, MA: MIT Press.

Shaywitz, S. E. (1998). Dyslexia. *New England Journal of Medicine, 338*(5), 307–312. doi:10.1056/NEJM199801293380507.

Shute, V. J. (2011). Stealth assessment in computer-based games to support learning. *Computer games and instruction, 55*(2), 503–524.

Singleton, C., Thomas, K., & Horne, J. (2000). Computer-based cognitive assessment and the development of reading. *Journal of Research in Reading, 23*(2), 158–180. doi:10.1111/1467-9817.00112.

Snowling, M. J. (2000). *Dyslexia* (2nd Rev. ed.). Hoboken, NJ: Wiley Blackwell.

Steenbeek-Planting, E. G., Boot, M., Boer, J. C. de, Ven, M. V. de, Swart, N. M., & Hout, D. van der. (2013). Evidence-based psycholinguistic principles to remediate reading problems applied in the playful app Letterprins: A perspective of quality of healthcare on learning to read. In B. Schouten, S. Fedtke, T. Bekker, M. Schijven, & A. Gekker (Eds.), *Games for health* (pp. 281–291). Springer Fachmedien Wiesbaden. Retrieved from http://link.springer.com. kuleuven.ezproxy.kuleuven.be/chapter/10.1007/978-3-658-02897-8_22.

Stein, J., & Walsh, V. (1997). To see but not to read; the magnocellular theory of dyslexia. *Trends in Neurosciences, 20*(4), 147–152.

Sweetser, P., & Wyeth, P. (2005). GameFlow: A model for evaluating player enjoyment in games. *Computers in Entertainment, 3*(3), 3. doi:10.1145/1077246.1077253.

Talcott, J. B., & Witton, C. (2002). A sensory linguistic approach to the development of normal and impaired reading skills. In *Neuropsychology and cognition series. Basic functions of language and language disorders*. Dordrecht, Netherlands: Kluwer Academic Publishers.

Talcott, J. B., Witton, C., McLean, M. F., Hansen, P. C., Rees, A., Green, G. G., & Stein, J. (2000). Dynamic sensory sensitivity and children's word decoding skills. *Proceedings of the National Academy of Sciences of the United States of America, 97*(6), 2952–2957. doi:10.1073/pnas.040546597.

Tallal, P., Miller, S. L., Bedi, G., Byma, G., Wang, X., Nagarajan, S. S., ... Merzenich, M. M. (1996). Language comprehension in language-learning impaired children improved with acoustically modified speech. *Science, 271*(5245), 81–84. doi:10.1126/science.271.5245.81.

Temple, E., Deutsch, G. K., Poldrack, R. A., Miller, S. L., Tallal, P., Merzenich, M. M., & Gabrieli, J. D. E. (2003). Neural deficits in children with dyslexia ameliorated by behavioral remediation: Evidence from functional MRI. *Proceedings of the National Academy of Sciences of the United States of America, 100*(5), 2860–2865. doi:10.1073/pnas.0030098100.

Vanden Abeele, V., Schutter, B., Geurts, L., Desmet, S., Wauters, J., Husson, J., ... Geerts, D. (2012). P-III: A player-centered, iterative, interdisciplinary and integrated framework for serious game design and development. In S. Wannemacker, S. Vandercruysse, & G. Clarebout (Eds.), *Serious games: The challenge* (Vol. 280, pp. 82–86). Berlin, Germany: Springer. Retrieved from http://www.springerlink.com/content/k66727215741j3t0/abstract/.

Vanden Abeele, V., & Van Rompaey, V. (2006). Introducing human-centered research to game design: designing game concepts for and with senior citizens. In *CHI'06 extended abstracts on Human factors in computing systems* (pp. 1469–1474). ACM, Montréal, Québec, Canada. doi:10.1145/1125451.1125721.

Visser, F. S., Stappers, P. J., van der Lugt, R., & Sanders, E. B.-N. (2005). Contextmapping: Experiences from practice. *CoDesign, 1*(2), 119–149. doi:10.1080/15710880500135987.

Wang, H., & Sun, C.-T. (2011). Game reward systems: Gaming experiences and social meanings. In *Proceedings of DiGRA 2011 Conference: Think Design Play* (pp. 1–12). Citeseer. Retrieved from http://citeseerx.ist.psu.edu/viewdoc/download?doi=10.1.1.221.4931&rep=rep1&type=pdf.

Witton, C., Talcott, J. B., Hansen, P. C., Richardson, A. J., Griffiths, T. D., Rees, A., ... Green, G. G. (1998). Sensitivity to dynamic auditory and visual stimuli predicts nonword reading ability in both dyslexic and normal readers. *Current Biology: CB, 8*(14), 791–797.

Zaman, B. (2008). Introducing contextual laddering to evaluate the likeability of games with children. *Cognition, Technology & Work, 10*(2), 107–117.

Zaman, B., & Abeele, V. V. (2010). Laddering with young children in user experience evaluations: Theoretical groundings and a practical case. In *Proceedings of the 9th International Conference on Interaction Design and Children* (pp. 156–165). New York, NY: ACM. doi:10.1145/1810543.1810561.

Zaman, B., & Vanden Abeele, V. (2007). Towards a likeability framework that meets child-computer interaction & communication sciences. In *Proceedings of the 6th international conference on Interaction design and children* (pp. 1–8). Aalborg, Denmark: ACM. doi:10.1145/1297277.1297279.

Part II
Empirical Studies on Serious Games

Performance in Educational Math Games: Is It a Question of Math Knowledge?

Marie Maertens, Mieke Vandewaetere, Frederik Cornillie, and Piet Desmet

Abstract In order to develop game-based learning environments (GBLEs) that accommodate to learners' needs and individual differences, GBLEs can be enriched with learner models that describe learner profiles from which adaptive instruction can be offered during gameplay. Learner models can encompass several parameters or learner characteristics derived from measurements taken either prior to play (e.g., already available knowledge of the subject matter of which the GBLE is comprised) or during gameplay (i.e., learner behavior in the GBLE). This study makes a case for two skills which may be relevant from the perspective of adaptive gameplay, namely (1) the knowledge or skills with respect to the learning content and (2) the gaming skills. The current study investigates the joint inclusion of both gaming skills and domain knowledge creating learner profiles. In addition, this study sheds light on how performance during gameplay can be attributed to certain learner profiles. To investigate this, a commercially available 3D educational game for primary school children was offered to 53 children of the third grade. Learners' behavior while playing in the GBLE was captured and logged. Prior to gameplay, math knowledge, and gaming skills were measured. Subsequently, learners' in-game performance was measured. Results revealed that learners with high or low gaming skills can be distinguished into two learner profiles. More specific, learners with

M. Maertens (✉) • M. Vandewaetere
ITEC—iMinds—KU Leuven—Kulak, Interactive Technologies,
Etienne Sabbelaan 53, Box 7654, Kortrijk 8500, Belgium

Center for Instructional Psychology and Technology, KU Leuven,
Etienne Sabbelaan 53, Box 7654, Kortrijk 8500, Belgium
e-mail: Marie.Maertens@kuleuven-kulak.be; Mieke.vandewaetere@kuleuven-kulak.be

F. Cornillie
ITEC—iMinds—KU Leuven—Kulak, Interactive Technologies,
Etienne Sabbelaan 53, Box 7654, Kortrijk 8500, Belgium
e-mail: Frederik.Cornillie@kuleuven-kulak.be

P. Desmet
ITEC—iMinds—KU Leuven—Kulak, Interactive Technologies,
Etienne Sabbelaan 53, Box 7654, Kortrijk 8500, Belgium

Franitalco, Research on French, Italian and Comparative Linguistics, KU Leuven,
Etienne Sabbelaan 53, Box 7654, Kortrijk 8500, Belgium
e-mail: Piet.Desmet@kuleuven-kulak.be

© Springer International Publishing Switzerland 2015   117
J. Torbeyns et al. (eds.), *Describing and Studying Domain-Specific Serious Games*,
Advances in Game-Based Learning, DOI 10.1007/978-3-319-20276-1_8

high gaming skills outperformed learners with low gaming skills in more complex mini-games. The findings of this study suggest that a learner's gaming skills can be taken into account in developing learner profiles and hence in the design and development of GBLEs.

Keywords Math game • GBLE • Gaming skills • Mathematic skills • Learner models

Adaptive GBLEs are designed to accommodate the needs and abilities of different learners (Shute & Zapata-Rivera, 2008). With respect to game-based learning and educational games, adaptive gameplay refers to adjusting/tuning the gaming experience to the individual learners, being more responsive to different player types and their individual needs (Lopes & Bidarra, 2011). In order to establish appropriate adaptive gameplay, GBLEs can apply learner models as to adjust gameplay to specific (groups of) learners.

Learner modeling stems from research on intelligent tutoring systems (ITS) in which tailored and on-time instruction is offered by means of artificial intelligence techniques (Park & Lee, 2003). The benefit of including learner models in GBLEs is that they can inform the instructional process, individualize, and hence optimize gameplay. The content of the learning materials or the order in which it is presented, can for example be adapted to the learners' inferred knowledge state, instructional feedback can be given when the learner model infers that a learner experiences difficulties, or affective feedback can be given when the learner model infers that a learner is likely to lose motivation (Vandewaetere, Desmet, & Clarebout, 2011). The research on effectiveness of certain learner models, and hence the effectiveness of adaptive learning environments, has a long tradition in investigating what parameters are worthwhile to be included in an effective learner model, that is, a model that assists in providing instruction that is tailored or adapted to learner characteristics that are deemed relevant in learning. Although there is an upward trend towards more systematic research about learner modeling in adaptive systems (for an overview, see Vandewaetere et al., 2011), there is little known about learner models in GBLEs and the learner characteristics they should comprise.

Learner models in GBLEs can encompass several parameters like learner characteristics (e.g., already available knowledge) and learners' behavior in the game. To create a learner model, first, learners' actions and outcomes on learning materials are monitored while interacting with the educational game. Second, the backend of the game stores and maintains data structures, based on learners' actions. Third, interferences can be made about learners' knowledge, attitudes, or motivation based on the stored data and adaptive gameplay can be offered (Shute, Masduki, & Donmez, 2010).

With respect to educational games, two parameters could be highly relevant from the perspective of adaptive gameplay and can therefore be included in the learner model: domain knowledge and gaming skills.

First, according to Graesser, Jackson, and McDaniel (2007) and Park and Lee (2003), cognitive characteristics like already available knowledge can have a central place in the learner model. In this study, we define the already available knowledge as how well a learner masters the domain knowledge or the learning content that is present in the GBLE. As such, optimal challenge can be offered by adjusting the difficulty of the learning content in the game to the learner's already available knowledge. When, for example, a learner with good math knowledge plays a math game, the difficulty of the math items may be high from the start of the game. If not, the learner could lose interest. Opposite, when a learner is not very good in math, a too difficult learning content can cause frustration, so the learning content of the game could be made less difficult.

Second, it can be argued that, next to the domain knowledge, the format in which the content is offered is also related to the experienced difficulty and hence to the outcomes of gameplay. We refer here to a learner's gaming skills, described as how well a learner can operate with the input devices (keyboard and mouse) and how well the learner can cope with elements of gameplay. For example, an experienced player could be experiencing too little challenge, increasing the risk of losing interest. On the other hand, an inexperienced player could become frustrated when the gameplay is experienced as too difficult or beyond the gaming skills. In addition, there is a link between a learner's gaming skills and his/her performance in the GBLE. For example, not all "errors" that are made in solving domain-related content (e.g., math items) can be attributed to a lack of, or erroneous domain knowledge. For example, if a learner is not able to fill the basket with the correct solution before the opponent shoots him, then this is recorded as a wrongly solved math item, while this error might be attributed to slow handling of the mouse or keys (Baker, Habgood, Ainsworth, & Corbett, 2007). Other research (Maertens, Vandewaetere, Cornillie, & Desmet, 2014) also focused on the confounding role of gameplay and gaming skills in assessing a learner's knowledge by demonstrating that offering the same content in a game environment was associated with lower scores as compared to a pen-and-paper test. This relation was even more pronounced when the GBLE was more complex and learners had to take into account multiple elements in addition to solving the math item. For example, a mini-game with high element interactivity or a lot of elements that need to be integrated simultaneously was likely to add more difficulty to math items as compared to a mini-game with only a small amount of to-be-integrated elements. This is in line with research on element interactivity that demonstrated that items with higher element interactivity are evaluated as more complex and more difficult (Sweller, 2010). To summarize, games are likely to add difficulty to the learning content and this added difficulty is likely to be associated with the complexity of game or mini-game (Maertens et al., 2014). Therefore, it can be suggested that learners with more gaming skills are likely to deal better with in-game complexity as they have more experience with game mechanics that require motor skills like simultaneously using keys and mouse.

In order to provide optimal challenge, adaptive gameplay could not only adjust the difficulty of the learning materials towards the learner's domain knowledge, but also adjust the complexity of the gameplay towards a learner's gaming skills. Including both parameters in the learner model might provide a way to further optimize adaptive GBLEs and provide more insights as to improve the effectiveness of game-based learning.

In this study, we will investigate whether domain knowledge and gaming skills could be used to group learners (research question 1). Furthermore, we want to see if these different learner groups, if any, are related to performance during gameplay (research question 2), in order to be used to develop learner models. Based on previous research from Maertens et al. (2014), where it was demonstrated that a game as such and in addition the format of mini-games add difficulty to learning content and that easy and difficult mini-games could be distinguished, we formulate two additional hypotheses. First, learners' gaming skills are positively related to in-game performance. More specific, we suggest that learners with higher gaming skills will outperform learners with low gaming skills during gameplay. Second, we suggest that mini-games with higher element interactivity ask a higher level of gaming skills from learners and that learners with higher gaming skills will perform better on more complex mini-games.

Method

Participants

Fifty-three pupils from the third grade of a primary school in a small town in Flanders participated in this experiment. Two pupils were removed from the dataset because they had not completed the entire experimental procedure. The mean age was 8 year and 10 months (SD = 1 year). There was a more or less equal distribution for gender: 54.72 % of the participants were boys and 45.28 % girls.

Game-Environment and Measurement Instruments

The educational game *Museum of Anything* (henceforth: *Museum*) from the *Monkey Tales* series (http://www.monkeytalesgames.com/) was used as GBLE. The *Museum* game is intended for learners of the third grade and offers rehearsal and additional practice of math content that was learned in the previous year (i.e., math content of the second grade). The commercial version of this game contains 5 tutorial levels on how to play the game and 48 regular levels. In these regular levels, puzzle games are offered in which the learner needs to overcome obstacles in order to advance to the next level. Each puzzle game also contains a mini-game in which a learner has to solve math items while playing against an artificially intelligent (AI) monkey character. If the learner wins the mini-game, he or she can move to the next puzzle game and hence to the next mini-game. If the learner loses the mini-game against the AI, he or she needs to retry, and an easier mini-game is offered (unless the learner was already at the easiest difficulty level). In general, six different types of mini-games are offered in the game: Number Cruncher, Math Cards, Pebble Rebel, Cannon Battle, Rocket Science, and Cypher shooter. Each mini-game features math items in accordance to one specific math rule (e.g., item "$8 \times 6 = \ldots$" for the math rule "Table of 6"). A more comprehensive description of the game environment can be found in Vandercruysse, Maertens, and Elen (2015).

For this particular study, the commercially released version of the game was adapted in order to measure domain knowledge and gaming skill. To accomplish unobtrusive measurement in the GBLE, learner behavior was captured and logged (such as learners' performance on item-level and reaction time). In the following section, a description is offered about the measurement of domain knowledge, gaming skills, and the performance in the mini-games.

Measurement of domain knowledge: As the *Monkey Tales* series contains only math items, we will focus on math knowledge. Math knowledge was operationalized as the ability to compute multi-digit additions and subtractions (i.e., the math items that are offered in the game). Math knowledge was measured with a multiple choice assignment in a separate level of the game called *Bridge of Death*. This level requires minimal gaming skills as learners answer the multiple choice questions by selecting the correct answer with a mouse-click. Also, there is no opponent, no time-pressure, no distracting game-elements, etc. in this type of assignment which makes this measurement feasible to use as an in-game measurement for learners' math knowledge.

In the *Bridge of Death*, the learner's avatar started on the left side of the bridge and moved forward tile by tile to the right side. There was only one way to move across the bridge, though, and the pathway across the bridge contained between 11 and 15 tiles (which was generated at runtime). At the start of the puzzle game, the avatar needed to step on a tile that was highlighted. The other tiles were traps: When the character stepped on a tile that was not highlighted, he or she fell through the bridge and had to start over. When the learner's character stepped on the first (highlighted) tile, a multiple choice assignment was displayed, containing one math item with three possible answers. When the learner selected the correct answer, no traps were offered and the next, safe tile was highlighted so learners could move forward one tile. When the learner selected an incorrect option, the bridge "lied": rather than surely highlighting the safe tile, surrounding tiles were highlighted that could or could not be a trap. In this scenario, a learner had to guess and could choose the correct, safe tile and move forward, or a learner made a wrong guess, stepped on a trap, and had to start all over again. As stepping on a tile and answering the multiple choice item required only a single mouse-click, the performance of learners on these questions can be assumed to be equal to the performance of computerized, non-game, math test.

The *Bridge of Death* level comprised between 11 and 15 multiple choice assignments to measure math knowledge, covering five math rules: division table of 6 (e.g., 36 : 6 = …), division table of 8 (e.g., 56 : 8 = …), division table of 9 (e.g., 9 : 9 = …), subtraction to 100 with bridge Ten Unit − Unit (e.g., 84 − 6 = …), and addition to 100 with bridge Ten Unit + Ten Unit (e.g., 16 + 28 = …) (for an illustration of this level, see Vandercruysse et al., 2015). From these math rules, items were randomly selected and offered to learners. For example, for the division table of 6, "6 : 6," "12 : 6," "18 : 6," "24 : 6," … up to "60 : 6" were randomly selected and offered in the *Bridge of Death*.

Learners' math knowledge was calculated for each learner by mining the logging data of all the attempts learners needed to cross the *Bridge of Death*, and counting, across all attempts, the number of incorrect responses a learner gave in the multiple choice assignments. A learner who gave no incorrect responses crossed the bridge successfully. His/her score for math knowledge was 0 (i.e., 0 incorrect responses). The math knowledge of a learner who gave one incorrect response was set to 1 (i.e., 1 incorrect response). The more attempts learners needed to cross the *Bridge of Death*, the lower learners' actual math knowledge. The reliability of the overall measurement of math knowledge was high, as determined in a previous experiment with participants of the same age ($\alpha = .83$; Maertens et al., 2014).

Measurement of gaming skills: When looking at the gaming skills learners were expected to use in the *Museum* game, each mini-game required learners to use different gaming skills (i.e., skills that are related to visuo-spatial performance, reaction times, motor performance). So gaming skill was operationalized as the skill required to deal with the overall game mechanics (like evading an opponent) and the element interactivity in each separate mini-game. A more detailed analysis of the different gaming skills needed to play the six different mini-games is given by Vandercruysse et al. (2015). As the six different mini-games require to apply different gaming skills, it is feasible to measure the outcomes of learners on a mini-game where both gaming and math knowledge are needed and to compare this with a version where no math knowledge is required (e.g., when learners have to solve problems that do not require to apply their math knowledge). Six adapted versions were created containing no math content (henceforth, no-math mini-game). The no-math mini-game *Number Crunchers* is discussed here as an example. Instead of solving a math equation and shooting on blocks that contained numbers as in the commercial version (see Vandercruysse et al., 2015), learners were instructed to shoot on blocks that contain the same symbol as was offered in the instruction (instead of the math equation; see Fig. 1). Learners' performance on this no-math mini-game could not be attributed to their math knowledge and was therefore an appropriate measurement of gaming skill for the *Number Cruncher* game. Similar no-math versions were created for the other mini-game types.

For each of these different mini-game types, we used the proportion of correct responses in the learner's first attempt on the no-math mini-game (resulting in six different variables) in order to infer learners' gaming skills.

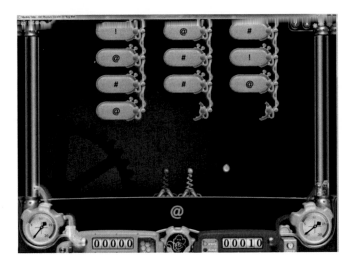

Fig. 1 No-math *Number Cruncher*

Performance on the mini-games with math content: Learners' performance on the mini-games with math content was measured in a way similar to the measurement of performance on the no-math mini-games; by computing the proportion of correct responses during the first attempt on completing a mini-game. Different math rules were offered in the distinct mini-games (see Table 1). For example, the rule subtraction to 100, Ten Unit–Unit (e.g., $36-7=\dots$) was offered in the *Number Cruncher* game.

In order to eliminate practice effects, the set of math rules offered in the mini-games was different from the math rules offered in the *Bridge of Death* to measure math knowledge. To measure learners' performance on mini-game with math content, we chose math rules with an average difficulty and which had the same difficulty (Maertens et al., 2014), whereas for the items offered in the *Bridge of Death*, we needed math rules with a wider variety of difficulty (from easy to difficult), in order to improve an accurate measurement of math knowledge.

Procedure

Learners' parents were asked permission to involve their child in this study. When parents approved, children played the game during class time, at their own pace, but with support of one of the researchers. Learners first saw a general video with the storyline, then played the *Bridge of Death* as a test to measure their math knowledge. Subsequently, learners played the six no-math mini-games in order to sketch their gaming skills after which they started the game play itself where the mini-games with math content were similar to those offered in the commercial version of the game.

Table 1 Math content offered in the mini-games

Mini-game	Math rule	Example
Number Cruncher	Subtraction to 100, Ten Unit – Unit	$36 - 7 = \ldots$
Cypher Shooter	Odd and even numbers	Shoot at the odd numbers
Rocket Science	Addition to 100, Ten Unit + Unit	$42 + 9 = \ldots$
Math Cards	Division table of 9	$81 : 9 = \ldots$
Pebble Rebel	Split	Split 36 in 6 equal parts
Cannon Battle	Understanding numbers to 100	What numbers are bigger than 35?

Results

Learners' math knowledge was operationalized as the number of incorrect responses across all attempts needed to cross the *Bridge of Death*. The mean math knowledge of all learners is 2.05 (SD = 1.63, min = 0, max = 7), indicating that, in order to cross the *Bridge of Death*, learners gave on average two incorrect responses or needed three attempts.

Gaming skill was measured as the proportion of correct responses on the first attempt on the no-math mini-game for each of the six different games separately. The proportion correct responses is .30 (SD = .13) for *Cypher Shooter*, .64 (SD = .22) for *Cannon Battle*, .28 (SD = .25) for *Math Cards*, .28 (SD = .15) for *Number Cruncher*, .31 (SD = .32) for *Pebble Rebel* and .43 (SD = .40) for *Rocket Science*. With respect to learners' gaming skills, the proportion of correct responses between the no-math mini-games ranges from .28 to .64. When first playing the no-math version of *Cannon Battle* and *Number Cruncher*, for example, the proportion correct is, respectively, .64 and .28. Therefore, *Cannon Battle* can be considered as a rather easy mini-game (i.e., high proportion correct) and not requiring high gaming skills, whereas *Number Cruncher* is a rather difficult mini-game (i.e., low proportion correct) requiring more gaming skills. In the next section, the results per research question are discussed.

Research Question 1: Could Domain Knowledge and Gaming Skills be Used to Group Learners?

In order to group learners, a hierarchical cluster analysis was performed on the standardized math knowledge and gaming skills variables, using Ward's method. In total, 7 variables were included: 1 variable for math knowledge, and 6 variables for gaming skill (i.e., the proportion of correct responses for each of the six no-math mini-games).

No fixed number of clusters was predefined. As to increase the robustness of the cluster solution, multiple cluster analyses were run with, for each run, a different order in which the variables were entered. The outcomes of the repeated cluster analyses (with the criterion that between-cluster distance should be maximized and within-cluster distances minimized) revealed that cluster 1 ($n = 28$) contains 28 learners and cluster 2 contains 22 learners.

The second step was to profile learners' gaming skills and math knowledge in the two clusters. To this end, a multivariate analysis of variance (MANOVA) was carried out, with all seven clustered variables as dependent variables and cluster membership (first or second cluster) as factor. Results reveal that learners from the different clusters indeed have overall different values for math and gaming skills, $F(7, 42) = 14.87$, $p < .001$. The values for gaming skills and math knowledge for the two different clusters are visualized in Fig. 2, and the exact values are included in Table 2.

Results of post hoc-tests show that the two clusters differ significantly from each other for the proportion of correct responses in five no-math mini-games: *Cypher Shooter* ($F(1, 48) = 17.70$, $p < .001$), *Cannon Battle* ($F(1, 48) = 10.22$, $p = .002$), *Number Cruncher* ($F(1, 48) = 3.96$, $p = .05$), *Pebble Rebel* ($F(1, 48) = 21.10$, $p < .001$), and *Rocket Science* ($F(1, 48) = 57.68$, $p < .001$). As shown in Fig. 2, there is no significant

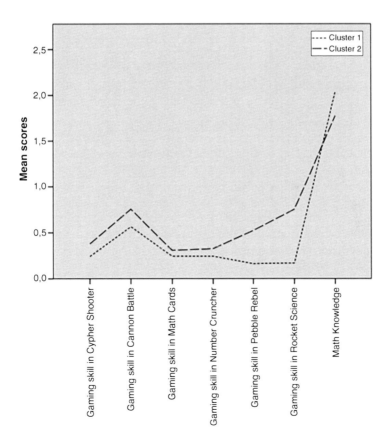

Fig. 2 The two obtained clusters

Table 2 Mean (standardized) values for gaming skill and math knowledge

	Cluster 1	Cluster 2	Overall mean
Gaming skill in *Cypher Shooter*	.24 (SD = .10)	.38 (SD = .13)	.30 (SD = .13)
Gaming skill in *Cannon Battle*	.56 (SD = .25)	.75 (SD = .13)	.65 (SD = .23)
Gaming skill in *Math Cards*	.24 (SD = .20)	.31 (SD = .28)	.27 (SD = .24)
Gaming skill in *Number Cruncher*	.24 (SD = .15)	.33 (SD = .14)	.28 (SD = .15)
Gaming skill in *Pebble Rebel*	.16 (SD = .20)	.52 (SD = .35)	.32 (SD = .33)
Gaming skill in *Rocket Science*	.17 (SD = .30)	.75 (SD = .22)	.43 (SD = .40)
Math knowledge[a]	2.04 (SD = 1.7)	1.77 (SD = 1.48)	1.92 (SD = 1.58)

[a]Math knowledge is operationalized as the number of incorrect responses across all attempts to cross the Bridge of Death. High values indicate low math knowledge

difference between cluster 1 and cluster 2 with respect to gaming skill in the mini-game *Math Cards*, nor is there a significant difference for learners' math knowledge. In addition, Fig. 2 shows that the proportion of correct responses on each no-math mini-game is higher for learners in cluster 2 than for learners in cluster 1, suggesting that learners in cluster 2 have higher gaming skills than learners in cluster 1.

Research Question 2: Are the Learner Groups Related to Performance During Gameplay?

To answer the second research question, a multivariate analysis of variance (MANOVA) was performed with six performance indicators (i.e., learners' proportion correct of the six mini-games with math content) as dependent variables and the cluster solution as a factor. Results reveal that cluster membership has no relation with performance on the six mini-games ($F(6, 37) = 2.24$, $p = .06$). This indicates that a learner's gaming skill (as measured by his or her performance in the mini-games without educational content) is not related to his or her success in mini-games with educational content. The performances of the learners from cluster 1 (low gaming skills) and cluster 2 (high gaming skills) on each mini-game are displayed in Fig. 3.

In an attempt to explain this nonexisting relation between gaming skills and in-game performance, the results of the post-hoc analyses were looked at in more detail. Results of post hoc-tests show that the difference in gaming skills has a significant effect on the performance in two mini-games: *Number Cruncher* ($F(1, 42) = 6.57$, $p = .01$) and *Rocket Science* ($F(1, 42) = 4.67$, $p = .04$). In these mini-games, the learners with high gaming skills outperform the learners with low gaming skills. For the other four mini-games, there is no significant difference in performance between learners with high and low gaming skills. So, our first hypothesis (learners with high gaming skills outperform learners with low gaming skills) is partly confirmed, as the learners with high gaming skills only outperform learners with low gaming skills in two mini-games.

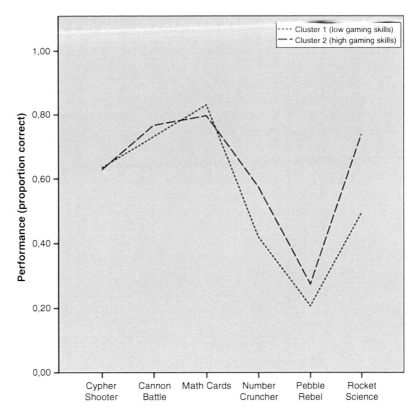

Fig. 3 Performance on mini-games with educational content, according to cluster

Discussion and Conclusion

This study first investigated whether learners' math knowledge and gaming skills could be used to group learners (research question 1). The results of the cluster analysis show that learners can be grouped into learners with high or low gaming skills based on in-game measurements of performance on no-math mini-games. Such in-game measurement of gaming skills is more ecologically valid as the measured skills are the same skills that a learner needs to apply in order to play the math mini-games. The results of the cluster analysis show how the different mini-games made appeal to learners' gaming skills. Three of the five mini-games where there is a significant difference between learners with high and low gaming skills contain obstacles which make the gameplay more complex: In *Number Cruncher*, players can get stuck under the green slime and have to quickly press two keys to get liberated. Players with low gaming skills are likely to experience more difficulties with quickly pressing these keys, resulting in lower scores on this mini-game. In *Cannon Battle*, purple chips are falling down from time to time. The first who hits this purple chip (the player or the opponent monkey) makes his antagonist immobile for a few seconds. Players with good gaming skills could make use of these purple chips to win the mini-game. In *Pebble Rebel*, tornados make players immobile for a few seconds. Players with low gaming skills are likely not able to avoid the tornados whereas players with high gaming skills have the required gaming skills (like motoric speed) to avoid the tornados. Besides the presence of obstacles in three mini-games, also *Cypher Shooter* and *Rocket Science* appeal in a stronger way on learners' gaming skills. In *Rocket Science*, players have to combine different tasks at the same time; decide fast where to navigate, answer the corresponding items correctly, confirm this answer and meanwhile, shoot hostile ships and hit accelerators to move more fast. The combination of solving a math items and subsequently executing different game mechanics is probably more intense for players with low gaming skills, compared to players with high gaming skills. Finally, in *Cypher Shooter*, the cards emerge at the same time, so learners have to quickly throw balls at the correct answers. Again, these quick and precise reactions appeal more on one's gaming skills, so it is conceivable that players with high gaming skills perform better. On the contrary, in *Math Cards*, no obstacles are used in this mini-game. This mini-game is similar to *Cypher Shooter*, except that the possible answers don't emerge at once but one by one. So, players have more time to look for the correct answer.

This study also investigated whether the two groups of learners showed different performance during gameplay (research question 2). Overall, having high or low gaming skills is not related to overall success on the mini-games with math content. However, for the performance on the mini-games *Number Cruncher* and *Rocket Science* gaming skills of learners might have played a role. More specifically, learners with high gaming skills outperformed learners with low gaming skills in these two mini-games, as stated in the first hypothesis. An earlier study showed that *Number Cruncher* is a difficult mini-game (Maertens et al., 2014) due to the green toxic drops falling from the roof. When learners got stuck under the green drops, they are immobile for a few seconds and they have to quickly press some keys to get mobile again. These motoric skills of pressing with a high frequency on some keys require the application of more advanced gaming skills. In line with this, the mini-game *Rocket Science* can be seen as a mini-game with high element interactivity because different elements need to be combined; learners have to decide fast if they want to navigate to the left or right, they have the answer the corresponding items correctly and confirm it and meanwhile, learners have to shoot hostile ships and hit accelerators to move more fast during gameplay. All these actions, and the integration of it, require high gaming skills and result in a rather high element interactivity of the game. Such environments are evaluated as more complex and more difficult (Sweller, 2010). So, also the second hypothesis could be confirmed, as the good gamers outperform the bad gamers in more complex mini-games.

To summarize, learners' gaming skills could be used to cluster learners and to distinguish between learners with high and low gaming skills. Moreover, the finding that learners' gaming skills are especially important in difficult and more complex mini-games is a strong argument to include gaming skills as a parameter in the construction of learner models and the development of adaptive gameplay. More concretely, the game's adaptivity engine could rely on an implementation of the above described clustering procedure in order to group learners and to create learner profiles. With respect to the measurements, unobtrusive tests for gaming skill in the beginning of the game could be implemented, and cut-off points can be used to distinguish between learners with high and low gaming skill. These cut-off points could be based on the average proportion of correct responses in the mini-games without educational content. Then, upon launching the first mini-games with educational content, the amount of element interactivity in these games (e.g., many or few additional challenges in *Number Cruncher*, many or few opponents in *Rocket Science*) could be set to high or low, adapted to the gaming skills of the learner.

Limitations and Suggestions for Future Research

Some limitations of this study are worthwhile to be mentioned. First, it is possible that a learner's results on the unobtrusive math knowledge test (the multiple choice assignments implemented in the *Bridge of Death*) still can be confounded by his/her gaming skills. Although the game mechanics were set to a minimum, gaming skills still can have played a role. A more pure measurement of learners' math knowledge could be a paper-and-pencil (P&P) math test. However, using a P&P math test does not meet the ecological validity of this study because it is not realistic that users of the commercial game first have to complete a P&P test in order to get access to the game. In addition, this study was industry-driven with the objective to investigate in-game measurements of learners' math knowledge as to adapt gameplay. From that point of view, it was also decided not to use a P&P test. However, a comparison between the in-game measurement of knowledge and a P&P test outcome would have been of added value to sketch the validity of the in-game measurement. Further research could therefore investigate the correlation between a P&P math test and the multiple choice assignments in the *Bridge of Death* to test the hypothesis that the measurement of math knowledge is not confounded by learners' gaming skills. In addition, the measurement of math knowledge could be not fully able to capture the different "types" of learners with respect to their math knowledge. This may be due to two reasons: (1) the math knowledge test was implemented in the *Bridge of Death* puzzle game and therefore minimal gaming skills are still required which confounds the measurement of math knowledge or (2) the number of incorrect responses given on the multiple choice assignments on the *Bridge of Death* is likely to be an overestimation of the actual math knowledge due to gambling behavior (as there were only three options and answers could be recognized rather than to be produced). More specific, when learners make an error, the bridge could "lie" and the learner had to guess which tile is safe taking the risk of falling through the *Bridge of Death*. Although we tried to ensure the validity of this test (e.g., by using items from earlier studies that distinguished well between learners with high and low math knowledge), this test might not represent learners' actual math knowledge very well. Thus, on the basis of these results, future research could design and develop other unobtrusive measurements of math knowledge. Other measurements of learners' math knowledge would be desirable, such as a version of the *Bridge of Death* with multiple choice assignments in which learners do not have to start all over again when they make a mistake and fall through the bridge, and in which all learners get an equal number of test items (rather than a random number of items that depends on the length of the pathway across the bridge), as well as the same items (rather than similar, generated items). This allows for a more reliable and valid measurement of math knowledge. Finally, the operationalization of math knowledge in this study is more limited than the commonly accepted definition of math knowledge. This study focused on arithmetic, whereas for example word problems and geometry also play an important role in determining learners' overall math knowledge. Generalizability could be improved in future research by using a more broad definition of math knowledge and investigating whether different math knowledge result in different conclusions about the link between gaming skills and in-game performance.

Second, it could be argued that behavioral variables related to gameplay actions other than selecting responses, such as evading slime (as displayed in Fig. 1, learners have to avoid the green slime falling from the roof because this slime makes learners immobile for a few seconds) or other obstacles in the mini-games, number of bonuses taken, as well as reaction times need to be taken into account in order to come to a more accurate measurement of gaming skill. However, the game mechanics of the different mini-games are different, and hence, different actions are required from learners in different mini-games, and different events are possible so comparing these actions and events among mini-games is impossible. Therefore, including other behavioral variables like gaining additional bonuses in, for example, *Math Card* makes mutual comparisons more difficult. However, future research could look at more complex formulae, including combinations of behavioral variables, to sketch learners' gaming skills.

Third, it must be acknowledged that maybe not all learners like playing educational games, so there might be other factors as well which result in differences in gameplay. For example, learners' interest in math could be a mediating variable for learners' gaming skills. If a learner is not motivated for math, he is probably less eager to perform well in an educational math game.

Conclusion

To conclude, in order to group learners and create learner profiles to realize adaptive gameplay in GBLEs, learners' gaming skills are a crucial learner variable. The findings of this study show that learners' gaming skills are crucial when playing educational games. If not, learners could get bored if the gameplay is too easy for them or frustrated is the needed gaming skills are too difficult. So, it is crucial to adapt the gameplay to learners' gaming skills.

Acknowledgement This study is based on a research project funded by iMinds-Flanders, called Games@School (2012–2014).

References

Baker, R. S., Habgood, J., Ainsworth, S. E., & Corbett, A. T. (2007). Modeling the acquisition of fluent skill in educational action games. In C. Conati, K. McCoy, & G. Paliouras (Eds.), *User modelling 2007* (pp. 17–26). Corfu, Greece: Springer.

Graesser, A., Jackson, G., & McDaniel, B. (2007). AutoTutor holds conversations with learners that are responsive to their cognitive and emotional states. *Educational Technology, 47*, 19–22.

Lopes, R., & Bidarra, R. (2011). Adaptivity challenges in games and simulations: A survey. *IEEE Transactions on Computational Intelligence and AI in Games, 3*(2), 85–99.

Maertens, M., Vandewaetere, M., Cornillie, F., & Desmet, P. (2014). From pen-and-paper content to educational math game content for children: A transfer with added difficulty. *International Journal of Child-Computer Interaction, 2*(2), 85–92. doi:10.1016/j.ijcci.2014.04.001.

Park, O., & Lee, H. (2003). Adaptive instructional systems. In D. H. Jonassen (Ed.), *Handbook of research on educational communications and technology* (2nd ed., pp. 651–684). Bloomington, IN: The Associates for Educational Communications and Technology (AECT).

Shute, V. J., Masduki, I., & Donmez, O. (2010). Conceptual framework for modeling, assessing and supporting competencies within game environments. *Technology, Instruction, Cognition and Learning, 8*(2), 137–161.

Shute, V. J., & Zapata-Rivera, D. (2008). Adaptive technologies. In J. M. Spector, M. D. Merill, J. J. G. van Merriënboer, & M. Driscoll (Eds.), *Handbook of research on educational communications and technology* (3rd ed., pp. 277–294). Hillsdale, NY: Lawrence Erlbaum.

Sweller, J. (2010). Element interactivity and intrinsic, extraneous, and germane cognitive load. *Educational Psychology Review, 22*, 123–138.

Vandercruysse, S., Maertens, M., & Elen, J. (2015). Description of the educational games 'Monkey Tales: The museum of Anything'. In L. Verschaffel (Ed.), *Research on serious games: Descriptions and findings*. New York, NY: Springer.

Vandewaetere, M., Desmet, P., & Clarebout, G. (2011). The value of learner characteristics in the development of computer-based adaptive learning environments. *Computers in Human Behavior, 27*, 118–130.

Integration in the Curriculum as a Factor in Math-Game Effectiveness

Sylke Vandercruysse, Elke Desmet, Mieke Vandewaetere, and Jan Elen

Abstract While numerous claims are made about the effectiveness of games, the studies that examine their educational effectiveness often contain flaws resulting in unclear conclusions. One possible solution for these shortcomings is to focus on separate game elements rather than on games as a whole. A second solution is to take into account students' perception as this is likely to affect students' interpretations and learning outcomes. This study investigated the effect of the integration of an educational game in the curriculum on students' motivation, perception, and learning outcomes. Forty-nine vocational track students participated, all working in a game-based learning environment for learning calculations with fractions. The results demonstrate that integrating the learning content in the game with the learning content in the classroom is related to students' in-game performance, but not to students' math performance on a paper-and-pencil test, postgame perception and postgame motivation. To conclude this chapter, practical and theoretical implications for the fields of instructional design and educational games research are discussed.

Keywords Educational game • Math game • Content integration • Curriculum integration • Game perception

Educational games have become a hot issue in the educational technology domain and are considered as a potential learning tool. Positive outcomes and effects have been claimed and educational effectiveness is expected from the use of games. Amongst others, educational games are expected to evoke intense engagement and

S. Vandercruysse (✉) • J. Elen
Center for Instructional Psychology and Technology, KU Leuven,
Etienne Sabbelaan 53, Box 7654, Kortrijk 8500, Belgium
e-mail: Sylke.Vandercruysse@kuleuven-kulak.be; jan.elen@ppw.kuleuven.be

E. Desmet • M. Vandewaetere
Faculty of Psychology and Educational Sciences, Campus Kortrijk @ Kulak, KU Leuven,
Kortrijk, Belgium
e-mail: desmetelke@hotmail.com; mieke.vandewaetere@kuleuven-kulak.be

© Springer International Publishing Switzerland 2015
J. Torbeyns et al. (eds.), *Describing and Studying Domain-Specific Serious Games*,
Advances in Game-Based Learning, DOI 10.1007/978-3-319-20276-1_9

133

motivation in the learning process (e.g., O'Neil, Wainess, & Baker, 2005; Vogel et al., 2006), to actively involve students in challenging situated problem solving (e.g., Becker, 2007; Garris, Ahlers, & Driskell, 2002), to enhance learning and understanding (Hayes & Games, 2008), and to improve student's performance (Liu & Chu, 2010). Notwithstanding the popularity of educational games in education and the optimistic stance that is taken towards the potentials of games in education, empirical research, and evidence for the claims and expectations remain limited (Connolly, Boyle, MacArthur, Hainey, & Boyle, 2012; Girard, Ecalle, & Magnan, 2013; Hays, 2005; O'Neil et al., 2005; Randel, Morris, Wetzle, & Whitehead, 1992; Sitzman, 2011; Tobias, Fletcher, Dai, & Wind, 2011; Vandercruysse, Vandewaetere, & Clarebout, 2012; Wouters, van der Spek, & van Oostendorp, 2009). There is lack of scientifically rigorous studies that pinpoint instructional design features that improve the instructional effectiveness of games (DeLeeuw & Mayer, 2011). This hampers drawing conclusions on the effectiveness of educational games but also results in insufficient guidance for game designers on how to develop effective games. In order to make a step forward with respect to this guidance, there is a need for studying specific characteristics of game-based learning environments (GBLEs)—rather than games as such (Aldrich, 2005)—as well as interactions between these characteristics and learner-related variables. Therefore, in this study we attempted to get more evidence on the assumed benefits of games by focusing on the effects of one specific characteristic related to the game (i.e., the type of game integration in the curriculum) on students' motivation, learning processes, and acquired knowledge.

Integration in the Curriculum

Multiple claims are made about the added value of gaming in the math curriculum and various factors have been mentioned to affect math-game effectiveness. Game integration is one of these factors. The notion of game integration, however, is multidimensional. On the one hand, game integration can be described as the integration of the learning content into the (story line of the) game. Habgood and Ainsworth (2011) define this integration as *intrinsic integration* or the more productive relationship between educational games and their learning content. Clark and colleagues (2011, p. 2180) distinguish between "conceptually integrated" and "conceptually embedded" games. In the former type of games, the learning goals are integrated into the actual movement and gameplay mechanics which has the potential advantage of engaging the player with the learning content in the game during a longer amount of time. In the latter type of games, this is not the case and also other interactions (with no referral to the learning content) are involved in the game.

On the other hand, game integration can refer to the use of the game (and thus its integration) in the classroom. In this study, we focus on this latter meaning of game integration, which is also multidimensional. For instance, Demirbilek and Turner (2010) found in their study that teachers utilize computer games during math lessons in different ways, for example, as evaluation purpose, as remediation stage, as reinforcement, distractor, or bonus. Various studies have investigated concrete ways of game integration. Most of these studies focus on cooperative and competitive gaming (Ke, 2008a, 2008b; Ke & Grabowksi, 2007; Vandercruysse, Vandewaetere, Cornillie, & Clarebout, 2013) and the degree of which free choice to play a game influenced learning results (Barendregt & Bekker, 2011). The results are interesting but do not pertain to the essence of this study. In this study, we investigate the effect of the integration of the learning content in the game in the curriculum of the students, and more specifically the effect of the absence or presence of an explicit link between the learning content in the game and the curriculum (i.e., the learning content in the classroom) of the students. In this study, the curriculum is interpreted based on the definition of Walker and Soltis (1997):

> The curriculum as we use the term, refers not only to the official list of courses offered by the school—we call that the 'official curriculum'—but also to the purposes, content, activities and organization of the educational program actually created in the school by teachers, students and administrators (p. 1).

The integration of the game in the curriculum refers to the integration of the game in the classroom activities. The literature reviews of Hays (2005) and Tobias and colleagues (2011) indicated that a stronger integration of games in the instruction program (or curriculum) promotes the learning process. Tobias and colleagues (2011) pointed to the fact that games that are not related to the instruction program might be fun, but probably do not promote the cognitive possibilities of the learners. This might be due to the fact that games don't appear to help students to make the leap from tacit understanding during gameplay to more formalized knowledge in the classroom (Clark et al., 2011). In order for students to make the connections between the game and the more formalized knowledge demanded in a school-based context, aids (or scaffolds) are required (Clark et al., 2011). In this study, aid is provided by linking the learning content in the game with the math content during math class. By linking the learning content in the game explicitly with the learning content in the classroom, the (learning) goal of the GBLE becomes clearer to the students. This might be beneficial for the students because clear goals are supposed to stimulate engagement and engage players' self-esteem (Akilli, 2007; Bergeron, 2006; Garris et al., 2002; Hays, 2005; Malone, 1980; Prensky, 2001). Hence, we might assume there is a relationship between the degree of integration of a game in the curriculum and the learning effect. Din and Calao (2001) already investigated the two extremes; being the difference between games that were integrated vs. games that were not integrated in the curriculum. In this study, we do not investigate the extremes, but more the continuum of integration: a strong integration vs. a weak integration in the curriculum. The effect of different degrees of integration (strong vs. weak integration) on mathematical performance and learners' motivation will be investigated.

Learners' Perception: Moderating the Influence of the Teachers' Instruction

"Learners are active actors in learning environments and not mere consumers of instructional designers' products" (Lowyck, Elen, & Clarebout, 2004, p. 429). The so-called mediational paradigm (Winne, 1982, 1987) is based on this thought and emphasizes the crucial impact of students' cognitive processes. This contrasts with the process-product paradigm from earlier days (but also nowadays in some research studies, cf. Vandercruysse et al., 2012), in which it was assumed that an instruction method (process) directly influences learning outcomes (product) of students. Now, researchers are more and more convinced that learners actively construct their own knowledge and interpret the teachers' instructions. The way students interpret the instruction evokes different cognitive processes (Lowyck et al., 2004) which then lead to different learning outcomes (Winne, 1987). Unintended interpretations of the instruction by students might lead to unintended learning results (Lowyck et al., 2004). Entwistle (1991), Salomon (1984), and Shuell and Farber (2001) share this thought of the moderating role of students' perception. More specific, Salomon (1984) demonstrated that students' differential learning may depend on what they perceive the learning material to be. If students perceive the material as "easy" leisure time activities, they invest less mental effort compared to students who perceive the material as more instructional (Salomon, 1984). Hence, although a teacher may decide to implement a game in the classroom, the perception of the students will determine to what extent and how this implementation will influence their learning.

From this point of view, we claim the importance of taking students' perception into account. In this study, students' perception is defined as (1) students' expectations about the goals of the environment and more specific whether the players think of the game as a leisure time activity (something fun) or an educational one (something more akin to work, perceived playfulness) and (2) the degree to which students believe that using GBLEs will enhance their performance on what the GBLE focuses on (perceived usefulness) (Vandercruysse et al., 2015).

Students' perception about learning environments is not only related to the instructional method (i.e., the way the educational game is introduced to the student and integrated in the curriculum) and performance, but also their intrinsic motivation (Lowyck et al., 2004). Intrinsic motivation gets stimulated when students perceive instruction as important and relevant (Kinzie, 1990; Ryan & Deci, 2000). The study of Herndon (1987) also concludes that students' intrinsic motivation is higher when students are confronted with relevant and interesting instruction for the students compared to instruction that does not take students' interest into account. Hence, we may assume that students, who perceive the game environment as more useful and effective, will show higher intrinsic motivation than students who perceive the environment as less useful and effective.

The Present Study

In this study, we investigate the impact of the integration of the game in the curriculum, by which we focus on the way this integration takes place. Two experimental conditions are set up. In the *weak integration* condition, students get the chance to play with the GBLE during 2 h as a reward for their efforts in the last lessons; during instruction time only the fun-part of the GBLE is mentioned. In the *strong integration* condition, students are told they need some extra exercises on the content they had during math class. For a change, the exercises are implemented in a GBLE and will help to improve their math skills. In the latter condition, the link between the learning content in the GBLE and the curriculum of the students is made explicit, while in the former condition this is not the case. The research focus of this study is the relation between on the one hand the explicitness of the link between GBLE learning content and curricular/classroom learning content and on the other hand students' performances, motivation, and perception.

Based on the literature, we suppose that, because of the explicit link between the learning content in the game and the learning content in the classroom, in the strong integration condition, students have a better idea about the goal of the GBLE. This might lead to greater (intrinsic) motivation for the strong integration condition (hypothesis 1) because clear goals are supposed to stimulate engagement and engage players' self-esteem (Akilli, 2007; Bergeron, 2006; Garris et al., 2002; Hays, 2005; Malone, 1980; Prensky, 2001). Additionally, students in the strong integration condition are supposed to perform better than students in the weak integration condition (hypothesis 2) because a stronger integration of games in the instruction program (or curriculum) is assumed to promote the learning process (Hays, 2005; Tobias et al., 2011) due to the fact that in the strong integration condition students will be more able to make the leap from tacit understanding during gameplay to the more formalized knowledge in the classroom (Clark et al., 2011). Additionally, a higher perceived usefulness and perceived playfulness (hypothesis 3) is assumed for the strong integration condition. This assumption is based on the mediational paradigm which assumes that the effect of game integration in the curriculum on students' motivation and performances is influenced by students' perception (Entwistle, 1991; Lowyck et al., 2004; Salomon, 1984; Shuell & Farber, 2001). In the strong integration condition, the GBLE might be more perceived as a useful means to learn math; while in the weak integration condition students might perceive the environment more as a leisure time activity. Additionally, we assume that this difference in perception will result in a difference in motivation and performance. We expect that students who perceive the environment as a useful means to learn math will be more intrinsically motivated (hypothesis 4) and perform better on the mathematical exercises (i.e., solve them more correctly) during the gameplay and afterwards (hypothesis 5) than students who perceive the environment as a pastime (Lowyck et al., 2004; Salomon, 1984). Finally, students that perceive the game environment as a useful tool to learn math before the gameplay, will keep this perception after the gameplay (hypothesis 6).

Table 1 Conditions with number of students who initially participated (and the amount of students who actually participated in the whole study)

	Specialization	Grade	n_{Boys}	n_{Girls}	n_{Total}
Condition 1	Hairdressing courses	4	0	12	**23**
Strong integration	Hairdressing courses	4	0	11	
Condition 2	Hairdressing courses	3	2	9 (8)	**26 (25)**
Weak integration	Hairdressing courses	4	0	15	
n_{Total}			**2**	**47 (46)**	**49 (48)**

Method

Participants

The sample of this study consisted of 49 vocational track students. Participants were selected from the third and fourth year of secondary vocational education in Flanders (Belgium). Five classes from one secondary school were selected. The students all followed hairdressing courses which resulted in an unbalanced gender division (only two male students). In Table 1, an overview is given of the conditions and the number of students that participated in the study. For all involved students, this research was organized during the course Project General Subjects (PGS).[1] The participants formed a homogeneous group with respect to cultural background; they lived in the same region and had similar educational background, computer access, and ICT knowledge. The age range varied between 15 and 18 years old ($M = 16.43$; $SD = .83$).

Because students who did not complete the whole study were discarded from the analyses, one student was removed from the dataset. This resulted in 48 participants for whom data on all measured variables were available.

Design

A prepost between subject design with experimental condition (weak integration vs. strong integration) as a between subjects variable was used. Two experimental conditions were defined. In the weak integration condition, students were told that as a reward for their intensive work during the math class, without specifically referring to the mathematical content, they got playtime. During the instruction, the fun and leisure component of the game instead of the learning goals were emphasized (i.e., "We organized a gameplay session because you did your best during the previous

---

[1] PGS [Project Algemene Vakken; PAV] breaks through subject-tied learning, and is based on an integrated approach. The students develop knowledge, skills, and attitudes in useful and recognizable contexts, making them more sufficiently resilient and socially skilled.

courses and you really deserve it. It's supposed to be fun, so we can get a fresh start afterwards with a new topic"). Hence, playing the game in the weak integration condition was not introduced as being part of the curriculum. In the strong integration condition, students were told they got some additional exercise time for practicing fractions. So students got the chance to practice their calculations with fractions in line with their math course, by playing the game. During the instruction, an explicit link between the math course and the exercises in the game was made and the learning goal and the opportunity for the students to have some extra exercises were emphasized (i.e., "We will practice a bit further on fractions similar to what we did in other mathematics lessons but now by playing a math game. Try to do your best because the exercises in the game will help to improve your fraction calculating skills"). Hence, playing the game in the strong integration condition was part of the curriculum.

Materials

GBLE: Monkey Tales. An existing 3D game was used as GBLE, namely the museum game[2] from the Monkey Tales series (LarianStudios).[3] In the game, players have to beat Carmine Pranquill, a huge dinosaur, which has conquered the museum. This can only succeed by passing through all the rooms in the museum. Every room contains two challenges: (1) solving a 3D puzzle-game and (2) winning a mathematical mini-game. A player can only win the mini-games by showing better math skills as compared to the opponent (a monkey).

Four different kinds of mini-games are implemented in the museum game. See Fig. 1 for an example of a challenge in the mini-game "balloons pop-up" which is a shooting gallery. The math-assignment appears at the bottom of the screen (i.e., "Shoot on the fractions that equal 1/5") and on the treadmill, cards with possible answers pop-up on the screen (i.e., 3/15 and a bonus card). By using the mouse to aim and throw a ball towards the cards (left click) with the correct answer, they gain points (blue/left score). By choosing—as fast as they can—all the right answers, they can beat the monkey (their opponent—red/right score).

The museum game is originally intended for third grade primary school children as rehearsal and additional practice of math content learned during math courses. For this experiment, the content was adapted to our target group and their curriculum (i.e., second grade vocational track students). All mini-games in the environment are related to comparing, adding, and multiplying fractions. Different difficulty levels concerning fractions are implemented (see Table 2) based on (1) the range of numbers of the denominator and nominator in the fractions and (2) the operations students have to conduct with the fractions.

---

[2] For a thorough description of the environment, see Vandercruysse, Maertens, and Elen (2015).

[3] A demo-version can be found on http://www.monkeytalesgames.com/UKen/games/2 (LarianStudios).

Fig. 1 Example comparison task: Which fractions equal 1/5?—Monkey Tales from Larian Studios

Measurements. The measurements in this study are threefold: We measured students' motivation, their performances, and their game perception.

Motivation. Students' premotivation (before the intervention started) was measured with subscales of the Dutch version of the motivated strategies for learning questionnaire (MSLQ; Pintrich, Smith, Garcia, & McKeachie, 1993). This self-report instrument assesses students' motivational orientations and their different learning strategies on a 6-point Likert scale. For this study, the subscales for intrinsic goal orientation (four items, e.g., "In class, I prefer course material that arouses my curiosity, even if it is difficult to learn," $\alpha = 0.78$), extrinsic goal orientation (four items, e.g., "Getting a good grade in this class is the most satisfying thing for me right now," $\alpha = 0.85$), and task value (four items, e.g., "I am very interested in solving fractions," $\alpha = 0.88$) were administered. The higher a student scores on these subscales, the higher his/her premotivation. Correlations between the three subscales are positively significant ($r_{\text{Task Value–Intrinsic Goal}} = .80$, $p < .001$; $r_{\text{Task Value–Extrinsic Goal}} = .81$, $p < .001$; $r_{\text{Intrinsic Goal–Extrinsic Goal}} = .78$, $p < .001$). Reliability of the MSLQ, measured by three subscales, is $\alpha = 0.94$. Students' premotivation was operationalized as the sum of the scores on the three subscales.

To measure students' intrinsic motivation during completion of the tasks (i.e., playing the educational game), a post-assessment of students' motivation was done wherein students were instigated to reflect on their motivation during task completion. Students filled in the Dutch version of the intrinsic motivation inventory (IMI; McAuley, Duncan, & Tammen, 1987; Plant & Ryan, 1985). Students completed two

Table 2 Overview of different types of exercises implemented in the game environment according to the different mini-games

Type	Mini-game	Specification	Operations	Example
Comparison fractions				
Type 1	Balloon pop-up	$x = 1$	$x/y > x/z$	1/3 > 1/6?
		$y = (2, 10, 1)$	$x/y < x/z$	1/4 < 1/2?
		$z = (2, 10, 1)$	$x/y = x/z$	1/7 = 1/8?
Type 2	Balloon pop-up	$x = (1, y - 1, 1)$	$x/y > a/b$	2/6 > 4/8?
		$y = (2, 10, 1)$	$x/y < a/b$	3/9 < 1/2?
		$a = (1, y - 1, 1)$	$x/y = a/b$	5/10 = 4/8?
		$b = (2, 10, 1)$		
Type 3	Balloon pop-up	$x = (1, y - 1, 1)$	$x/y > a/b$	10/15 > 1/5?
		$y = (2, 16, 1)$	$x/y < a/b$	1/2 < 4/16?
		$a = (1, y - 1, 1)$	$x/y = a/b$	2/4 = 5/10?
		$b = (2, 16, 1)$		
Type 4	Balloon pop-up	$x = (1, 10, 1)$	$x/y > a/b$	6/2 > 8/4?
		$y = (2, 10, 1)$	$x/y < a/b$	3/9 < 1/2?
		$a = (1, 10, 1)$	$x/y = a/b$	2/1 = 5/10?
		$b = (2, 10, 1)$		
Type 5	Balloon pop-up	$x = (1, 15, 1)$	$x/y > a/b$	15/10 > 5/1?
		$y = (2, 16, 1)$	$x/y < a/b$	1/2 < 16/4?
		$a = (1, 15, 1)$	$x/y = a/b$	4/2 = 10/5?
		$b = (2, 16, 1)$		
Operations—equal denominator				
Type 1	Mathcards	$x = (1, 9, 1)$	$x/y + z/y = [x + z]/y$	1/4 + 2/4 = 3/4
	Number-Invader	$y = (2, 9, 1)$	$x/y - z/y = [x - z]/y$	6/3 − 2/3 = 4/3
		$z = (1, 9, 1)$		
Type 2	Mathcards	$x = (1, 15, 1)$	$x/y + z/y = [x + z]/y$	6/12 + 4/12 = 10/12
	Number-Invader	$y = (2, 16, 1)$	$x/y - z/y = [x - z]/y$	15/10 − 8/10 = 7/10
		$z = (1, 9, 1)$		
Operations—simple fractions				
Type 1	Mathcards	$x = (1, 10, 1)$	$x/a + y/b = [[x \times b] + [y \times a]]/[a \times b]$	2/3 + 2/6 = 18/18
	Number-Invader	$y = (1, 10, 1)$	$x/a - y/b = [[x \times b] - [y \times a]]/[a \times b]$	5/7 − 1/2 = 3/14
		$a = (2, 10, 1)$	$x/a \times y/b = [x \times y]/[a \times b]$	1/3 × 2/5 = 2/15
		$b = (2, 10, 1)$		
Type 2	Mathcards	$x = (1, 10, 1)$	$x/a + y/b = [[x \times b] + [y \times a]]/[a \times b]$	4/15 + 2/5 = 50/75
	Number-Invader	$y = (1, 10, 1)$	$x/a - y/b = [[x \times b] - [y \times a]]/[a \times b]$	10/14 − 1/2 = 6/28
		$a = (2, 16, 1)$	$x/a \times y/b = [x \times y]/[a \times b]$	5/11 × 4/7 = 20/77
		$b = (2, 10, 1)$		

(continued)

Table 2 (continued)

Type	Mini-game	Specification	Operations	Example
Operations—fraction of number				
Type 1	Mathcards	$x=(2, 10, 1)$	$1/y$ of $[x \times y] = x$	1/5 of 35 = 7
	PebbleRebel	$y=(2, 10, 1)$		
	Number-Invader			
Type 2	Mathcards	$x=(2, 10, 1)$	z/y of $[x \times y] = [x \times z]$	3/4 of 12 = 9
	PebbleRebel	$y=(2, 10, 1)$		
	Number-Invader	$z=(1, y-1, 1)$		
Type 3	Mathcards	$x=(2, 12, 1)$	z/y of $[x \times y] = [x \times z]$	2/11 of 22 = 4
	PebbleRebel	$y=(2, 16, 1)$		
	Number-Invader	$z=(1, y-1, 1)$		
Type 4	Mathcards	$x=(2, 10, 1)$	z/y of $[x \times y] = [x \times z]$	6/3 of 24 = 48
	PebbleRebel	$y=(2, 10, 1)$		
	Number-Invader	$z=(1, 10, 1)$		
Type 5	Mathcards	$x=(2, 12, 1)$	z/y of $[x \times y] = [x \times z]$	15/10 of 20 = 30
	PebbleRebel	$y=(2, 16, 1)$		
	Number-Invader	$z=(1, 15, 1)$		

Note: The digits between brackets for example (2, 10, 1) shows that this denominator or nominator has a range from 2 (first digit) to 10 (second digit) with jumps of 1 (third number). Concrete, in this example, it concerns a number of the following series: 2, 3, 4, 5, 6, 7, 8, 9, or 10. The game generates at random which number of the series is selected

IMI subscales: the interest/enjoyment subscale (seven items, e.g., "I enjoyed playing this game very much," $\alpha=0.91$) and the perceived competence subscale (six items, e.g., "I think I am pretty good at playing this game," $\alpha=0.87$). The correlation between the interest/enjoyment subscale and perceived competence subscale was positively significant ($r=.57$, $p<.001$). Again—and in line with the MSLQ—both subscales are taken together ($\alpha=0.91$) and the sum of both subscales is used for analyses.

Performance. In a self-developed pre- and posttest students' math performance concerning calculating factions was measured. Both tests, with comparable difficulty level, contained 30 questions (30 items, $\alpha_{pretest}=.83$ and $\alpha_{posttest}=.87$) with only one possible correct answer. There was no time-limit. In Table 3, an overview is given of the test-items. As Table 3 shows, there is a considerable overlap between the questions in the tests and the exercise types in the mini-games (i.e., questions concerning comparing, adding, subtracting, and multiplying fractions). Additionally, three transfer questions are presented to the pupils, more specific, these questions concern proportional reasoning problems.

Next to this pen-and-paper math performance during the pre- and postphase, also in-game math performance is taken into account. Therefore, the score students received in the mini-games and the amount of mini-games students were able to win were used as indicators. These in-game score parameters, however, are possibly an underestimation of students' math ability because of the difficulty of the mini-games which also require gaming- and puzzle-solving skills of the students.

Table 3 Overview of different types of questions presented in pre- and posttest

Question in test (*example*)	# Questions	Type of question (see Table 2)	Mini-game
Fill in following exercises. (*1/6 of 54 = ?*)	5	Operations—fraction of number Type 1–5	Mathcards
			PebbleRebel
			NumberInvader
Which fractions equal *x*? (*Which fractions equals 1/2? 4/8, 2/6, 5/10, 4/9, or 2/4?*)	4	Comparison—fractions Type 1, 2 and 3	Balloon pop-up
Which fractions are bigger than *x*? (*Which fractions are bigger than 1/4? 3/8, 1/6, 1/2, 4/5, or 2/10?*)	4	Comparison—fractions Type 1, 2 and 3	Balloon pop-up
Which fractions are smaller than *x*? (*Which fractions are smaller than 1/4? 3/8, 1/6, 1/2, 4/5, or 2/10?*)	4	Comparison—fractions Type 1, 2 and 3	Balloon pop-up
Solve the following exercises. (*2/6 + 5/6 = ?*)	4	Operations—equal denominator	Mathcards
			NumberInvader
Solve the following exercises. (*2/6 + 4/5 = ?*)	6	Operations—simple fractions	Mathcards
			NumberInvader
Solve the following problems. (*Dylan and Larissa are talking about their scooter. Dylan's tank use for 30 km equals 1 L. Larissa is driving 360 km with a tank of 12 L. Who is driving the most economical?*)	3	Proportional reasoning problem	–

Game perception. The game perception scale (GPS; Vandercruysse, Vandewaetere et al., 2015) was used to measure students' perception of the GBLE. This questionnaire measures (1) students' expectations about the playfulness of the GBLE and (2) the degree to which a student believes that using a GBLE will enhance his or her performance. Both aspects are represented in a subscale of the GPS: the perceived playfulness subscale (three items, as suggested by Vandercruysse et al., 2015; for example, "I was playing the game rather than working/learning," $\alpha_{pre} = 74$ and $\alpha_{post} = .85$) and the perceived usefulness subscale (five items, e.g., "I think that playing this game is useful for learning fractions," $\alpha_{pre} = .77$ and $\alpha_{post} = .91$).

Procedure

The study started with a pretest session of 1 h. During this session, a short refresher course on math was given as introduction. Although calculating fractions is part of the curriculum, this activated their prior knowledge (Merrill, 2002). In line with the mathematical content that was implemented in the game for this experiment (see Table 2), some general information concerning fractions and instruction related to comparing, adding, subtracting, and multiplying fractions was focused on . This introduction was followed by the questionnaire which measured students' premotivation (MSLQ) and perception of the GBLE (GPS). Also the pretest, which students had to fill in individually and without using a calculator, was presented to the students.

After this pretest session, students received their instructions which varied depending on the condition they were assigned to (see design). This was followed by a playtime session which lasted for 2 h.

After the playtime session, students received the 30-item posttest and postquestionnaire which measured postexperimental motivation (IMI) and game perception (GPS). Again students were stimulated to work individually and without the aid of a calculator (for the posttest). This session took approximately 1 h.

As previously mentioned, the experiment organized during the PGS course of the participants. Since students in vocational education weekly have 6 h of PGS, we strived for a maximum time interval between the pretest, intervention, and posttest of 1 week.

Results

For all analyses, a significance level of $\alpha = 0.05$ was set. After detecting for outliers, one participant was excluded, which resulted in 47 participants. To investigate possible significant differences between the classes, multilevel analyses were conducted for all the dependent variables of the analyses. None of the analyses revealed a significant difference between the classes. Hence, the differences between classes were not taken into account in the following analyses.

Initial Differences Between the Two Experimental Conditions

To identify possible initial differences between both conditions, two ANOVAs were conducted with condition as independent variable and score on the pretest and premotivation questionnaire (MSLQ) as dependent variables. Additionally a MANOVA, with the two subscales of the GPS as dependent variables and condition as independent variable was done. Concerning the pretest, the mean scores were 61.47 % ($SD = 19.32$ %; with a minimum of 26.67 % and maximum score of 90.00 %) for the weak integration condition and 65 % ($SD = 13.28$ %; with a minimum of 36.67 % and a maximum of 90.00 %) for the strong integration condition, which is quite high for our target group. There was no significant difference between both conditions ($F(1, 45) = .52, p = .48$) with respect to students' score on the pre-test. Also for students' premotivation as measured by the sum of the score on the subscales of the

MSLQ ($M_{\text{weak integration condition}}$ = 38.09; $M_{\text{strong integration condition}}$ = 30.05) with a minimum of 12 and a maximum score of 72, no significant difference was found ($F(1, 39) = 3.52$, $p = .07$). The MANOVA, using Wilks's statistics, showed a significant initial difference between both conditions (Wilks's $\lambda = .80$; $F(2, 40) = 4.98$; $p = .012$, $\eta^2 = .20$) concerning their GPS-subscale scores. Separate univariate ANOVAs on the outcome variables revealed no significant difference for their perceived playfulness of the GBLE ($F(1, 41) = 2.59$, $p = .12$), but we did find a significant difference between both conditions for their perceived usefulness ($F(1, 41) = 8.46$, $p = .006$). The weak integration condition ($M = 18.65$, $SD = 4.99$; with a minimum of 8 and a maximum score of 48) scored higher for their perceived usefulness than the students in the strong integration condition ($M = 14.55$, $SD = 4.14$) and perceived the GBLE as more useful before the intervention took place. Therefore, and because we assumed that students' game perception would influence students' motivation, performance, and perception, we corrected for students' pregame perception (more specific their perceived usefulness and perceived playfulness) in the following analyses.

Effect of Curriculum Integration on Students' Motivation (Hypothesis 1 and 4)

Because we supposed that students in the strong integration condition would show greater (intrinsic) motivation (hypothesis 1) the relation between curriculum integration and students' intrinsic motivation was investigated with an ANCOVA. Condition was used as factor and motivation, measured by the sum of the scores on the interest/enjoyment subscale and perceived competence subscale, as dependent variable. Students' GPS score on the perceived usability subscale and perceived playfulness subscale were used as covariates.

Results show that curriculum integration, controlled for both GPS subscales, is not significantly related to students' postexperimental intrinsic motivation ($F(1, 35) = .45$, $p = .51$). The weak integration condition ($M = 45.42$, SE = 2.47) is not significantly different from the strong integration condition ($M = 42.92$, SE = 2.54) regarding their intrinsic motivation. Hypothesis 1, which expected a relation between the degree of curriculum integration and students' (intrinsic) motivation during gameplay (and more specific that the strong integration condition would show greater intrinsic motivation), was not confirmed.

Hypothesis 4, in which we expected that students who perceived the environment as a useful means to learn math would be more intrinsically motivated, was partly confirmed since a significant effect was found between students' perceived usability score and their postexperimental intrinsic motivation ($F(1, 35) = 14.12$, $p = .001$, $\eta^2 = 0.29$). More specifically, students who perceived the game as more useful for their learning, prior to the gameplay showed higher scores on self-reported intrinsic motivation as measured after gameplay. However, no significant relation was found between students' perceived playfulness and their postexperimental intrinsic motivation ($F(1, 35) = .002$, $p = .96$).

Effect of Curriculum Integration on Students' Performance (Hypothesis 2 and 5)

Math performance. An ANCOVA with condition as factor, the posttest score as dependent variable and perceived usefulness and perceived playfulness as covariates was conducted because a stronger integration of games in the instruction program (or curriculum) was assumed to promote the learning process (hypothesis 2). The ANCOVA revealed no significant effect of curriculum integration on students' performance on the posttest after controlling for their perceived usefulness and perceived playfulness ($F(1, 39) = .34$, $p = .56$). After playing the game with a different instruction, and thus a different integration in the curriculum, students in the strong integration condition ($M = 67.03$ %, $SE = 4.43$ %) scored not significantly higher than students in the weak integration condition ($M = 63.31$ %, $SE = 4.10$ %). Hypothesis 2, in which a difference was expected, was not confirmed. As was the case with the pretest, a large variation in scores was found which indicated that some students scored very low on the posttest (minimum = 33.33 %) and other students scored very high (maximum = 100 %).

The relation between the perceived usefulness and the posttest score (hypothesis 5) of the students was not significant ($F(1, 39) = .16$, $p = .69$). Also the relation between the perceived playfulness and the posttest score of the students was not significant ($F(1, 39) = .95$, $p = .34$). The way students perceived the game (concerning its usefulness and playfulness) before the intervention was not related to their performance on the posttest after playing the game. Hypothesis 5, in which we assumed that the game perception would be positively related to students' performance, was not confirmed.

Game performance. To investigate the relation between the curriculum integration of the game and students' game performance (hypothesis 2), two ANCOVAs were conducted with condition as factor, perceived playfulness and perceived usefulness as covariates and the performance (measured with the total game-score and amount of mini-games won) as dependent variables.

The first ANCOVA with the amount of mini-games won as dependent variable, revealed no significant effect of curriculum integration, controlled for perceived usefulness and perceived playfulness, on students' game performance ($F(1, 36) = 3.74$, $p = .06$). Students in the strong integration condition ($M = 10.30$, $SE = 0.76$) finished not significantly more mini-games than students in the weak integration condition ($M = 8.16$, $SE = 0.72$) and thus progressed not significantly further in the game.

The results of the second ANCOVA in which the total game-score is the dependent variable revealed a significant effect of the curriculum integration, controlled for pregame perception, on students' performance in the game ($F(1, 35) = 6.43$, $p = .02$, $\eta^2 = .16$). The strong integration condition ($M = 25\ 050.76$, $SE = 2049.22$) scored significantly higher in the game than the weak integration condition ($M = 17\ 653.16$, $SE = 1882.83$). Hence, hypothesis 2 was only partly confirmed for the in-game performance of the students.

Further, the relation between the perceived playfulness and the amount of mini-games won ($F(1, 36) = .12$, $p = .73$) and the relation between the perceived usefulness and the amount of mini-games won ($F(1, 36) = .49$, $p = .49$) were both not significant. Also the relation between the perceived playfulness and the total game-score ($F(1, 35) = .99$, $p = .33$) and the relation between the perceived usefulness and the total game-score ($F(1, 35) = .01$, $p = .93$) was not significant. The way students perceived the game (concerning its usefulness and playfulness) before the intervention was not related to their in-game performance. Hypothesis 5, in which we assumed that game perception would be positively related to students' performance, was not confirmed.

Effect of Curriculum Integration on Students' Game Perception (Hypothesis 3 and 6)

Finally, the relation between curriculum integration and students' perception of the environment after gameplay was investigated (hypothesis 3). A MANCOVA with condition as factor and students' perceived usefulness (post) and perceived playfulness (post) as dependent variables was conducted. The scores on the two GPS subscales measured before the game-play were used as two covariates. The results showed no significant difference between both conditions related to their score on the two post GPS subscales (Wilks's $\lambda = .97$; $F(2, 35) = .50$; $p = .61$). Hence, hypothesis 3 was not confirmed.

Hypothesis 6 instead was partly confirmed because a significant relation was found between the preperceived usefulness score and the postperceived usefulness score ($F(1, 36) = 11.57$, $p = .002$, $\eta^2 = 0.24$). As was expected, the more students perceived the environment as a useful game environment before gameplay ($b = 0.62$), the more they perceived the environment as a useful game environment after gameplay. No significant relation was found between the preperceived usefulness and the postperceived playfulness ($F(1, 36) = .05$, $p = .83$), between the preperceived playfulness and postperceived usefulness ($F(1, 36) = .40$, $p = .53$) and between the preperceived playfulness and postperceived playfulness ($F(1, 36) = 2.68$, $p = .11$).

Discussion

This study investigated the influence of the (weak or strong) integration of an educational game in the curriculum, and more specific the absence or presence of an explicit link between the learning content in the game and the learning content in classroom/curriculum, on students' motivation, (in-game) math performance, and perception. Based on the literature, we expected that the condition in which the game was strongly integrated in the curriculum would show greater intrinsic motivation and better performances (Hays, 2005; Tobias et al., 2011). Additionally, the mediational paradigm (Winne, 1982, 1987) assumed that learners' perception of the environment influenced the effect of curriculum integration on motivation and performance. The results showed that the strong integration condition indeed outperformed the weak integration condition for the in-game performances, more specific for the game-score (but not for the progress through the game, i.e., the amount of mini-games won). The other hypotheses however could not be confirmed.

The first finding confirms the assumption that students in the condition in which the learning content in the game (i.e., mathematics; operations with fractions) was strongly integrated (i.e., explicitly linked) in the curriculum, scored better during gameplay than students in the condition in which this integration was more weakly present. More concrete, the students from the strong integration condition obtained a higher game-score than the students in the weak integration condition. This is in line with the expectations (Hays, 2005; Tobias et al., 2011) that game integration in the curriculum enhances students' game performances (which is a reflection of students' math performances and their puzzle solving and gaming skills). However, one of the striking findings of this study is that, although learners in the strong integration condition were significantly more successful in the game (as indicated by their high game-score), their ability to solve fraction exercises measured with the posttest, which related to the game content, was not significantly different from the students in the weak integration condition. The scores on the pretest were already quite high for this target group, and only a slight progression was found for both conditions after the gameplay (i.e., approximately 2 %). A possible explanation is that the students did not make a connection between the content in the game and the content that was presented in the tests (Barzilai & Blau, 2014) and that the operationalization of the integration in the curriculum could be more explicitly elaborated (see further). Additionally, the time interval of the experiment was limited to 1 week. It might be interesting in future research to implement a long-term measurement, with multiple measurement moments, to investigate whether the students in the strong integration condition would continue to outperform the students in the weak integration condition after a longer period of time. Furthermore, it might also be interesting to investigate if a longer implementation of the GBLE in the classroom has an(other) effect on students' (in-game) performances.

In contrast to our expectations, the strong or weak integration of the game environment in the classroom was not related to students' motivation. A possible explanation for these findings is the low premotivation of the participants. Students in the weak integration condition had a mean premotivation score of 38.09 and students in the strong integration condition of 30.05 while the maximum score they could reach was 72 (and a minimum of 12). According to Winne (1987) insufficient (pre-)motivation can lead to ineffective instructional methods. Another possible explanation is that in both conditions different processes were influencing students' intrinsic motivation. In the literature, it seems that students' intrinsic motivation is influenced (and stimulated) when they perceive the game as more relevant (Herndon, 1987; Kinzie, 1990; Ryan & Deci, 2000). Students who belonged to the strong integration condition, perceived the game as more relevant and were more intrinsically motivated. In the weak integration condition however, students might also be intrinsically motivated, not because of the perceived relevance of the game, but because of the reward they received, that is, the game was introduced as a reward for their hard work during previous lessons (Deci, Koestner, & Ryan, 1999). So in both conditions, intrinsic motivation might have been stimulated, although only slightly, but as a result of two different processes.

Again unlike the expectations (Winne, 1982, 1987), no significant difference between students' perception was found. More specific, integrating the game in the curriculum did not reveal any significant differences in students' perception about the usefulness and playfulness of the educational game. A possible explanation here is that students' perception were influenced by other factors than we intended to. Possibly the fact that students knew they participated in scientific research influenced their expectations and consequently their results (Grabinger, 2009; Vandercruysse et al., 2013). Because students participated in our study, they might not perceive the game as a part of the curriculum (in the strong integration condition) which may explain the lack of difference in perception. An additional possible explanation might be the study procedure, more specific the moment of measurement. Students needed to fill in the premotivation and preperception questionnaire before they received the introduction and instruction. This might have led to unintended misunderstanding of the students about the GBLE used in the study because they only saw the environment after filling in the questionnaires. Previous experiences (or the lack of such experiences) with other GBLEs might have influenced their responses.

However, the study revealed support for the supposed relation between the pre- and postperceptions of the students. Additionally, students who perceived the GBLE as an environment that was useful to learn solving fractions (i.e., their perceived usefulness) were more intrinsically motivated and perceived the environment as more useful after the gameplay. These findings emphasize the importance of students' perception in game-based learning processes. Unfortunately, this effect was not found for students' (in-game and posttest) performances.

A limitation of this study might be the operationalization of the integration in the curriculum. The limited link between the learning content in the game and the curriculum (even in the strong integration condition) might explain the lack of significant differences between both conditions. Therefore in a subsequent study, the operationalization of the integration of the GBLE will be based on the suggestions of Felicia (2011) who suggests based on Gagné's "nine events of instruction" that game integration in the curriculum contains three steps (Felicia, 2011). Before the students start to play the game, teachers need to identify learning objectives, explain the objectives, demonstrate the game, and explain how common tasks are performed. A second step is the gameplay session. During this gameplay, teachers explain or clarify possible confusions and intervene shortly during "mini-teaching moments" to have an input that is essential for the understanding of the curriculum and to progress in the game. In the third and last step, a debriefing is organized.

During this session, a connection is made between the curriculum and the game after play. This operationalization is more explicit than the operationalization in this study which only contained the first step. A link between learning content in the game and curriculum was only made explicit before the gameplay. The link during and after gameplay was lacking. Also Watson, Mong, and Harris (2011) and Charsky and Mims (2008) emphasized the importance of a short debriefing after gameplay during which students are learning to comprehend their mistakes and are stimulated to reflect which heightens the chance on transfer (Watson, Mong, & Harris, 2011).

Another limitation is the limited amount of participants. Although 51 participants were recruited, some analyses were only conducted with 36 participants because of incompletely filled-in questionnaires. This might be a possible additional explanation for a substantial decrease of the power of the study which reduces the chance for finding significant effects. Furthermore, the small group of participants seemed to be a heterogeneous group because of the high standard deviations and big range of the scores. It might be that, because of this heterogeneity, we did not find significant effects with an F-test because the denominator was very high. Another possible disadvantage of the participants in this study is the over-representation of girls. It is argued that girls have less initial computer and game knowledge, possibly resulting in a greater difficulty in using a game application (Vandercruysse et al., 2012). Also the learning time may have been too short in order to support deep learning (i.e., one-shot). Mean playtime was 80 min which might be too short for finding learning and motivational effects. In the next study, we will try to take into account these limitations.

In sum, this study only partly answers the question how the integration of an educational game is related to students' motivation, performance, and perception. We only found a significant difference in students' in-game performance. Although teachers are often convinced that using games with a stronger integration is advisable (Demirbilek & Tamer, 2010; Kebritchi, 2010; Koh, Kin, Wadhwa, & Lim, 2012), this study indicates that the integration of the game in the curriculum is only significantly related to students' in-game performance and thus yields no influence on their score on a regular paper-and-pencil test, their intrinsic motivation and their game perception. Obviously, further research is warranted in which a more thorough operationalization of the game integration is used. Additionally, in this study only one operationalization of game integration was investigated. As mentioned in the introduction, game integration might also be operationalized in a completely different way. Further research could also focus on intrinsically integrated games and the effect this type of integration has on students' performance, motivation, and perception.

Acknowledgments This work was sponsored by a research project funded by iMinds Flanders (ICON, Games@School (G@S), 2012–2013) and a research project funded by the Fund of Scientific Research (FWO—G.O.516.11.N.10). Additionally, the authors would like to express their great appreciation to Martin Vanbrabant, for the technical support concerning the customization options of the game-based learning environment.

References

Akilli, G. K. (2007). Games and simulations: A new approach in education? In D. G. Gibson, C. A. Aldrich, & M. Prensky (Eds.), *Games and simulations in online learning: Research and development frameworks* (pp. 1–20). Hershey, PA: Information Science Publishing.

Aldrich, C. (2005). *Learning by doing: The comprehensive guide to simulations, computer games, and pedagogy in e-learning and other educational experiences.* San Francisco, CA: Pfeiffer.

Barendregt, W., & Bekker, T. M. (2011). The influence of the level of free-choice learning activities on the use of an educational computer game. *Computers & Education, 56*, 80–90. doi:10.1016/j.compedu.2010.08.018.

Barzilai, S., & Blau, I. (2014). Scaffolding game-based learning: Impact on learning achievements, perceived learning, and game experiences. *Computers & Education, 70*, 65–79. doi:10.1016/j.compedu.2013.08.003.

Becker, K. (2007). Pedagogy in commercial video games. In D. G. Gibson, C. A. Aldrich, & M. Prensky (Eds.), *Games and simulations in online learning: Research and development frameworks.* Hershey, PA: Information Science Publishing. doi:10.4018/978-1-59904-304-3.ch002.

Bergeron, B. (2006). *Developing serious games.* Hingham, MA: Charles River Media.

Charsky, D., & Mims, C. (2008). Integrating commercial off-the-shelf video games into school curriculums. *TechTrends, 52*, 38–44.

Clark, D. B., Nelson, B. C., Chang, H.-Y., Martinez-Garza, M., Slack, K., & D'Angelo, C. M. (2011). Exploring Newtonian mechanics in a conceptually-integrated digital game: Comparison of learning and affective outcomes for students in Taiwan and the United States. *Computers & Education, 57*, 2178–2195. doi:10.1016/j.compedu.2011.05.007.

Connolly, T. M., Boyle, E. A., MacArthur, E., Hainey, T., & Boyle, J. M. (2012). A systematic literature review of empirical evidence on computer games and serious games. *Computers & Education, 59*(2), 661–686.

Deci, E. L., Koestner, R., & Ryan, R. M. (1999). A meta-analytic review of experiments examining the effects of extrinsic rewards on intrinsic motivation. *Psychological Bulletin, 125*, 627–668.

DeLeeuw, K. E., & Mayer, R. E. (2011). Cognitive consequences of making computer-based learning activities more game-like. *Computers in Human Behaviour, 27*, 2011–2016. doi:10.1016/j.chb.2011.05.008.

Demirbilek, M., & Tamer, S. L. (2010). Math teachers' perspectives on using educational computer games in math education. *Procedia Social and Behavioral Sciences, 9*, 709–716. doi:10.1016/j.sbspro.2010.12.222.

Din, F. S., & Calao, J. (2001). The effects of playing educational video games on kindergarten achievement. *Child Study Journal, 31*, 95–102.

Entwistle, N. J. (1991). Approaches to learning and perceptions of the learning environment: Introduction to the special issue. *Higher Education, 22*, 201–204.

Felicia, P. (2011). *How can digital games be used to teach the school curriculum?* Retrieved from http://linked.eun.org/c/document_library/get_file?p_l_id=22779&folderId=24664&name=DLFE-783.pdf

Garris, R., Ahlers, R., & Driskell, J. E. (2002). Games, motivation, and learning: A research and practice model. *Simulation & Gaming, 33*, 441–467. doi:10.1177/1046878102238607.

Girard, C., Ecalle, J., & Magnan, A. (2013). Serious games as new educational tools. How effective are they? A meta-analysis of recent studies. *Journal of Computer Assisted Learning, 29*, 207–219. doi:10.1111/j.1365-2729.2012.00489.x.

Grabinger, R. S. (2009). Discussion. *Computers in Human Behavior, 25*, 836–840.

Habgood, M. P. J., & Ainsworth, S. E. (2011). Motivating children to learn effectively: exploring the value of intrinsic integration in educational games. *Journal of the Learning Sciences, 20*, 169–206. doi:10.1080/10508406.2010.508029.

Hayes, E., & Games, I. (2008). Learning through game design: a review of current software and research. *Games and Culture, 3*, 309–332.

Hays, R. T. (2005). *The effectiveness of instructional games: A literature review and discussion* (Report No. 2005-004). Orlando, FL: Naval Air Warfare Center Training Systems Division.

Herndon, J. N. (1987). Learner interests, achievement, and continuing motivation in instruction. *Journal of Instructional Development, 10*, 11–14.

Ke, F. (2008a). Alternative goal structures for computer game-based learning. *International Journal of Computer-Supported Collaborative Learning, 3*, 429–445. doi:10.1007/s11412-008-9048-2.

Ke, F. (2008b). Computer games application within alternative classroom goal structures: Cognitive, metacognitive, and affective evaluation. *Educational Technology Research and Development, 56*, 539–556. doi:10.1007/s11423-008-9086-5.

Ke, F., & Grabowksi, B. (2007). Gameplaying for maths learning: Cooperative or not? *British Journal of Educational Technology, 38*, 249–259. doi:10.1111/j.1467-8535.2006.00593.x.

Kebritchi, M. (2010). Factors affecting teachers' adoption of educational computer games: A case study. *British Journal of Educational Technology, 41*, 256–270. doi:10.1111/j.1467-8535.2008.00921.x.

Kinzie, M. B. (1990). Requirements and benefits of effective interactive instruction: Learner control, self-regulation, and continuing motivation. *Educational Technology Research and Development, 38*, 5–21.

Koh, E., Kin, Y. G., Wadhwa, B., & Lim, J. (2012). Teacher perceptions of games in Singapore schools. *Simulation & Gaming, 43*, 51–66. doi:10.1177/1046878111401839.

Liu, T. Y., & Chu, Y. L. (2010). Using ubiquitous games in an English listening and speaking course: Impact on learning outcomes and motivation. *Computers & Education, 55*, 630–643. doi:10.1016/j.compedu.2010.02.023.

Lowyck, J., Elen, J., & Clarebout, G. (2004). Instructional conceptions: Analyses from an instructional design perspective. *International Journal of Educational Research, 41*, 429–444.

Malone, T. (1980). What makes things fun to learn? Heuristics for designing instructional computer games. In *Proceedings of the 3rd ACM SIGSMALL symposium and the 1st SIGPC symposium on small systems*, Palo Alto, CA (pp. 162–169).

McAuley, E., Duncan, T., & Tammen, V. V. (1987). Psychometric properties of the intrinsic motivation inventory in a competitive sport setting: a confirmatory factor analysis. *Research Quarterly for Exercise and Sport, 60*(1), 48–58. doi:10.1080/02701367.1989.10607413.

Merrill, M. D. (2002). First principles of instruction. *Educational Technology Research and Development, 50*(3), 43–59.

O'Neil, H. F., Wainess, R., & Baker, E. L. (2005). Classification of learning outcomes: evidence from the computer games literature. *The Curriculum Journal, 16*, 455–474. doi:10.1080/09585170500384529.

Pintrich, P. R., Smith, D. A. F., Garcia, T., & McKeachie, W. J. (1993). Reliability and predictive validity of the motivated strategies for learning questionnaire (MSLQ). *Educational and Psychological Measurement, 53*, 801–813.

Plant, R. W., & Ryan, R. M. (1985). Intrinsic motivation and the effects of self-consciousness, self-awareness, and ego-involvement: An investigation of internally controlling styles. *Journal of Personality, 53*, 435–449. doi:10.1111/j.1467-6494.1985.tb00375.x.

Prensky, M. (2001). *Digital game-based learning*. New York, NY: McGraw-Hill.

Randel, J. M., Morris, B. A., Wetzle, C. D., & Whitehead, B. V. (1992). The effectiveness of games for educational purposes: A review of recent research. *Simulation & Gaming, 23*, 261–276.

Ryan, R. M., & Deci, E. L. (2000). Intrinsic and extrinsic motivations: Classic definitions and new directions. *Contemporary Educational Psychology, 25*, 54–67. doi:10.1006/ceps.1999.1020.

Salomon, G. (1984). Television is "easy" and print is "tough": The differential investment of mental effort in learning as a function of perceptions and attributions. *Journal of Educational Psychology, 76*, 647–658.

Shuell, T. J., & Farber, S. L. (2001). Students' perceptions of technology use in college courses. *Journal of Educational Computing Research, 24*, 119–138.

Sitzman, T. (2011). A meta-analytic examination of the instructional effectiveness of computer-based simulation games. *Personnel Psychology, 64*, 489–528.

Tobias, S., Fletcher, J. D., Dai, D. Y., & Wind, A. P. (2011). Review of research on computer games. In S. Tobias & J. D. Fletcher (Eds.), *Computer games and instruction* (pp. 127–221). Charlotte, NC: Information Age Publishing.

Vandercruysse, S., Maertens, M., & Elen, J. (2015). Description of the educational math game "Monkey Tales: The museum of anything". New York, NY: Springer

Vandercruysse, S., Vandewaetere, M., Cornillie, F., & Clarebout, G. (2013). Competition and students' perceptions in a game-based language learning environment. *Educational Technology Research and Development, 61*(6), 927–950.

Vandercruysse, S., Vandewaetere, M., Maertens, M., ter Vrugte, J., Wouters, P., de Jong, T., … Elen, J. (2015). Development and validation of the game perception scale (GPS). *Journal of Educational Media and Hypermedia, 24*(1), 43–74.

Vandercruysse, S., Vandewaetere, M., & Clarebout, G. (2012). Game based learning: A review on the effectiveness of educational games. In M. M. Cruz-Cunda (Ed.), *Handbook of research on serious games as educational, business, and research tools*. Hershey, PA: IGI Global.

Vogel, J. J., Vogel, D. S., Cannon-Bowers, J., Bowers, C. A., Muse, K., & Wright, M. (2006). Computer games and interactive simulations for learning: A meta-analysis. *Journal of Educational Computing Research, 34*, 229–243. doi:10.2190/FLHV-K4WA-WPVQ-H0YM.

Walker, D. F., & Soltis, J. F. (1997). *Curriculum and aims*. New York, NY: Teachers College Press.

Watson, W. R., Mong, C. J., & Harris, C. A. (2011). A case study of the in-class use of a video game for teaching high school history. *Computers & Education, 56*, 466–474.

Winne, P. H. (1982). Minimizing the black box problem to enhance the validity of theories about instructional effects. *Instructional Science, 11*, 13–28.

Winne, P. H. (1987). Why process-product research cannot explain process-product findings and a proposed remedy: The cognitive mediational paradigm. *Teaching & Teacher Education, 3*, 333–356.

Wouters, P., van der Spek, D., & van Oostendorp, H. (2009). Current practices in serious game research: A review from a learning outcomes perspective. In T. M. Connolly, M. Stansfield, & L. Boyle (Eds.), *Games based learning advancements for multisensory human computer interfaces: Techniques and effective practices* (pp. 232–255). Hershey, PA: IGI Global. doi:10.4018/978-1-60566-360-9.ch014.

Developing Adaptive Number Knowledge with the Number Navigation Game-Based Learning Environment

Boglárka Brezovszky, Gabriela Rodríguez-Aflecht, Jake McMullen,
Koen Veermans, Nonmanut Pongsakdi, Minna M. Hannula-Sormunen,
and Erno Lehtinen

Abstract Research suggests that adaptivity with arithmetic problem solving can be developed by placing more focus on developing students' understanding of the underlying numerical characteristics and connections during problem solving. For this reason, the present study aimed to explore how primary school students' game performance using the "Number Navigation Game" (NNG) game-based learning environment was related to their development of adaptive number knowledge. NNG provides extensive opportunities for working strategically with various number patterns and number–operation combinations. Sixth grade students ($N = 23$) played NNG in pairs, once a week, for 7 weeks during math class. Students completed measures of adaptive number knowledge and arithmetic fluency during pre- and post-testing. Results show that students' game performance had a unique contribution to explaining students' adaptive number knowledge during post-test. This suggests that NNG is a promising game-based learning environment for developing adaptivity with arithmetic problem solving by enhancing students' adaptive number knowledge.

Keywords Adaptive number knowledge • Arithmetic problem solving • Numerical relations • Game-based learning environment

B. Brezovszky (✉) • G. Rodríguez-Aflecht • J. McMullen
K. Veermans • N. Pongsakdi • E. Lehtinen
Department of Teacher Education, Centre for Learning Research,
University of Turku, Turku 20014, Finland
e-mail: bogbre@utu.fi; gabriela.rodriguez@utu.fi; jake.mcmullen@utu.fi;
koen.veermans@utu.fi; nopong@utu.fi; erno.lehtinen@utu.fi

M.M. Hannula-Sormunen
Department of Teacher Education, Turku Institute for Advanced Studies,
University of Turku, Turku 20014, Finland
e-mail: mimarha@utu.fi

© Springer International Publishing Switzerland 2015
J. Torbeyns et al. (eds.), *Describing and Studying Domain-Specific Serious Games*,
Advances in Game-Based Learning, DOI 10.1007/978-3-319-20276-1_10

The development of adaptive expertise with arithmetic has long been stated as foundational for developing proficient future skills in all areas of mathematics and is a goal of curricula all over the world (National Council of Teachers of Mathematics, 2000). By placing too much focus on training solution algorithms, traditional arithmetic instruction has often been criticized as encouraging the development of routine rather than adaptive expertise, where students become highly efficient in applying different algorithms for very specific types of problems but fail to transfer these skills into new contexts and problem types (Blöte, Klein, & Beishuizen, 2000; Hatano & Oura, 2003).

Adaptive expertise with arithmetic refers to students' ability to adaptively and flexibly use arithmetic strategies in solving mathematical tasks. There are only a few practical suggestions offered by research on how adaptivity with arithmetic problem solving can be developed. One general guideline is to provide students practice with different combinations of numbers and operations in order to develop a better understanding of the underlying numerical characteristics and relations in their problem-solving process (Baroody, 2003). The aim of the present study was to explore the affordances of the Number Navigation Game-based learning environment (NNG) in developing a richly connected mental representation of numbers which underlies and supports the development of adaptivity with arithmetic problem solving.

Literature Overview

Adaptive Number Knowledge

Adaptive and flexible arithmetic problem solving can be described by the ability to select the most "optimal" (fast and efficient) problem-solving methods for a given mathematical task. However, it is fairly relative what can be defined as "optimal" problem solving for a given problem, as this can depend on many factors such as problem characteristics, personal characteristics, and preferences, and also the norms and rules of a given social context (Verschaffel, Luwel, Torbeyns, & Van Dooren, 2009). There are several underlying factors to consider when exploring adaptivity with arithmetic problem solving. One such factor is the ability to notice and use numerical characteristics and relations when performing calculations on novel tasks where just recalling arithmetic facts is not sufficient. Based on the density and strength of numerical relations available for a person, different numerical connections can be noticed leading to various solution methods (Dowker, 1992). Thus, adaptivity with arithmetic problem solving can be described as involving the noticing and use of numerical characteristics and relations in order to arrive at efficient problem-solving strategies in mental calculations (Threlfall, 2002, 2009). Accordingly, efficiently noticing and using these connections requires a well-connected mental representation of numerical characteristics and relations. The knowledge of these characteristics and relations is a key component of adaptivity with arithmetic problem solving and is referred to as *adaptive number knowledge* in the present study.

The importance of numerical characteristics and relations has been explored in a number of studies on students' adaptivity with arithmetic problem solving. Children with a well-connected representation of numbers use more flexible procedures in their mental computations (Heirdsfield & Cooper, 2004). Mathematical experts have been found to have more rich numerical connections and can flexibly use them in their mental problem solving (Dowker, 1992). Students who can understand the principles of commutativity or associativity are also more efficient and more flexible in their mental computations (Canobi, Reeve, & Pattison, 2003). However, even if students are able to report on a variety of procedures to solve a problem, this knowledge is often not used during problem solving, especially with novel problem types (Blöte et al., 2000; Canobi et al., 2003).

In previous studies, adaptivity with arithmetic problem solving was mainly measured using (a) measures of specific strategies, such as indirect addition and direct subtraction (e.g. Torbeyns, Ghesquière, & Verschaffel, 2009), (b) case studies, interviews, detailed analyses of problem-solving procedures (e.g. Heirdsfield & Cooper, 2004), or (c) language-intensive tests (e.g. Schneider, Rittle-Johnson, & Star, 2011). In this study, a measure of adaptive number knowledge is presented which aims to assess individual differences in students' available mental connections of numerical characteristics and relations while solving novel types of arithmetic problems (McMullen, Brezovszky, Rodríguez Padilla, Pongsakdi, & Lehtinen, 2015). The Adaptive Number Knowledge Task is a timed paper-pencil measure that can be applied in a classroom setting. In this task, given a certain set of numbers, students need to look for various combinations of these numbers and the four arithmetic operations that would lead to a given outcome. The amount and complexity of different combinations provided by the students is considered to reflect students' recognition and use of numerical connections in their problem-solving process, and thus represent a measure of students' adaptive number knowledge.

Integrating Adaptive Number Knowledge Training and Game Mechanics

For developing stronger adaptive number knowledge, it is suggested, that more emphasis should be placed on providing students with contexts for discovering the underlying relations between numbers and operations. Working with various combinations of numbers and operations can aid the development of rich networks of numerical relations and help student to recognize and use these relations in their arithmetic problem solving (Baroody, 2003; Threlfall, 2002, 2009; Verschaffel et al., 2009). Game-based learning environments can provide an optimal context for discovery learning and exploration without the fear of failure (Devlin, 2011; Gee, 2003), which makes them promising tools for supporting extensive playful practice with various number–operation combinations.

Despite the educational potential of game-based learning environments, even recently published review studies report inconclusive evidence regarding the effectiveness of this medium (Girard, Ecalle, & Magnan, 2013; Wouters, van Nimwegen, van Oostendorp, & van der Spek, 2013; Young et al., 2012). This pattern is similar in the domain of mathematics instruction; although the literature suggests a growing trend in using games for developing different mathematical skills (Hwang & Wu, 2012), the number of empirically tested game-based learning environments is low and even published studies are often methodologically problematic (Cheung & Slavin, 2013; Heirdsfield & Cooper, 2004; Seo & Bryant, 2009). Additionally, many of the existing empirically tested game-based learning environments in mathematics are playful drill-and-practice training environments that aim to strengthening basic arithmetic skills, the results of which are hard to transfer in new contexts (e.g. Kucian et al., 2011; Räsänen, Salminen, Wilson, Aunio, & Dehaene, 2009; Wilson, Revkin, Cohen, Cohen, & Dehaene, 2006).

A further problem with existing game-based learning environments in mathematics is the inability to adequately integrate their core game mechanics and educational content (Devlin, 2011; Habgood & Ainsworth, 2011; Young et al., 2012). Game mechanics are crucial mechanisms through which players make choices and progress in the game (Salen & Zimmerman, 2004). The difference between an integrated and non-integrated game design is that in the first case, the player progresses through the game by doing math while in the second case the player is forced to do math in order to progress. Thus, when developing NNG used in the present study, the aim was to design a game which offers more than just the drill and practice of calculation fluency, but which aids the development of adaptive number knowledge through the core game mechanics where students work with number patterns and numerical relations.

The Relationship of Learning Goals and Game Performance

The NNG integrates the hundred-square representation of the natural number system with game mechanics in which players are required to use their knowledge of numerical characteristics and relations. This allows players to gain extensive practice with various number–operation connections. The core concept of the game is the external representation of base ten systems as a number square and the basic unit of the game is a map, which is a 10×10 number square superimposed over varying landscapes of sea and islands (see Fig. 1).

Because the aim of NNG is to go beyond the basic understanding of natural numbers, the hundred square was selected as the core representation of the number system (see a detailed theoretical rationale in Lehtinen et al., this volume). Compared to the linear number line, the hundred square provides students with a representation of the base ten system which better highlights the abstract, systemic nature of natural numbers. Thus, it is often used in activities where the aim is finding number

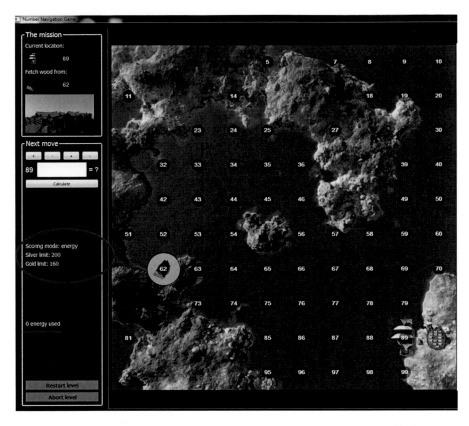

Fig. 1 Example of an NNG map in the energy scoring mode (harbour at number 89, first target material at number 62)

patterns and numerical relations within the framework of natural numbers (Beishuizen, 1993). Additionally, recent research suggests that in addition to board games which use the number line as a basic representation (Siegler & Booth, 2004; Siegler & Ramani, 2009), using the 10×10 number square as the basis of a regular children's board game also shows promising results in developing mathematical understanding (Laski & Siegler, 2014).

In NNG, within each map, the player has to navigate a ship in order to retrieve different target materials and build settlements, which means selecting certain combinations of numbers and operations as a result of which the ship will move from one location to the next (see Fig. 1). Within each map, players have to collect four types of target materials placed in different locations and return them to the starting harbour. Players need to choose their moves strategically in order to avoid islands, and adapt their strategies according to the two scoring modes of the game. With a total of 64 maps and a variety of rules and challenges, as well as different scoring modes, the game provides ample opportunities for working with various combinations of numbers and operations. For a more detailed description of the relation between different scoring modes and strategies used by the players, see the game design description by Lehtinen and colleagues (this volume) or Brezovszky, Lehtinen, McMullen, Rodriguez, and Veermans (2013).

In studying the effects of different learning environments such as game-based learning environments, one crucial issue is how students interpret the learning tasks and how they orient to the learning processes in these environments (Järvelä, Lehtinen, & Salonen, 2000; Lowyck, Lehtinen, & Elen, 2004). When analysing the effectiveness of learning environments, Engle and Conant (2002) have used the term "productive disciplinary engagement" to describe the kind of approach which results in productive learning. When discussing the educational effectiveness of a gaming environment, it is not enough that students are playing the game. Instead, what matters is how they focus on the core ideas of the learning tasks and the quality of their engagement in productive activities or productive learning behaviour (Chen, Liao, Cheng, Yeh, & Chan, 2012).

In NNG, the basic unit of the game is a map. Although players are free to access, close and return to any maps in any order, a meaningful game goal is to complete the maps by collecting the four target materials within each map. Only by completing maps can players collect the reward coins, which allow them to gain access to further maps and difficulty levels. Integrating the learning aims and the core game mechanics in a game-based learning environment is important as this method can aid students to meaningfully engage with the core learning aims (Devlin, 2011; Habgood & Ainsworth, 2011). When domain-specific content is integrated into the gameplay, as in the case of NNG, students' game performance, or the amount of practice students have with the game, is a good representation of the amount of productive engagement with the targeted learning content. In the present study, the number of maps completed was considered as a measure of players' game performance and a representation of their productive engagement with the learning content within the game context.

Aim of the Present Study

The aim of the present study is to explore if and how game performance is related to the development of adaptive number knowledge in primary school children using the NNG game-based learning environment. Providing students with environments to work with various combinations of numbers and operations is expected to be beneficial for developing their adaptivity with arithmetic problem solving (Baroody, 2003; Threlfall, 2002, 2009; Verschaffel et al., 2009). NNG provides vast opportunities for working strategically with various number patterns and number–operation combinations using an integrated game design where the learning gains and game performance should be highly related. Thus, we hypothesize that differences in students' game performance in NNG predict the development of their adaptive number knowledge.

Method

Participants

Participants were 23 Finnish speaking sixth grade primary school students (11 female, $M_{age} = 12.2$, age range: 11–13 years) from a single classroom. Students played NNG in pairs, though due to the odd number of students in the class one of them was using the game individually. The game data of the individual player was lost and one student was missing during post-test. Informed consents from parents and students were obtained before the start of the study. Ethical guidelines of the University of Turku were followed.

Procedure

A pre-test, intervention, and post-test design was used. Starting at the beginning of the autumn semester, students took part in a 12-week long intervention playing NNG for 8 consecutive weeks with a 1-week school holiday break. Pre-tests of mathematical skills were administered 2 weeks before the first playing session, and the post-tests were completed 2 weeks after the last playing session. Students played the game seven times in total, each Friday at school during math class. The whole 45 min long class period was afforded for playing. From these 45 min, the average time on actual playing the game during a class period was 26 min (SD = 2 min, 22 s), and average total time on task across the seven play sessions was 3 h and 3 min (SD = 18 min, 47 s). Play sessions took place in the classroom (three pairs) and in a computer lab just next to the classroom (eight pairs). Students only played the game during these 45 min sessions in class. The teacher and one to three teacher assistants were present during each playing session.

Students were playing in pairs, each pair having their own computer. The study did not impose any restrictions on the selection of pairs; the teacher was free to select pairs the way he wanted. More information on the player pairs is provided in Table 2 in the "Results" section. Pair play was chosen as the results of similar studies in game-based learning environments and mathematics suggest that collaborative play might lead to better attitudes towards mathematics and also better learning outcomes (Ke, 2008; Plass et al., 2013) and because a previous pilot study with NNG suggests that using the game collaboratively can enhance game-strategy-related discussion (Brezovszky et al., 2013).

Measures

Parallel versions of the paper-pencil measures of adaptive number knowledge (Adaptive Number Knowledge Task) and the same measure of arithmetic fluency (Woodcock-Johnson Math Fluency) were administered during pre- and post-test.

Fig. 2 Example item of the Adaptive Number Knowledge Task

Table 1 Items of the Adaptive Number Knowledge Task during pre- and post-test

Pre-test	Post-test
/2, 4, 8, 12, 32/ = 16	/2, 4, 6, 16, 24/ = 12
/1, 2, 3, 5, 30/ = 59	/1, 2, 4, 5, 40/ = 79
/2, 4, 8, 10/ = 22	/3, 5, 30, 120, 180/ = 12
/3, 4, 5, 6/ = 63	/3, 4, 5, 6/ = 126

Additionally, students' game performance was saved in the game log data and students' grades in mathematics from the previous semester were provided.

Adaptive Number Knowledge Task. The aim of the Adaptive Number Knowledge Task is to measure students' ability to recognize and use different numerical characteristics and relations in their arithmetic problem solving. The test was developed based on the results of previously conducted pilot studies (McMullen et al., 2015). The task consists of four items and for each item students were given four or five numbers and a target number. Using the given numbers and the four arithmetic operations, the task was to produce as many solutions as they could which equalled the target number (see Fig. 2). The students had 90 s to complete each item. Tests were administered by a trained researcher during pre-test and by the class teacher with the help of a trained researcher during post-test.

The format of the task was the same at both time points. Items were changed across time points but the given numbers and target numbers were selected so that similar types of number–operation combinations could be used in order to reach correct solutions. Table 1 shows the items in order for the two time points.

Solutions were scored on the criteria of quantity and complexity of correct arithmetic sentences. Quantity was defined as the total number of correct solutions across all trials (*correct* solutions). Complexity was defined as the total number of solutions in which both additive and multiplicative operations were used (*multi-operational* solutions); for example, $6+4+2=12$ or $8+8-4=12$ was not considered to be multi-operational, but $2*3+6=12$ was considered multi-operational.

Pre-test Cronbach's alpha reliability scores were $\alpha = .55$ for the number of correct solutions and $\alpha = .67$ for the number of multi-operation solutions. Cronbach's alpha reliability scores of all items were low on the post-test. Therefore, based on item analysis aimed at identifying a reliable uni-dimensional adaptive number knowledge score (Metsämuuronen, 2006), only the first two post test items of the Adaptive Number Knowledge Task were used for analysis. For the post-test, the reliability score was $\alpha = .74$ for correct solutions and $\alpha = .72$ for multi-operation solutions.

Woodcock-Johnson Math Fluency. In order to measure students' basic arithmetic skills, the Woodcock-Johnson Math Fluency sub-test (WJ III® Test of Achievement) was administered after the Adaptive Number Knowledge Task at both time points. The test was selected as it is a highly reliable and validated instrument measuring arithmetic fluency (Schrank, McGrew, & Woodcock, 2001). Following the original instructions, students had to complete as many arithmetic problems (simple addition, subtraction, and multiplication) as possible during 3 min. The test consists of two pages with a total of 160 items. Calculations become gradually more difficult as the test progresses.

Game performance. All data regarding players' game activity was logged and saved. The number of maps completed was selected to be used as a measure of game performance in the present study. A map is completed when all the four target materials are collected within a map and the player receives a reward coin.

General math achievement. Students' grades in mathematics from the previous semester were provided by the class teacher. Grades in the Finnish system range between 4 and 10.

Results

Detailed information on the composition of pairs, their gender, general math achievement (math grades), and game performance (maps completed) is presented in Table 2. Average sum scores for the number of total correct solutions and multi-operation solution on the Adaptive Number Knowledge Task, as well as students' sum scores on the Math Fluency task for the two time points are presented in Table 3.

Table 2 Gender, general math achievement, and game performance of the 11 player pairs

Pair no	Gender	Math grades	Maps completed
1	F–F	9–8	19
2	M–M	7–7	29
3	M–M	8–8	26
4	F–M	9–9	19
5	F–M	8–9	14
6	F–F	8–8	18
7	F–F	8–7	11
8	F–F	7–6	24
9	M–M	5–6	20
10	M–M	5–5	14
11	M–M	7–6	16

Table 3 Descriptive statistics for the Adaptive Number Knowledge Task and the Woodcock-Johnson math fluency test at the two time points

Variable	Pre-test ($N=23$)			Post-test ($N=22$)		
	M	SD	Range	M	SD	Range
Adaptive Number Knowledge Task						
Total correct solutions	1.30	0.75	0.25–3.25	2.73	1.13	0.50–6.00
Total multi-op. solutions	0.42	0.40	0.00–1.25	0.75	0.74	0.00–3.00
Math fluency	70.50	17.50	44–106	78.40	16.75	45–105

Table 4 Intercorrelations (Pearson product-moment correlation) of adaptive number knowledge, Woodcock Johnson math fluency, and game performance

Variable	1	2	3	4	5	6	7
1. Correct solutions pre-test	–						
2. Correct solutions post-test	.68**	–					
3. Multi-op. solutions pre-test	.59**	.62**	–				
4. Multi-op. solutions post-test	.69**	.87**	.72**	–			
5. Math fluency pre-test	.10	.16	.43*	.22	–		
6. Math fluency post-test	.34	.38	.63**	.43*	.86**	–	
7. Maps completed	.22	.37	.17	.47*	.39	.40	–

Note: $*p<.05$, $**p<.01$ (2-tailed)

With regard to overall game performance, out of the total 64 maps, students completed between 11 and 29 maps ($M=19.05$, SD$=5.3$).

Independent samples t-test showed no gender differences in students' game performance $t(20)=1.12$, $p=.28$. Pearson product-moment correlation showed no relation between students' general math achievement and their game performance $r(22)=.02$, $p=.918$.

Overall, results show that there was substantial improvement in participants' performance on the Adaptive Number Knowledge Task and Math Fluency measure during the period when NNG was used in the classroom. Paired samples t-test showed differences from pre- to post-test with medium to large effect sizes for the total number of correct solutions, $t(21)=-7.97$, $p<.001$, $d=1.49$; total number of multi-operations used, $t(21)=-2.72$, $p=.013$, $d=0.55$, as well as math fluency scores, $t(21)=-4.10$, $p<.001$, $d=0.46$. Pearson product-moment correlation was conducted in order to explore the relationship between students' game performance and their adaptive number knowledge and arithmetic fluency (Table 4).

In order to investigate the specific impact of game performance on the development of adaptive number knowledge multiple stepwise linear regression analyses were run. Two regressions were calculated, first with the number of correct solutions on the Adaptive Number Knowledge post-test as the dependent variable and second with the number of multi-operational solutions on the Adaptive Number Knowledge post-test as the dependent variable. For both regressions, participants' pre-test scores of total correct and total multi-operational solutions and number of maps

Table 5 Stepwise linear
regression analysis: specific
effects of multi-operation
solutions pre-test, correct
solutions pre-test and maps
completed on multi-operation
solutions post-test

	Multi-op. post test			
Variable	β	B	95 % CI for B	R^2 change
Multi-op. pre-test	.45*	0.83	[0.20, 1.46]	.49***
Maps completed	.30*	0.04	[0.002, 0.08]	.12*
Correct pre-test	.35*	0.34	[0.01, 0.68]	.08*
Total				.70+

Note: $^+F(3, 17) = 12.92$, $p < .001$. $*p < .05$, $**p < .01$, $***p < .001$

completed were entered stepwise as independent variables. No multicollinearity was detected for the three independent variables.

For total correct solutions, the final model was significant, $F(1, 19) = 15.64$, $p = .001$, $R^2 = .45$ with pre-test scores as the only significant predictor of post-test correct solutions ($\beta = .67$, $p = .001$). For total multi-operational solutions, the final model was fairly informative (Table 5), with 70 % of post-test scores being explained by participants' pre-test correct and multi-operational solutions and the number of maps completed.

A third stepwise linear regression analysis was run in order to examine the possible impact of gameplay on the development of math fluency, with math fluency post-test scores as the dependent variable and math fluency pre-test scores and number of maps completed entered stepwise as independent variables. The final model was significant, $F(1, 19) = 61.79$, $p = .001$, $R^2 = .77$ with pre-test scores as the only significant predictor of math fluency post-test scores ($\beta = .88$, $p < .001$).

Discussion

The aim of the present study was to explore how students' game performance in NNG predicts the development of their adaptive number knowledge. Results show that students' game performance was a unique predictor of their post-test multi-operation solutions on the Adaptive Number Knowledge Task. Findings of the study are in line with the theoretical assumption that providing extensive practice with various combinations of numbers and operations can aid students' noticing of numerical characteristics and relations, as indexed by their adaptive number knowledge (Baroody, 2003; Threlfall, 2002, 2009; Verschaffel et al., 2009).

From the point of view of the design of game-based learning environments, the results of the present study are promising. In order for a game-based learning environment to be efficient and effective players need to be engaged in productive activities which are relevant to the learning outcomes (Chen et al., 2012; Engle & Conant, 2002). Integrating the learning content and the core game mechanics is considered to help this process, resulting in higher engagement and better learning gains (Devlin, 2011; Habgood & Ainsworth, 2011). However, in practice it often happens that even if students are engaged with the game, they are engaged with aspects that are irrelevant to the educational content and learning goals (Garris, Ahlers, & Driskell, 2002; Martens, Gulikers, & Bastiaens, 2004). The relation between students' game performance and their development in noticing and using complex numerical relations in their arithmetic problem solving suggests that working with the NNG could promote aspects relevant to the development of adaptive number knowledge. Thus, engaged gameplay in the NNG seems to be related to activities relevant to the intended learning goals.

The number of maps completed by the student pairs was selected as the basic indicator of students' active engagement with the mathematical content in NNG. In order to complete maps and progress in the game students needed to be continuously working with various combinations of numbers and operations. These combinations needed to be strategically selected, taking into consideration the available numbers, target positions, and the different scoring modes of the game (moves or energy mode). Thus, measuring students' game performance by the amount of maps completed during the seven playing sessions was sufficient for the goals of the present study. However, future studies could address alternative and more in-depth aspects of students' game performance such as changes in players' adaptive problem-solving procedures while playing the NNG.

Although the use of student pairs has pedagogical benefits (Hufferd-Ackles, Fuson, & Sherin, 2004), it also causes some problems for interpreting the findings. Differences in prior knowledge, gaming experience, or attitudes towards mathematics and games in general could all affect how students play in pairs, and how they share responsibilities during the game play. Thus, pair scores of game performance might not represent the true game performance of individual players and as a result, using pair game performance scores can be an underestimation of the effect of gameplay on the learning outcomes. Results should be confirmed with a substantially larger sample. Likewise, differences between playing in pairs versus playing individually need to be addressed in future studies.

In the present study, recognizing and using numerical characteristics and relations is described by the term adaptive number knowledge and is considered as a key component of adaptivity with arithmetic problem solving. The results of the present study suggest that NNG promotes the development of adaptive number knowledge. However, due to the small sample size and problems with the low reliability of the Adaptive Number Knowledge Task, these results have to be taken with caution. Although, students' game performance explains variance in students' post-test multi-operational solutions on the Adaptive Number Knowledge Task, the largest amount of variance was explained by students' pre-test scores. In interpreting these results, it is also important to take into account that adaptive number knowledge was measured with far transfer tasks which were not directly practiced during the gameplay.

Results showed no relationship between students' game performance and the development of their correct solutions on the Adaptive Number Knowledge Task. It is possible that playing NNG can only be associated with the task-specific development in students' noticing and using complex numerical relations. As the Adaptive Number Knowledge Task is timed, it is possible that after playing the NNG students are more prone to invest effort in finding complex types of numerical relations; as a result, students would come up with fewer solutions overall compared to the pre-test. However, the lack of a relation between the number of correct solutions in the Adaptive Number Knowledge Task and students' game performance may be explained by reliability issues and the small sample size. It is possible that by increasing the reliability of items, finding more appropriate indicators of adaptive number knowledge on these tasks (McMullen et al., 2015), and having a larger sample size, results would also show a relationship between students' game performance and their development in the number of correct solutions on the Adaptive Number Knowledge Task.

Math fluency was used as a control measure in the present study. The lack of relation between students' game performance and their math fluency is in line with the theoretical expectations that playing with NNG can be associated to a larger extent with the development of more adaptive aspects of arithmetic problem solving than number facts (e.g. Baroody, 2003). However, given the lack of statistical power in the present study, it is also possible that a significant relation could be identified in a larger sample.

There is an extensive theoretical framework describing the advantages of mathematics instruction which aims at developing adaptivity with arithmetic problem solving (Baroody, 2003; Blöte et al., 2000; Hatano & Oura, 2003; Threlfall, 2002, 2009). However, there are very few empirical studies which would offer practical guidelines on how this type of adaptivity could be operationalized and enhanced through classroom activities. Results of the present study suggest that the NNG is a promising game-based learning environment which can develop students' adaptive number knowledge by enhancing noticing and using numerical characteristics and relations in arithmetic problem solving. NNG provides a novel type of game-based learning environment which offers more than just the drill and practice of already acquired mathematical skills, as students' engagement with the core game mechanics is intrinsically connected to meaningful practice with skills and knowledge underlying adaptivity with arithmetic problem solving.

Acknowledgment The present study was funded by grant 274163 awarded to the last author by the Academy of Finland.

References

Baroody, A. J. (2003). The development of adaptive expertise and flexibility: The integration of conceptual and procedural knowledge. In A. J. Baroody & A. Dowker (Eds.), *The development of arithmetic concepts and skills: Constructing adaptive expertise* (pp. 1–33). London, England: Lawrence Erlbaum.

Beishuizen, M. (1993). Mental strategies and materials or models for addition and subtraction up to 100 in Dutch second grades. *Journal for Research in Mathematics Education, 24*, 294–323. doi:10.2307/749464.

Blöte, A. W., Klein, A. S., & Beishuizen, M. (2000). Mental computation and conceptual understanding. *Learning and Instruction, 10*, 221–247. doi:10.1016/S0959-4752(99)00028-6.

Brezovszky, B., Lehtinen, E., McMullen, J., Rodriguez, G., & Veermans, K. (2013). Training flexible and adaptive arithmetic problem solving skills through exploration with numbers. The development of Number Navigation Game. In C. Vaz de Carvalho, & P. Escuderio (Eds.), *Proceedings of the 7th European Conference on Game Based Learning (ECGBL2013)* (pp. 626–634). Retrieved from http://issuu.com/acpil/docs/ecgbl2013-issuu_vol_2

Canobi, K. H., Reeve, R. A., & Pattison, P. E. (2003). Patterns of knowledge in children's addition. *Developmental Psychology, 39*, 521–534. doi:10.1037/0012-1649.39.3.521.

Chen, Z. -H., Liao, C. C. Y., Cheng, H. N. H., Yeh, C. Y. C., & Chan, T. -W. (2012). Influence of game quests on pupils' enjoyment and goal-pursuing in math learning. *Educational Technology & Society, 15*, 317–327. Retrieved from http://dblp.uni-trier.de/db/journals/ets/ets15.html#ChenLCYC12

Cheung, A. C., & Slavin, R. E. (2013). The effectiveness of educational technology applications for enhancing mathematics achievement in K-12 classrooms: A meta-analysis. *Educational Research Review, 9*, 88–113. doi:10.1016/j.edurev.2013.01.001.

Devlin, K. (2011). *Mathematics education for a new era: Video games as a medium for learning.* Natick, MA: AK Peters.

Dowker, A. (1992). Computational estimation strategies of professional mathematicians. *Journal for Research in Mathematics Education, 23*, 45–55. Retrieved from http://www.jstor.org/stable/749163.

Engle, R. A., & Conant, F. R. (2002). Guiding principles for fostering productive disciplinary engagement: Explaining an emergent argument in a community of learners classroom. *Cognition and Instruction, 20*, 399–483. doi:10.1207/S1532690XCI2004_1.

Garris, R., Ahlers, R., & Driskell, J. E. (2002). Games, motivation, and learning: A research and practice model. *Simulation & Gaming, 33*, 441–467. doi:10.1177/1046878102238607.

Gee, J. P. (2003). *What video games have to teach us about literacy and learning.* Hampshire, England: Palgrave Macmillan.

Girard, C., Ecalle, J., & Magnan, A. (2013). Serious games as new educational tools: How effective are they? A meta-analysis of recent studies. *Journal of Computer Assisted Learning, 29*, 207–219. doi:10.1111/j.1365-2729.2012.00489.x.

Habgood, M. P. J., & Ainsworth, S. E. (2011). Motivating children to learn effectively: Exploring the value of intrinsic integration in educational games. *Journal of the Learning Sciences, 20*, 169–206. doi:10.1080/10508406.2010.508029.

Hatano, G., & Oura, Y. (2003). Commentary: Reconceptualizing school learning using insight from expertise research. *Educational Researcher, 32*, 26–29. Retrieved from http://www.jstor.org/stable/3700083.

Heirdsfield, A. M., & Cooper, T. J. (2004). Factors affecting the process of proficient mental addition and subtraction: Case studies of flexible and inflexible computers. *The Journal of Mathematical Behavior, 23*, 443–463. doi:10.1016/j.jmathb.2004.09.005.

Hufferd-Ackles, K., Fuson, K. C., & Sherin, M. G. (2004). Describing levels and components of a math-talk learning community. *Journal for Research in Mathematics Education, 35*, 81–116. doi:10.2307/30034933.

Hwang, G., & Wu, P. (2012). Advancements and trends in digital game-based learning research: A review of publications in selected journals from 2001 to 2010. *British Journal of Educational Technology, 43*, E6–E10. doi:10.1111/j.1467-8535.2011.01242.x.

Järvelä, S., Lehtinen, E., & Salonen, P. (2000). Socio-emotional orientation as a mediating variable in teaching learning interaction: Implications for instructional design. *Scandinavian Journal of Educational Research, 44*, 293–306. doi:10.1080/713696677.

Ke, F. (2008). A case study of computer gaming for math: Engaged learning from gameplay? *Computers & Education, 51*, 1609–1620. doi:10.1016/j.compedu.2008.03.003.

Kucian, K., Grond, U., Rotzer, S., Henzi, B., Schönmann, C., Plangger, F., …von Aster, M. (2011). Mental number line training in children with developmental dyscalculia. *NeuroImage, 57*, 782–795. doi:10.1016/j.neuroimage.2011.01.070

Laski, E. V., & Siegler, R. S. (2014). Learning from number board games: You learn what you encode. *Developmental Psychology, 50*, 853–864. doi:10.1037/a0034321.

Lehtinen, E., Brezovszky, B., Rodríguez Padilla, G. Lehtinen, H. Hannula-Sormunen, M. M, McMullen, J., ... Jaakkola, T. (2015). Number Navigation Game (NNG): Design principles and game description. In J. Torbeyns, E. Lehtinen & J. Elen (Eds.), *Developing competencies in learners: From ascertaining to intervening* (pp. xx-xx). New York, NY: Springer.

Lowyck, J., Lehtinen, E., & Elen, J. (2004). Editorial: Students' perspectives on learning environments. *International Journal of Educational Research, 41*, 401–406. doi:10.1016/j.ijer.2005.08.008.

Martens, R., Gulikers, J., & Bastiaens, T. (2004). The impact of intrinsic motivation on e-learning in authentic computer tasks. *Journal of Computer Assisted Learning, 20*, 368–376. doi:10.1111/j.1365-2729.2004.00096.x.

McMullen, J., Brezovszky, B., Rodríguez Padilla, G., Pongsakdi, N., & Lehtinen, E. (2015). *Adaptive number knowledge: Exploring the foundations of adaptivity with whole-number arithmetic.* Manuscript submitted for publication.

Metsämuuronen, J. (2006). *Tutkimuksen tekemisen perusteet ihmistieteissä.* [Principles of conducting scientific research in humanities]. Jyväskylä, Finland: Gummeruksen kirjapaino Oy.

National Council of Teachers of Mathematics. (2000). *Principles and standards for school mathematics.* NCTM (Ed.), Reston, VA: National Council of Teachers of Mathematics. Retrieved from http://www.nctm.org/

Plass, J. L., O'Keefe, P. A., Homer, B. D., Case, J., Hayward, E. O., Stein, M., & Perlin, K. (2013). The impact of individual, competitive, and collaborative mathematics gameplay on learning, performance, and motivation. *Journal of Educational Psychology, 105*, 1050–1066. doi:10.1037/a0032688

Räsänen, P., Salminen, J., Wilson, A. J., Aunio, P., & Dehaene, S. (2009). Computer-assisted intervention for children with low numeracy skills. *Cognitive Development, 24*, 450–472. doi:10.1016/j.cogdev.2009.09.003.

Salen, K., & Zimmerman, E. (2004). *Rules of play: Game design fundamentals.* Cambridge, MA: MIT Press.

Schneider, M., Rittle-Johnson, B., & Star, J. R. (2011). Relations among conceptual knowledge, procedural knowledge, and procedural flexibility in two samples differing in prior knowledge. *Developmental Psychology, 47*, 1525–1538. doi:10.1037/a0024997.

Schrank, F. A., McGrew, K. S., & Woodcock, R. W. (2001). *Technical abstract (Woodcock-Johnson III Assessment Service Bulletin No. 2).* Itasca, IL: Riverside Publishing. Retrieved from http://www.riverpub.com/clinical/pdf/WJIII_ASB2.pdf

Seo, Y., & Bryant, D. P. (2009). Analysis of studies of the effects of computer-assisted instruction on the mathematics performance of students with learning disabilities. *Computers & Education, 53*, 913–928. doi:10.1016/j.compedu.2009.05.002.

Siegler, R. S., & Booth, J. L. (2004). Development of numerical estimation in young children. *Child Development, 75*, 428–444. doi:10.1111/j.1467-8624.2004.00684.x.

Siegler, R. S., & Ramani, G. B. (2009). Playing linear number board games—But not circular ones—Improves low-income preschoolers' numerical understanding. *Journal of Educational Psychology, 101*, 545–560. doi:10.1037/a0014239.

Threlfall, J. (2002). Flexible mental calculation. *Educational Studies in Mathematics, 50*, 29–47. doi:10.1023/A:1020572803437.

Threlfall, J. (2009). Strategies and flexibility in mental calculation. *ZDM—International Journal on Mathematics Education, 41*, 541–555. doi:10.1007/s11858-009-0195-3.

Torbeyns, J., Ghesquière, P., & Verschaffel, L. (2009). Efficiency and flexibility of indirect addition in the domain of multi-digit subtraction. *Learning and Instruction, 19*, 1–12. doi:10.1016/j.learninstruc.2007.12.002.

Verschaffel, L., Luwel, K., Torbeyns, J., & Van Dooren, W. (2009). Conceptualizing, investigating, and enhancing adaptive expertise in elementary mathematics education. *European Journal of Psychology of Education, 24*, 335–359. doi:10.1007/BF03174765.

Wilson, A. J., Revkin, S. K., Cohen, D., Cohen, L., & Dehaene, S. (2006). An open trial assessment of "The number race", an adaptive computer game for remediation of dyscalculia. *Behavioral and Brain Functions, 2*, 1–16. doi:10.1186/1744-9081-2-20.

Wouters, P., van Nimwegen, C., van Oostendorp, H., & van der Spek, E. D. (2013). A meta-analysis of the cognitive and motivational effects of serious games. *Journal of Educational Psychology, 105*, 249–265. doi:10.1037/a0031311.

Young, M. F., Slota, S., Cutter, A. B., Jalette, G., Mullin, G., Lai, B., … Yukhymenko, M. (2012). Our princess is in another castle. A review of trends in serious gaming for education. *Review of Educational Research, 82*, 61–89. doi:10.3102/0034654312436980

Number Navigation Game (NNG): Experience and Motivational Effects

Gabriela Rodríguez-Aflecht, Boglárka Brezovszky, Nonmanut Pongsakdi,
Tomi Jaakkola, Minna M. Hannula-Sormunen, Jake McMullen,
and Erno Lehtinen

Abstract Number Navigation Game-based learning environment (NNG) is a mathematical game-based learning environment designed to enhance students' adaptivity with arithmetic problem solving and to increase their motivation towards math. Fourth through sixth grade classrooms were randomly assigned into either an experimental group (students $n = 642$) which played NNG during a 10-week period or into a control group (students $n = 526$) which continued with a traditional textbook-based mathematics curriculum. The aims of the present study were to investigate the effects of the intervention on students' motivation and to explore how students' differing game experiences were related to changes in their motivation and, as an indicator of cognitive outcomes, their arithmetic fluency. Results indicate the intervention resulted in small decreases in the math motivation expectancy-values of interest, utility, and attainment value. Students had mixed game experiences which varied by gender and grade level. When looking at the role of these game experiences on post-test motivation and arithmetic fluency, corresponding pre-test values were the strongest predictive variables. Out of game experiences, only competence was a significant predictor of post-test motivational scores; however, no game experience variable was a predictor of post-test arithmetic fluency.

Keywords Game-based learning • GEQ • Motivation • Expectancy-value model • Arithmetic fluency

G. Rodríguez-Aflecht (✉) • B. Brezovszky • N. Pongsakdi • T. Jaakkola
M.M. Hannula-Sormunen • J. McMullen • E. Lehtinen
Department of Teacher Education, Centre for Learning Research, University of Turku,
Assistentinkatu 7, Turku 20014, Finland
e-mail: gabriela.rodriguez@utu.fi; bogbre@utu.fi; nopong@utu.fi; tomi.jaakkola@utu.fi;
mimarha@utu.fi; jake.mcmullen@utu.fi; erno.lehtinen@utu.fi

© Springer International Publishing Switzerland 2015
J. Torbeyns et al. (eds.), *Describing and Studying Domain-Specific Serious Games*,
Advances in Game-Based Learning, DOI 10.1007/978-3-319-20276-1_11

There has been an increasing interest in applying digital games in teaching mathematics. In many countries, teachers and educational authorities are concerned about a decreasing motivation to study mathematics, and educational games are considered to be a solution which would make mathematics education more fun and motivating. For example, a survey carried out amongst Finnish school teachers by Klemmetti and colleagues (2009) revealed that 99 % of respondents believed game-based learning environments would motivate students' learning. Despite this assumption, there is a lack of empirical studies providing evidence that game-based learning environments are able to significantly increase motivation towards learning (Connolly, Boyle, MacArthur, Hainey, & Boyle, 2012), at least not when compared to conventional instruction methods (Wouters, van Nimwegen, van Oostendorp, & van der Spek, 2013).

A prototype game-based learning environment, Number Navigation Game (NNG), was developed to enhance students' adaptivity with arithmetic (see NNG description by Lehtinen et al., in this volume). NNG is based on an integrated game design (Habgood & Ainsworth, 2011) in which the game mechanics offer extensive and situated practice through which flexible and adaptive arithmetic problem-solving skills can be strengthened. The tasks players have to solve during gameplay are increasingly demanding and substantially differ from the tasks used in regular mathematics education. In the prototype game-based learning environment used for this study there are still few external motivating elements so students' engagement derived from the gaming mechanics itself. The aim of the present study was to find out the effects of playing NNG on students' motivation towards mathematics as well as on their arithmetic fluency, and whether these effects are related to students' game experiences.

Expectancy-Value Model as a Comprehensive Measure for Studying Motivation

Motivation is a broad concept for which numerous and sometimes overlapping theories exist (De Brabander & Martens, 2014). Motivation is often described as a set of cognitive motives which, together with emotions (which are alternately considered as a subset of motivation or as something separate from it) influence behavior; these motives can include beliefs, values, expectancies, intentions, or goals (Wegge, 2001). In this study, motivation was looked at from the theoretical perspective of the expectancy-values model, more specifically, Eccles and colleagues' (2002) expectancy-values model. The expectancy-values model is particularly suitable for this study because its usefulness in predicting students' future performance, persistence, and task choice has been demonstrated in educational studies (Berger & Karabenick, 2011; Eccles & Wigfield, 2002; Wigfield & Cambria, 2010). In this model, the expectation to succeed and the value given to succeeding will determine a person's motivation to perform tasks (Wigfield, 1994). The development of expectancy-values is influenced by psychological, sociocultural, and contextual factors, such as the feedback a child receives from parents, schools, and peers (Wigfield & Cambria, 2010). Expectancy-values are already distinct in young children (Wigfield & Eccles, 2000).

Expectancy refers to how well a person believes they will perform a task whereas values refer to a person's reasons for engaging in a task (Wigfield & Cambria, 2010). Expectancy is understood as a personal expectation or belief in one's own ability to succeed at a task. Value is task-subjective and composed of four aspects: intrinsic value, attainment value, utility value, and cost. Intrinsic value refers to interest, or how enjoyable a person finds the task, and is linked to Ryan and Deci's (2000) concept of intrinsic motivation (Wigfield & Eccles, 2000). Attainment value is determined by how important it is for a person's identity to perform well at the task. Utility value is defined as how useful the task is for a person's life. Cost, the least studied of these values, focuses on the perceived price a person feels they must pay in order to perform well on a task, both in terms of effort and time. Throughout the present study, motivation towards math is studied through the expectancy-value model, focusing on the variables of self-efficacy and interest, utility, attainment value, and cost.

Game Experience

Students' experiences during gaming depend on game features and on students' individual interpretations of these features. These interpretations may be related to age and gender. Interindividual differences in experiencing the game and gaming situations can mediate motivational and cognitive effects of educational games (Järvelä et al., 2000; Lowyck, Lehtinen, & Elen, 2004). Nevertheless, a common understanding of game experience has yet to be found (IJsselsteijn, de Kort, Poels, Jurgelionis, & Bellotti, 2007; Kiili, Lainema, De Freitas, & Arnab, 2014; Nacke & Drachen, 2011), though different frameworks and models have been proposed (see review by Nacke & Drachen, 2011). IJsselsteijn and colleagues (2007) argued this is because the field is relatively young, and the great variety of games makes it difficult to find a "one-size-fits-all" method to study all experiences elicited by games.

For the purposes of this study, game experience was considered from the framework developed by Poels and colleagues (2007). Their framework is composed of seven dimensions which are measured post-play through the Game Experience Questionnaire (GEQ). Although originally developed to measure users' experiences with commercial games for entertainment, the GEQ has also been used for game-based learning environments (De Grove, Van Looy, & Courtois, 2010; Gajadhar, Nap, De Kort, & IJsselsteijn, 2008; IJsselsteijn et al., 2007; Nacke, Stellmach, & Lindley, 2011; Oksanen, 2013; Poels, IJsselsteijn, de Kort, & Van Iersel, 2010). The seven dimensions of this framework are competence, challenge, flow, (sensory and imaginative) immersion, negative affect, positive affect, and tension.

The first four of the dimensions are highly interconnected. Flow is a key aspect of most existing game experience frameworks, and it is deeply related to the dimensions of challenge and competence. In Csikszentmihalyi's flow theory (1991), one of the characteristics of flow is the balance between challenge and ability. Challenge must be neither too low, which would result in boredom, nor too high, which would result in frustration. In the flow theory, the balance of "challenge-skill" is considered to be one out of several components of flow and is crucial in educational games (Kiili et al., 2014). IJsselsteijn and colleagues (2007) characterize flow as a form of immersion which results from a player feeling there is balance between how challenging the game is and how competent they are. Jennett and colleagues (2008) distinguish between immersion and flow in that the latter leads to optimal experiences whereas the former does not necessarily do so. However, they admit these concepts may overlap. According to Ermi and Mäyrä (2005), immersion is seen as a broad concept in which (a) flow, or challenge-immersion, is separate from (b) sensory immersion and (c) imaginative immersion. Sensory immersion refers to audiovisual characteristics of the game, such as graphics or sound, whereas imaginative immersion refers for instance to the game's narration or characters. Whereas Ermi and Mäyrä (2005) look at these three types of immersion independently from one another, in the framework of Poels and colleagues (2007) used for the present study both sensory and imaginative immersion together conform one sole dimension, which refers to the absorption a player might feel towards game features such as story, game world, graphics, or sound.

The other dimensions included in the GEQ—positive affect, negative affect, and tension—focus on post-play affective states which indicate how enjoyable the game experience was. Nacke and Lindley (2009) argue that affect is an essential part of game experience, as it influences the cognitive decisions players take while playing. Based also on physiological responses, they report a correlation between flow and positive affect. Complementing this framework of game experience, our study included an additional dimension of "positive value," which measures students' belief that the game is helpful to them. Whitton (2010b) has argued that in order to benefit from game-based learning, users must first believe in the positive value of these games. While she was speaking of adult learners, it is here considered equally relevant for children who are playing games for educational purposes in school.

It is necessary to understand the types of game experiences students have when playing NNG, as it is clear that positive game experiences foster engagement while negative ones hinder it. An unengaged student might stop playing or only continue reluctantly (Oksanen, 2013), which might have repercussions on the effectiveness of NNG in enhancing students' motivation expectancy-values and arithmetic skills. Thus, examining the effect of students' game experiences on NNG's motivation expectancy-values and arithmetic fluency was part of the study's main aim.

Arithmetic Skills

In testing motivational effects of game-based learning, it is also important to compare them with possible cognitive gains. The objective of NNG is to enhance students' adaptivity with arithmetic problem solving and adaptive number knowledge (see Brezovszky et al., in this volume; Lehtinen et al., in this volume). However, in the present study about the motivational effects of the game, arithmetic fluency measures are used as an indicator of arithmetic skill development because the adaptive number knowledge results are not yet available. Arithmetic fluency refers to the quick and accurate retrieval of basic number facts and combinations and is a requisite for further conceptual and procedural development (Baroody, Bajwa, & Eiland, 2009; Canobi, 2009). While enhancing arithmetic fluency is not the main goal of NNG, given its relation to adaptive number knowledge (McMullen, Brezovszky, Rodríguez-Aflecht, Pongsakdi, & Lehtinen, 2015), it is used in the present study as a proximal indicator of the game's mathematical impact.

Research Questions

This study focuses on the following research questions:

1. What is the effect of the playing NNG on students' motivation towards mathematics, as framed by the expectancy-value model?
   Prior evidence on the motivational effects of game-based learning environments is mixed (Connolly et al., 2012). Thus, we assume that there is no strong overall development in math motivation, particularly when taking into account that the game-based learning environment used is a prototype that includes few externally motivating elements typical for commercial games. However, as gaming itself is already different from regular mathematics education, we assume that this, together with the nonstandard tasks to be solved within NNG, will produce a novelty effect and result in a slight increase in interest in mathematics.
2. What are students' experiences with the game and how do these experiences differ by gender and grade level?
   Considering that NNG is a prototype still lacking many externally motivating features common in the commercial games children are accustomed to (sound, advanced graphics, etc.), we expect students to rate their experiences close to the scales' midpoints. Gender differences have been much examined, often focusing on frequency of play, types of games preferred, and self-efficacy beliefs (Bourgonjon, Valcke, Soetaert, & Schellens, 2010; Carr, 2005; Jenson & de Castell, 2010). While NNG is meant to be gender-neutral, based on findings of earlier studies (e.g., Lucas & Sherry, 2004) we assume boys might report more positive game experiences. As the same version with the same difficulty level of NNG was used for children in different grade levels and different stages of their arithmetical development, we expect differences by grade level in game experiences, particularly those of challenge and competence.
3. How are students' game experiences with NNG related to changes in (a) motivation expectancy-values and (b) arithmetic fluency?
   Empirical studies directly analyzing the relationship between game experience and motivational effects are still rare. Based on earlier studies (e.g., the seminal work of Lepper & Malone, 1987) Paras and Bizzocchi (2005) concluded that if

games foster play and challenge, which produces a state of flow, then gameplay can result in increases in motivation, which supports the learning process. Students who have more positive experiences with the game are probably more engaged, and this might result in positive motivational and cognitive consequences. There was no systematic scaffolding or teacher support in this experiment and the "energy maps" (see NNG description by Lehtinen and colleagues, in this volume) are demanding, which can have diverse effects on students' mathematics self-efficacy beliefs. Students who did not experience competence during gameplay might report lower mathematics self-efficacy at post-test, whereas those who felt competent during gameplay might report stronger mathematics self-efficacy.

Method

Participants

In this study, 1168 students from 61 fourth through sixth grade classrooms spread across four cities in Finland participated. Participation was voluntary both for teachers and students, and informed consent was acquired in writing from the parents of all participants. Ethical guidelines of Turku University were followed. From the total, 546 participants were female, 620 were male, and there was missing data on the gender of two participants. As for grade level, 135 participants were fourth graders, 606 were fifth graders, and 427 were sixth graders. The mean ages for the fourth, fifth, and sixth grade participants were 10 years and 2 months, 11 years and 2 months, and 12 years and 3 months, respectively. Classes were randomly assigned into control and experimental groups, with 642 participants belonging to the experimental group and 526 to the control group.

Procedure

During the spring term 2014, the experimental group played NNG for a 10-week period as part of their regular math classes and curriculum, while the control group continued only with their regular textbook-based mathematics curriculum. Afterwards, conditions were reversed. While the present study only encompasses this first phase of the experiment, it is relevant to mention the reversal of conditions not only because it would have been ethically questionable to deny participants in the control group the chance to play, but also because the control group's knowledge about the upcoming play sessions could have an impact on some post-test measures. It was asked that students play for at least 10 h. Teachers were invited for a training session in which they were informed about NNG's learning aims and play mechanics. As part of their training, teachers were told sessions needed to last at least 30 min in order to give their students enough time to make significant progress in the game. Nevertheless, teachers were free to decide how long play sessions would extend, how to space these sessions throughout the intervention, what kind of support they would provide their students, and whether students would play individually or in pairs. There were no instructions for teacher support during the gaming processes. In case students played in pairs, teachers chose the criteria under which pairs would be formed.

Measures

Data used for this study was collected by questionnaires and math tests completed by students before the 10-week intervention and immediately after the 10 weeks. Students in the experimental group received a copy of the game immediately upon completing the pre-test, and class teachers were free to schedule game sessions as they saw fit. Game log data was collected upon completing the post-test, but it is not analyzed in the current study. Both pre- and post-tests were rigorously timed and structured, and were imparted by trained testers following standardized procedures. Both pre- and post-questionnaires were filled out by students during regular class time under the guidance of their teachers. The pre-questionnaire was identical for all participants, containing demographic items and items measuring their math motivation expectancy-values, while the experimental group's post-questionnaire included additional items concerning their game experiences playing NNG.

Math Motivation Expectancy-Values: Fourteen items measuring math expectancy-values were completed before and after the intervention by all participants. The test was modified on the basis of the motivation scale used by Berger and Karabenick (2011), with items being translated into Finnish and adapted to the ages of respondents. Three items were used to measure interest (for example, "I like math"). Three items measured utility ("Math is useful for me in everyday life"). Three items measured attainment value ("It is important to me to be a student who is good at math"). Two items were used to measure cost ("I believe that success in math requires that I give up other activities that I enjoy"). Three items were used to measure self-efficacy, ("I am certain I can do difficult math tasks"). Participants responded to each item using a 5-point Likert scale ranging from 1 (*completely disagree*), 2 (*disagree*), 3 (*neutral*), 4 (*agree*), to 5 (*completely agree*). These items were studied through principal component analysis with varimax rotation. Five separate factors (interest, utility, attainment value, self-efficacy, and cost) were found, upholding the 5-factor model developed by Eccles and Wigfield (2002). The explained variance of the model was 75.90 %. Data was adequate for factor analysis with a 0.90 Kaiser–Meyer–Olkin Measure, and Barlett's test of sphericity showed a significance of $p < 0.001$. All but one factor were shown to have good internal consistency and to be reliable across the two tests. At pre-test: interest Cronbach's $\alpha = .91$, utility: $\alpha = .80$, attainment value: $\alpha = .82$, cost: $\alpha = .50$, and self-efficacy $\alpha = .81$. At post-test: interest Cronbach's $\alpha = .91$, utility: $\alpha = .79$, attainment value: $\alpha = .83$, cost: $\alpha = .58$, and self-efficacy $\alpha = .81$. The poor reliability of cost compared to the other measures can be due to this dimension only having two items—consequently, the expectancy-value of cost was not used for any further analyses. Correlations of the variables at pre-test can be found in the Appendix.

Game Experience: Only participants in the experimental group were asked to fill the Game Experience Questionnaire (GEQ) after the intervention. The Finnish translations used by Oksanen (2013) were used, although the questionnaire was further modified by removing 15 of the 42 items and changing some of the phrasings to better suit our game and the age of our participants. Each item consisted of a statement and a 1–5 scale to indicate level of agreement, with answers ranging from 1 (*not at all*) to 5 (*extremely*), with the mid-scale 3 being neutral. The factor structure of the 31 items of GEQ was studied through principal component analysis with varimax rotation. Data was adequate for factor analysis with a 0.95 Kaiser–Meyer–Olkin Measure and Barlett's test of sphericity showed a significance of $p < .001$. Seven separate factors were found and used as basis for the subscales. The explained variance of the model was 69.60 %. The reliability of subscales was as follows: Challenge, (e.g., "I thought playing this game was hard"), $\alpha = .66$. Competence, ("I was good at playing"), $\alpha = .81$. Flow, ("I forgot everything around me when I played"), $\alpha = .79$. Immersion, ("I felt imaginative when I played"), $\alpha = .77$. Negative affect, ("I thought playing was boring"), $\alpha = .78$. Positive Affect, ("I thought playing was fun"), $\alpha = .92$. Positive value, ("This game helped me learn math"), $\alpha = .82$. Tension, ("I felt irritable when I played"), $\alpha = .77$. The reliability for challenge is low, which could be due to the removal of three items, although Oksanen (2013) also reported similar results. However, according to Clark and Watson (1995), this reliability is within the limits which can be used. As suggested by the theory, there are high correlations between flow, challenge, and competence (Appendix).

Arithmetic Fluency: Students' fluency in solving basic arithmetic tasks is used in this study as a basic measure of cognitive outcomes. The test was adapted from the Mathematical Fluency test of the Woodcock-Johnson Tests of Achievement (Woodcock, McGrew, & Mather, 2001), in which students have three minutes to answer as many simple arithmetic problems as they can. The minimum score was 0 and the maximum score 160. Changes made to the original test include replacing the multiplication symbol with its equivalent in Finland, that is, · was used instead of x.

Results

Results are organized into three subsections. The first subsection presents the effects of the intervention on math motivation expectancy-values. The second subsection describes the experimental group's game experiences with NNG as well as gender and grade level differences in these experiences. Finally, the third subsection explores how the experimental group's game experiences with NNG related to changes in their (a) math motivation expectancy-values and (b) arithmetic fluency.

The Effects of Intervention on Math Motivation and Arithmetic Skills

Descriptive statistics on pre- and post-test math expectancy-values subscales are presented in Table 1. A repeated measures ANOVA analyzing the effects of time (pre- and post-test) and condition (experimental or control) on math motivation expectancy-values measures was conducted. Overall, there was no main effect of time on interest or utility but there was a slight decrease in attainment value, $F(1, 1166) = 8.80$, $p = .003$, $\eta p^2 = 0.01$ and in self-efficacy, $F(1, 1166) = 5.14$, $p = .02$, $\eta p^2 = 0.004$. There was a small interaction effect of time and condition on interest, $F(1, 1166) = 13.21$, $p = .000$, $\eta p^2 = 0.011$, on utility, $F(1, 1166) = 7.15$, $p = .008$, $\eta p^2 = 0.01$, and on attainment value, $F(1, 1166) = 7.51$, $p = .006$, $\eta p^2 = 0.01$, showing a small decrease in these motivational aspects amongst the experimental group when compared with the control group.

There was no difference in the arithmetic fluency scores in the pre-test (experimental group $M = 70.56$; control group $M = 70.23$). Arithmetic fluency scores increased significantly in the post-test (experimental group $M = 80.15$; control group $M = 77.87$), $F(1,1166) = 589.52$, $p = .000$. There was a significant interaction effect of time and condition, $F(1,1166) = 5.99$, $p = .015$, $\eta p^2 = 0.01$, showing a small positive intervention effect on arithmetic fluency.

Game Experiences with NNG

Mean scores (Table 2) for the different dimensions of the GEQ averaged between 2 and 3. An independent samples t-test was run to determine whether there were differences in game experiences between girls and boys. Results showed significant differences between girls' and boys' experiences of challenge and competence while playing NNG; however, effect sizes were small (Table 2). Girls rated the game as more challenging than boys did, which means they were more likely to find the game difficult and that they had to make an effort when playing. Boys had higher competence scores than girls did, which means they were more likely to report feeling good, successful, and skillful while playing.

A one-way ANOVA was carried out to look at grade level differences in game experiences (Table 3). There were significant differences between the class levels in Flow, Immersion, Negative Affect, Positive Value, and Tension. Post hoc comparisons using Bonferroni correction indicated that fifth graders' experiences of immersion was significantly higher than sixth graders' (Mean difference = 0.18, $p = .033$). This means that fifth graders reported higher feelings of being imaginative, liking the story, and being able to explore.

The scores of students' belief in the positive value of the game also significantly differed between fourth graders and sixth graders, with fourth graders seeing more benefit in playing NNG (Mean difference = 0.30, $p = .049$) and feeling the game

Table 1 Descriptive statistics on motivation expectancy-values

Variable	All participants (N = 1168)					Experimental (n = 642)					Control (n = 526)				
	M	SD	Range	Skew.	Kurt.	M	SD	Range	Skew.	Kurt.	M	SD	Range	Skew.	Kurt.
Pre-test interest	3.13	0.96	1–5	−0.74	−0.15	3.14	0.94	1–5	−0.03	−0.07	3.11	0.98	1–5	−0.12	−0.25
Post-test interest	3.11	0.93	1–5	−0.09	−0.03	3.05	0.96	1–5	−0.04	−0.22	3.18	0.88	1–5	−0.13	0.28
Pre-test utility	4.19	0.73	1–5	−1.31	2.51	4.18	0.70	1–5	−1.13	2.05	4.21	0.78	1–5	−1.47	2.84
Post-test utility	4.20	0.69	1–5	−1.07	1.49	4.14	0.70	1–5	−0.96	1.20	4.28	0.67	1–5	−1.25	2.099
Pre-test attainment value	3.50	0.83	1–5	−0.29	−0.00	3.53	0.80	1–5	−0.29	0.12	3.46	0.87	1–5	−0.27	−0.15
Post-test attainment value	3.42	0.83	1–5	−0.23	−0.33	3.40	0.84	1–5	−0.24	0.37	3.45	0.82	1–5	−0.22	0.29
Pre-test self-efficacy	3.70	0.80	1–5	−0.58	0.51	3.68	0.78	1–5	−0.53	0.52	3.72	0.82	1–5	−0.65	0.53
Post-test self-efficacy	3.65	0.79	1–5	−0.53	0.65	3.63	0.82	1–5	−0.49	0.49	3.67	0.76	1–5	−0.57	0.88

Table 2 Game experiences of the experimental group, by gender, and gender differences

Variable	All experimental students (n = 642)					Girls (n = 299)		Boys (n = 343)		T-test of gender effects		
	M	SD	Range	Skew.	Kurt.	M	SD	M	SD	t(640)	p	Cohen's d
Challenge	2.34	0.82	1–5	0.37	0.05	2.43	0.79	2.25	0.85	2.75	.006	0.22
Competence	3.06	0.90	1–5	−0.07	−0.14	2.88	0.85	3.22	0.92	−4.78	.000	−0.38
Flow	2.07	0.79	1–5	0.71	0.38	2.08	0.74	2.06	0.83	0.42	.68	0.03
Immersion	2.04	0.87	1–5	0.75	0.19	2.03	0.84	2.05	0.91	−0.32	.75	−0.03
Negative affect	3.03	0.96	1–5	0.25	−0.53	3.00	0.94	3.05	0.99	−0.55	.58	−0.04
Positive affect	2.31	1.00	1–5	0.56	−0.27	2.27	0.93	2.35	1.06	−0.91	.36	−0.07
Positive value	2.31	0.91	1–5	0.50	−0.02	2.29	0.84	2.33	0.96	−0.63	.53	−0.05
Tension	2.52	1.20	1–5	0.59	−0.55	2.50	1.16	2.54	1.23	−0.45	.65	−0.04

Table 3 Game experiences of experimental group by grade level

Variable	Fourth grade ($n=63$)		Fifth grade ($n=309$)		Sixth grade ($n=270$)		$F(2, 639)$	p
	M	SD	M	SD	M	SD		
Challenge	2.37	0.87	2.34	0.81	2.33	0.84	0.05	.949
Competence	3.05	0.94	3.15	0.90	2.97	0.90	2.87	.057
Flow	2.22	0.90	2.11	0.79	1.98	0.75	3.22	.041
Immersion	2.12	1.03	2.12	0.88	1.94	0.81	3.45	.031
Negative affect	2.67	0.94	3.03	0.92	3.11	1.00	5.25	.005
Positive affect	2.48	1.12	2.36	1.00	2.21	0.97	2.60	.075
Positive value	2.50	1.03	2.37	0.91	2.20	0.86	4.33	.014
Tension	2.16	1.15	2.62	1.19	2.48	1.21	4.25	.015

helped them learn math. Scores for negative affect significantly differed both between fourth graders, with fifth graders having a higher score in negative affect (Mean difference $=0.36$, $p=.021$) and between fourth and sixth graders, with sixth graders having a higher score in negative affect (Mean difference $=0.44$, $p=.004$). That is, the youngest students were less likely to report feelings of boredom while playing. However, fourth graders were more likely to feel annoyed or irritable while playing than fifth graders, with the scores for tension significantly differing between fifth and fourth graders (Mean difference $=0.46$, $p=.014$). There were no significant differences between grade levels in the experiences of challenge, competence, or positive affect.

Effects of Game Experiences on Math Motivation Expectancy-Values and Arithmetic Fluency

In order to determine how the experimental group's game experiences related to their post-test scores for (a) math motivation expectancy-values and (b) arithmetic fluency, multiple linear regression analyses were conducted. As dependent variables, the post-test sum scores of the math motivation expectancy-values of interest, utility, attainment value, and self-efficacy were used, as well as arithmetic fluency post-test scores. For each dependent variable, its corresponding variable at pre-test as well as all game experience variables and arithmetic fluency were included as independent variables. Table 4 provides the results of these analyses.

Models were sufficient for explaining the post-test (Total R^2s $>.33$). For all the math motivation expectancy-values of interest, utility, attainment value, and self-efficacy, the corresponding pre-test variables proved to be the strongest predictive variables. In all these cases, the only other significant predictor of post-test scores was the game experience of competence (βs $>.12$). In the case of arithmetic fluency, $F(9, 997)=236.82$, $p<.001$, $R^2=.68$, only pre-test arithmetic fluency was a predictor ($\beta=.82$, $p<.001$), with game experiences not playing any role on post-test results.

Table 4 Regression analyses on post-test math motivation expectancy-values

	β			
	Interest	Utility	Attainment	Self-efficacy
Pre-test value	.58***	.48***	.48***	.47***
Challenge	−.01	.04	.04	−.03
Competence	.15***	.12**	.21***	.33***
Flow	.00	−.03	.06	−.02
Immersion	.01	.00	−.05	−.09
Negative affect	−.05	−.02	−.06	−.04
Positive affect	.04	.03	.01	−.01
Positive value	.05	.09	.06	.06
Tension	−.04	−.06	.00	−.00
R^2	.52	.33	.40	.45
F	113.78***	53.01***	72.04***	86.34***

Note: **$p < .01$, ***$p < .001$

Discussion

The aim of the present study was to investigate the effects of gameplay on students' math motivation as measured by using the expectancy-value model, and to explore how students' differing game experiences were related to the changes in their math motivation and arithmetic fluency.

There was a slight decrease in two of the motivation dimensions, attainment value and self-efficacy, for all participants in both experimental and control groups, which is in line with previous research reporting a general decrease of expectancy-values throughout the school term (Berger & Karabenick, 2011; Wigfield & Cambria, 2010). The control group's interest and utility slightly increased from pre-test to post-test. This could possibly be explained by the fact that participants in the control group anticipated the reversal of conditions and their interest and beliefs in the utility of math were sparked by the upcoming NNG intervention, although data is not sufficient to determine this. For the most part, playing NNG did not have a large impact on students' math motivation expectancy-values. Compared to the control group, the experimental group showed a slight decrease in three of the dimensions of the expectancy-value model (interest, utility, and attainment value), but all these effects were quite small. In spite of this, there was a slightly positive intervention effect on arithmetic fluency.

When focusing on the game experiences of the experimental group, results show that participants rated their game experiences in a predominantly negative or only slightly positive way. The game experience with the lowest mean score was immersion while the one with the highest mean score was competence. Participants reported higher feelings of competence than of challenge. Thus, the challenge-skill balance necessary to produce the game experience of flow, which leads to positive affect, was not reached. The high scores for competence suggest that the game might have been perceived as too simple, although it is unclear whether this was due to the game's form (gameplay) or content (arithmetic strategies needed) or both.

Results support Whitton's (2010a) claim that it cannot be assumed that a game dynamic will automatically make something interesting to learners who have no interest in the subject itself. More studies are needed to explore the impact of background factors, such as interest in math and in games, on game experiences. It is also important to further study to what extent improving the design of the game can foster positive game experiences.

There were some differences in students' game experiences depending on gender and grade level. Girls had higher mean scores for the dimension of challenge while boys had higher mean scores for the dimension of competence. However, it is not clear whether this is due to different perceptions of math skills or gaming skills between genders. Previous research suggests that boys have higher competence beliefs than girls for math even when controlling for skill level, although the gap in gender differences narrows with age (Wigfield & Eccles, 2002). Altogether, competence and challenge significantly differ by gender but not by grade level. Other dimensions such as immersion, positive value, negative affect, and tension differ by grade level, with the mean scores of fourth graders showing the most substantial differences when compared with students from other grade levels. It seems that younger students overall had more positive game experiences than older students. Here, it is important to note the much smaller number of participants in the fourth grade. Finally, the dimension of positive affect is the only dimension of game experience that shows no significant differences by gender or grade level.

Pre-test math motivation expectancy-values played a larger role in predicting post-test math motivation expectancy values than the different dimensions of game experiences, suggesting that there was little change in expectancy-values due to gameplay. Amongst game experiences, competence was the strongest predictor of post-test expectancy-values in all cases. However, this raises some questions about the validity of the dimension of competence as currently measured by the GEQ. It is not clear whether students interpreted the competence items of the GEQ as referring to their math competence or their gaming competence or both. If the former, then it seems that the items for competence and self-efficacy might have overlapped. However, as the correlation between the variables is only moderate ($r=.44$), this needs to be further explored. Similarly, game experiences did not predict post-test arithmetic fluency, suggesting that game experiences may not play a role in mathematical learning outcomes.

Implications

It seems that NNG's mechanics as such were not motivating for the majority of students, even though gameplay resulted in improvement in mathematical skills. Math motivation expectancy-values remained mostly stable, and although the experimental group showed a slight decrease in interest, utility, attainment value, and self-efficacy, these effect sizes were very small. The changes in expectancy-values of the experimental group could partly be predicted by their experience of competence during gameplay, which in turn differs by gender. As the basic mechanics of the game seems to work and resulted in improved mathematical skills, a next step would be to analyze whether new features of later versions of the game will lead to meaningful improvements in gaming experiences. It is encouraging that regardless of the quality of gaming experience, NNG is still effective in improving arithmetic fluency.

Limitations and Future Directions

Conditions could somewhat vary between classrooms, and there is no detailed information what the role of the teacher was in, for example, debriefing, feedback, support activities, or reflection. However, giving teachers the freedom to use the game as they saw fit allowed for testing the effectiveness of the game in the most natural school settings possible. The detailed log data which will be analyzed in the future will give some information of these differences, but in future studies it is important to collect detailed data of teachers' roles during gameplay.

A major limitation of this study is its dependence on subjective and self-reported data. Informal feedback from teachers paints a different picture of students' experiences, as many teachers claimed their students were very engaged while playing and enjoyed the experience. This will be remedied in the future with the addition of a feedback feature within the game itself, which will make it possible for players to give feedback on their affective states upon completing a map, in a situated way that does not disrupt flow.

When looking at game-based learning environments, it's important to acknowledge their oxymoronic nature (Abt, 1987). Jenkins (2011) brings up the contradictory relationship of playing—a "freely chosen irresponsibility"—and learning—an "assigned responsibility." Along similar lines, it has been argued that having teachers decide what games will be played, for how long, and under which circumstances, will have repercussions on the level of control felt by students and consequentially on their motivation (Wouters et al., 2013). Different results may be achieved when play is free and voluntary, as opposed to a formal and prescribed school activity (Islas Sedano, Leendertz, Vinni, Sutinen, & Ellis, 2013), as it has been reported that playing in a different context, such as at home, increases players' enjoyment, identification, and learning experiences (De Grove, Van Looy, Neys, & Jansz, 2012). An important next step could be to study the effects on motivation and core gaming experiences of having students play voluntarily at their homes.

Acknowledgments Gabriela Rodríguez-Aflecht, Centre for Learning Research, Department of Teacher Education, University of Turku; Boglárka Brezovszky, Centre for Learning Research, Department of Teacher Education, University of Turku, Finland; Finland; Nonmanut Pongsakdi, Centre for Learning Research, Department of Teacher Education, University of Turku; Tomi Jaakkola, Centre for Learning Research, Department of Teacher Education, University of Turku; Minna M. Hannula-Sormunen Department of Teacher Education, University of Turku, Finland and Turku Institute for Advanced Studies, University of Turku, Finland; Jake McMullen, Centre for Learning Research, Department of Teacher Education, University of Turku, Finland; Erno Lehtinen, Department of Teacher Education, University of Turku, Finland.

The present study was funded by grant 274163 awarded to the last author by the Academy of Finland.

Appendix

Correlations of pre-test expectancy-values and the GEQ

	1	2	3	4	5	6	7	8	9	10	11	12
1. Pre-test interest	–											
2. Pre-test utility	.46**	–										
3. Pre-test attainment value	.60**	.57**	–									
4. Pre-test self-efficacy	.56**	.42**	.56**	–								
5. Challenge	-.04	-.01	-.11*	-.21**	–							
6. Competence	.29**	.10*	.32**	.41**	-.00	–						
7. Flow	.20**	.01	.18**	.07	.49**	.38**	–					
8. Immersion	.20**	.01	.17**	.12*	.45**	.47**	.73**	–				
9. Negative affect	-.22**	-.01	-.07	-.01	-.28**	-.25**	-.57**	-.55**	–			
10. Positive affect	.26**	.02	.18**	.14**	.44**	.53**	.77**	.79**	-.64**	–		
11. Positive value	.19**	.04	.08	.06	.54**	.44**	.66**	.72**	-.51**	.73**	–	
12. Tension	-.13**	-.07	-.07	.00	-.18**	-.21**	-.36**	-.39**	.69**	-.52**	-.39**	–

*$p<.05$, **$p<.01$

References

Abt, C. (1987). *Serious games*. Boston, MA: University Press of America.

Baroody, A. J., Bajwa, N. P., & Eiland, M. (2009). Why can't Johnny remember the basic facts? *Developmental Disabilities, 15*, 69–79. doi:10.1002/ddrr.45.

Berger, J., & Karabenick, S. A. (2011). Motivation and students' use of learning strategies: Evidence of unidirectional effects in mathematics classrooms. *Learning and Instruction, 21*, 416–428. doi:10.1016/j.learninstruc.2010.06.002.

Bourgonjon, J., Valcke, M., Soetaert, R., & Schellens, T. (2010). Students' perceptions about the use of video games in the classroom. *Computers & Education, 54*, 1145–1156. doi:10.1016/j.compedu.2009.10.022.

Brezovszky, B., Rodríguez-Aflecht, G., McMullen, J., Veermans, K., Pongsakdi, N., Hannula-Sormunen, M. M. & Lehtinen, E. (2015). Developing adaptive number knowledge with the Number Navigation game-based learning environment. In J. Torbeyns, E. Lehtinen & J. Elen (Eds.), *Developing competencies in learners: From ascertaining to intervening* (pp. xx–xx). New York, NY: Springer.

Canobi, K. H. (2009). Concept–procedure interactions in children's addition and subtraction. *Journal of Experimental Child Psychology, 102*, 131–149. doi:10.1016/j.jecp.2008.07.008.

Carr, D. (2005). Contexts, gaming pleasures, and gendered preferences. *Simulation & Gaming, 36*, 464–482. doi:10.1177/1046878105282160.

Clark, L. A., & Watson, D. (1995). Constructing validity: Basic issues in objective scale development. *Psychological Assessment, 7*(3), 309–319.

Connolly, T. M., Boyle, E. A., MacArthur, E., Hainey, T., & Boyle, J. M. (2012). A systematic literature review of the empirical evidence on computer games and serious games. *Computers & Education, 59*, 661–686. doi:10.1016/j.compedu.2012.03.004.

Csikszentmihalyi, M. (1991). *Flow: The psychology of optimal experience*. New York, NY: Harper Perennial.

De Brabander, C., & Martens, R. L. (2014). Towards a unified theory of task-specific motivation. *Educational Research Review, 11*, 27–44. doi:10.1016/j.edurev.2013.11.001.

De Grove, F., Van Looy, J., Neys, J., & Jansz, J. (2012). Playing in school or at home? An exploration of the effects of context on educational game experience. *Electronic Journal of e-Learning, 10*, 83–208. Retrieved from http://files.eric.ed.gov/fulltext/EJ985422.pdf.

De Grove, F., Van Looy, J., & Courtois, C. (2010). Towards a serious game experience model: Validation, extension and adaptation of the GEQ for use in an educational context. In L. Calvi, K. Nuijten, & H. Bouwknegt (Eds.), *Playability and player experience* (Vol. 10, pp. 47–61). Breda, The Netherlands: Breda University of Applied Sciences.

Eccles, J. S., & Wigfield, A. (2002). Motivational beliefs, values, and goals. *Annual Review of Psychology, 53*, 109–132. Retrieved from http://www.rcgd.isr.umich.edu/garp/articles/eccles02c.

Ermi, L., & Mäyrä, F. (2005). Fundamental components of the gameplay experience: Analysing immersion. In S. de Castell & J. Jenson (Eds.), *Changing views: Worlds in play: Selected papers of the 2005 digital games research Association's second international conference* (pp. 15–27). Vancouver, British Columbia, Canada: Digital Interactive Games Research Association.

Gajadhar, B., Nap, H., De Kort, Y., & IJsselsteijn, W. (2008). Shared fun is doubled fun: Player enjoyment as a function of social setting. In P. Markopoulos, B. Ruyter, W. IJsselsteijn, & D. Rowland (Eds.), *Proceedings of the 2nd International Conference on Fun and Games* (pp. 106–117). Berlin, Germany: Springer.

Habgood, M. P. J., & Ainsworth, S. E. (2011). Motivating children to learn effectively: Exploring the value of intrinsic integration in educational games. *Journal of the Learning Sciences, 20*, 169–206. doi:10.1080/10508406.2010.508029.

IJsselsteijn, W., de Kort, Y., Poels, K., Jurgelionis, A., & Bellotti, F. (2007). Characterising and measuring user experiences in digital games. *Proceedings from the 2007 International*

Conference on Advances in Computer Entertainment Technology, Workshop 'Methods for Evaluating Games—How to measure Usability and User Experience in Games'. ACM Digital Library. Retrieved from http://alexandria.tue.nl/openaccess/Metis215134

Islas Sedano, C., Leendertz, V., Vinni, M., Sutinen, E., & Ellis, S. (2013). Hypercontextualized learning games: Fantasy, motivation, and engagement in reality. Simulation & Gaming, 44, 821–845. doi:10.1177/1046878113514807.

Järvelä, S., Lehtinen, E., & Salonen, P. (2000). Socio-emotional orientation as a mediating variable in teaching learning interaction: Implications for instructional design. Scandinavian Journal of Educational Research, 44, 293–306. http://dx.doi.org/10.1080/713696677.

Jenkins, H. (2011). Foreword. In S. de Freitas & P. Maharg (Eds.), Digital games and learning (pp. xxiii–xxvi). New York, NY: Continuum.

Jennett, C., Cox, A. L., Cairns, P., Dhoparee, S., Epps, A., Tijs, T., & Walton, A. (2008). Measuring and defining the experience of immersion in games. International Journal of Human-Computer Studies, 66, 641–661. doi:10.1016/j.ijhcs.2008.04.004.

Jenson, J., & de Castell, S. (2010). Gender, simulation, and gaming: Research review and redirections. Simulation & Gaming, 41(1), 51–71. doi:10.1177/1046878109353473.

Kiili, K., Lainema, T., De Freitas, S., & Arnab, S. (2014). Flow framework for analyzing the quality of educational games. Entertainment Computing, 5, 367–377. doi:10.1016/j.entcom.2014.08.002.

Klemetti, M., Taimisto, O., & Karppinen, P. (2009). The attitudes of Finnish school teachers towards commercial educational games. In M. Kankaanranta & P. Neittaanmäki (Eds.), Design and use of serious games (pp. 97–106). Jyväskylä, Finland: Springer.

Lehtinen, E., Brezovszky, B., Rodríguez-Aflecht, G., Lehtinen, H., Hannula-Sormunen, M., M., McMullen, J., … Jaakkola, T. (2015). Number Navigation Game (NNG): Design principles and game description. In J. Torbeyns, E. Lehtinen & J. Elen (Eds.), Developing competencies in learners: From ascertaining to intervening (pp. xx–xx). New York, NY: Springer.

Lepper, M. R., & Malone, T. W. (1987). Intrinsic motivation and instructional effectiveness in computer-based education. In R. E. Snow & M. J. Farr (Eds.), Aptitude, learning, and instruction (Cognitive and affective process analysis, Vol. 3, pp. 255–286). Hillsdale, NJ: Erlbaum.

Lowyck, J., Lehtinen, E., & Elen, J. (2004). Editorial: Students' perspectives on learning environments. International Journal of Educational Research, 41, 401–406. doi:10.1016/j.ijer.2005.08.008.

Lucas, K., & Sherry, J. L. (2004). Sex differences in video game play: A communication-based explanation. Communication Research, 31, 499–523. doi:10.1177/0093650204267930.

McMullen, J., Brezovszky, B., Rodríguez-Aflecht, G., Pongsakdi, N. & Lehtinen, E. (2015). Adaptive Number Knowledge: Exploring the foundations of adaptivity with whole-number arithmetic. Manuscript submitted for publication.

Nacke, L. E., & Drachen, A. (2011). Towards a framework of player experience research. In Proceedings of the Second International Workshop on Evaluating Player Experience in Games at FDG (Vol. 11). Retrieved from http://hciweb.usask.ca/uploads/230-Nacke DrachenPXFramework

Nacke, L. E., & Lindley, C. A. (2009). Affective ludology, flow and immersion in a first-person shooter: Measurement of player experience. Loading, 3. Retrieved from http://journals.sfu.ca/loading/index.php/loading/article/view/72/71.

Nacke, L. E., Stellmach, S., & Lindley, C. A. (2011). Electroencephalographic assessment of player experience: A pilot study in affective ludology. Simulation & Gaming, 42, 632–655. doi:10.1177/1046878110378140.

Oksanen, K. (2013). Subjective experience and sociability in a collaborative serious game. Simulation & Gaming, 44, 767–793. doi:10.1177/1046878113513079.

Paras, B., & Bizzocchi, J. (2005). Game, motivation, and effective learning: An integrated model for educational game design. Proceedings of DiGRA 2005 Conference: Changing Views: Worlds in Play. Retrieved from http://www.digra.org/wp-content/uploads/digital-library/06276.18065.pdf

Pavlas, D., Heyne, K., Bedwell, W., Lazzara, L. L., & Salas, E. (2010). Game based learning: The impact of flow state and videogame self-efficacy. *Proceedings of the Human Factors and Ergonomics Society Annual Meeting, 54,* 2398–2402. doi:10.1177/154193121005402808.

Poels, K., de Kort, Y. A. W., & IJsselsteijn, W. A. (2007). It is always a lot of fun!—Exploring dimensions of digital game experience using focus group methodology. In B. Kapralos, M. Katchabaw, & J. Rajnovich (Eds.) *Proceedings of the 2007 Conference on Future Play* (pp. 83–89). ACM Press. Retrieved from http://alexandria.tue.nl/openaccess/Metis215146

Poels, K., IJsselsteijn, W., de Kort, Y., & Van Iersel, B. (2010). Digital games, the aftermath. Qualitative insights into post game experiences. In R. Bernhaupt (Ed.), *Evaluating user experiences in games.* Berlin, Germany: Springer.

Ryan, R. M., & Deci, E. L. (2000). Intrinsic and extrinsic motivations: Classic definitions and new directions. *Contemporary Educational Psychology, 25,* 54–67.

Wegge, J. (2001). Motivation, information processing, and performance: Effects of goal setting on basic cognitive processes. In A. Efklides, J. Kuhl, & R. M. Sorrentino (Eds.), *Trends and prospects in motivation research* (pp. 269–296). Dordrecht, The Netherlands: Kluwer. doi:10.1007/0-306-47676-2.

Whitton, N. (2010a). Game engagement theory and adult learning. *Simulation & Gaming, 42,* 597–610. doi:10.1177/1046878110378587.

Whitton, N. (2010b). *Learning with digital games: A practical guide to engaging students in higher education.* New York, NY: Routledge.

Wigfield, A. (1994). Expectancy-value theory of achievement motivation: A developmental perspective. *Educational Psychology Review, 6*(1), 49–78.

Wigfield, A., & Cambria, J. (2010). Expectancy-value theory: Retrospective and prospective. In T. Urdan & S. A. Karabenick (Eds.), *Advances in motivation and achievement. The next decade of research in motivation and achievement* (pp. 35–70). London, England: Emerald.

Wigfield, A., & Eccles, J. S. (2000). Expectancy-value theory of achievement motivation. *Contemporary Educational Psychology, 25,* 68–81. doi:10.1006/ceps.1999.1015.

Wigfield, A., & Eccles, J.S. (2002).The Development of Competence Beliefs, Expectancies for Success, and Achievement Values from Childhood through Adolescence. In A. Wigfield, & J. S. Eccles (Eds.), *Development of achievement motivation* (pp. 91–120). Academic. Retrieved from http://www.rcgd.isr.umich.edu/garp/articles/eccles02o

Woodcock, R., McGrew, K., & Mather, N. (2001). *Woodcock-Johnson tests of achievement.* Itasca, IL: Riverside.

Wouters, P., van Nimwegen, C., van Oostendorp, H., & van der Spek, E. D. (2013). A meta-analysis of the cognitive and motivational effects of serious games. *Journal of Educational Psychology, 105,* 249–265. doi:10.1037/a0031311.

The Role of Curiosity-Triggering Events in Game-Based Learning for Mathematics

Pieter Wouters, Herre van Oostendorp, Judith ter Vrugte,
Sylke Vandercruysse, Ton de Jong, and Jan Elen

Abstract In this study, we investigate whether cognitive conflicts induced by curiosity-triggering events have a positive impact on learning and motivation. In two experiments, we tested a game about proportional reasoning for secondary prevocational students. Experiment 1 used a curiosity-triggering vs. control condition pretest–posttest design. The control condition received the game without curiosity-triggering events. The results provided evidence that the game improves proportional reasoning skills. Although game performance was positively related to posttest performance, the hypothesized higher increase in learning and motivation after curiosity-triggering events was not found. Based on the results of Experiment 1, the game was adapted. Experiment 2 showed basically the same pattern of results, but we did not find a learning effect after playing the game. In the Discussion, we suggest additional research with think-aloud and/or eye-tracking to map the actual thoughts after the curiosity-triggering events. In addition, we propose some alternative implementations to evoke cognitive conflicts.

Keywords Curiosity • Game-based learning • Cognition • Motivation • Mathematics

The last decade shows an increasing attention for the use of computer games in learning and instruction, often referred to as serious games or game-based learning (GBL). However, recent meta-analytic reviews have shown that GBL is only moderately more effective and not more motivating than traditional instruction (Sitzmann, 2011; Wouters, van Nimwegen, van Oostendorp, & van der Spek, 2013).

P. Wouters (✉) • H. van Oostendorp
Institute of Information and Computing Sciences, Utrecht University,
P.O. Box 80.089, Utrecht 3508 TB, The Netherlands
e-mail: p.j.m.wouters@uu.nl; H.vanoostendorp@uu.nl

J. ter Vrugte • T. de Jong
Department of Instructional Technology, University of Twente, Enschede, The Netherlands
e-mail: j.tervrugte@utwente.nl; A.J.M.deJong@utwente.nl

S. Vandercruysse • J. Elen
Center for Instructional Psychology & Technology, KU Leuven, Leuven, Belgium
e-mail: sylke.vandercruysse@kuleuven-kulak.be; jan.elen@ppw.kuleuven.be

© Springer International Publishing Switzerland 2015
J. Torbeyns et al. (eds.), *Describing and Studying Domain-Specific Serious Games*,
Advances in Game-Based Learning, DOI 10.1007/978-3-319-20276-1_12

For example, Wouters et al. reviewed 39 empirical studies for their meta-analysis and found a moderate effect size for learning of $d = .29$ in favor of GBL. Likewise, they found a moderate, but statistically nonsignificant, effect for motivation in favor of GBL.

A plausible explanation for the limited effect of GBL on learning is that players act in computer games and see the outcome of their actions directly in changes in the game world. This may lead to a kind of intuitive learning: players know how to apply knowledge, but they cannot explicate it. In other words: they don't necessarily acquire the underlying rules (Leemkuil & de Jong, 2011). It is possible that studies therefore find no relation between success in the game and success on an explicit knowledge test. Yet, it is important that learners articulate and explain their knowledge because it urges them to *organize* new information and *integrate* it with their prior knowledge (Mayer, 2011, Wouters, Paas, & van Merriënboer, 2008).

Sense of control regarding decisions during game play (e.g., when to leave the game, go back in the game, conduct specific actions in the game) is deemed an important determinant for intrinsic motivation (Deci, Koestner, & Ryan, 1999; Ryan, Rigby, & Przybylski, 2006). It is neglected that GBL often lacks control because the game that is used and the playing time are generally defined by the curriculum and not by the player (Wouters et al., 2013), resulting in low motivation. In addition, it is plausible that the lack of motivational appeal in GBL environments is a reflection of the fact that the world of game design and instructional design are not yet integrated (Wouters, van Oostendorp, Boonekamp, & van der Spek, 2011). Take, for example, the situation in which a designer uses a pop-up screen with a message that prompts the player to reflect. From an instructional design perspective such a focus may yield learning, but it is also likely that such an intervention will disturb the flow of the game and consequently undermine the entertaining nature of the game and reduce motivation and learning as well.

The question raised in this study is how we can stimulate players to engage in relevant cognitive processes that foster learning without jeopardizing the motivational appeal of the game. In this respect, the role of curiosity is often neglected in GBL. It is interesting for two reasons. To start with, curiosity is regarded as a motivator for active (cognitive) explorative behavior (cf. Berlyne, 1960; Litman, 2005; Loewenstein, 1994). Second, active exploration is a key aspect of contemporary computer games (Dickey, 2011) which might be beneficial for learning.

Curiosity

In his review, Loewenstein (1994) proposes an information-gap theory in which curiosity is supposed to arise when attention becomes focused on a gap in one's knowledge. Such an information gap produces the feeling of deprivation labeled curiosity. The curious individual is motivated to obtain the missing information in order to reduce the gap and to eliminate the feeling of deprivation.

An information gap can be interpreted in two ways. The first interpretation is related to conceptual change which can be defined as the process of connecting prior knowledge (ideas, beliefs, knowledge) with new knowledge (Limón, 2001; Merenluoto & Lehtinen, 2004). From an information gap perspective a cognitive conflict can be used as a strategy to promote conceptual change. Such a cognitive conflict can be induced by presenting information that is incongruent with the prior knowledge (e.g., it contradicts prior knowledge). The cognitive conflict is supposed to be a drive for information-seeking questions in order to reconcile the conflict between prior knowledge and new incongruent information (Graesser & McMahen, 1993; Graesser & Olde, 2003).

The second interpretation is related to Berlyne's concept of a cognitive conflict (Berlyne, 1960; Loewenstein, 1994). This construct encompasses "collative" variables such as complexity, novelty, and surprisingness. The presence of these stimulus characteristics would arouse cognitive conflict and stimulate curiosity. In this case, an information gap occurs when stimuli present contradictory or incongruent information. For example, in the game a learner is told that a presented problem can be solved but the game environment appears to offer no opportunities to solve the problem. Although this interpretation is not related to conceptual change, it can also be regarded as a cognitive conflict namely the conflict in the current mental representation of the learner between:

1. The expectations of the learner (based on the assurance that the problem can be solved).
2. The affordances in the learning environment to solve the problem.

The assumption—in line with Jirout and Klahr (2012)—is that this information gap will motivate students to explore the environment and find relevant information for constructing appropriate solution methods. More specifically, we assume that based on Loewenstein (1994) and Berlyne (1960) ideas that externally inducing the information gap will stimulate curiosity, raise arousal, and consequently enhance explorations in the game environment and in this way improve learning.

The advantage of curiosity induced by an information gap is that individuals are cognitively active in an engaging way. Scholars have emphasized the potential of curiosity in GBL (Dickey, 2011; Malone, 1981; Wouters et al., 2011), but empirical research is rather scarce. In this study, we present the results of two experiments in which we investigate the impact of curiosity-triggering events on learning. We expect that these events will improve learning because they will motivate learners to engage in explorative behavior. We used the GBL environment "Zeldenrust" that was specifically developed for learning proportional reasoning in secondary prevocational education (see Vandercruysse et al., this volume). Proportional reasoning was chosen because it is a relevant and well-defined domain and existing methods for proportional reasoning are often ineffective (Rick, Bejan, Roche, & Weinberger, 2012). Furthermore, secondary prevocational education students are often associated with lower levels of motivation for school which makes this population particularly suitable for GBL.

Experiment 1

In this experiment, we examine three hypotheses:

1. Playing the game yields learning in proportional reasoning.
2. Game performance is predictive for (off-line) posttest performance.
3. The game with curiosity-triggering events improves learning and increases motivation more than the game without these events.

Method

Participants and Design

The participants were 67 students (28 male, 39 female) from third-year prevocational education with a mean age of 15.5 (SD = .75) recruited from four classes of four schools.

We adopted a pretest–posttest design with a control ($N=34$) and a curiosity ($N=33$) group. Participants were randomly assigned to the conditions. Dependent variables were proportional reasoning skill, motivation, and game performance.

Materials

Domain. The domain of proportional reasoning comprises three problem types: comparison problems, missing value problems, and transformation problems (cf., Tourniaire & Pulos, 1985). In comparison problems, learners have to find out whether one proportion is "more than," "lesser-than," or "equal to" another proportion. In missing value problems, one value in one of two proportions is missing. Learners have to find this "missing value" in order to ensure that both proportions are equal. Transformation problems involve two proportions as well and all values are known, but the proportions are not equal. Learners have to find out how much has to be added to one or more of the proportions in order to make both proportions equal (for a more extensive description, see Vandercruysse et al., 2014).

Game environment. In the game Zeldenrust students have a summer job in a hotel. By doing different tasks the students can earn money that they can use to select a holiday destination during the game: the more money they earn, the further they can travel. During the game, the player is accompanied by the manager, a non-playing character, who provides information about the task and gives feedback regarding the performance on the task. The game comprises a base game and several subgames. The base game provides the structure from which the subgames can be started. It allows the player to select an avatar, it presents the context of the game in a sort of animation and features the "Student room" from which the student can control the game (e.g., by choosing a specific subgame). Each task is implemented as a subgame and covers a specific problem type in the domain of proportional reasoning. The tasks are directly related to proportional reasoning (e.g., mixing two drinks to make a cocktail according to a particular ratio directly involves proportional reasoning skills). In addition, mental operations with respect to proportional reasoning are connected with the game mechanics (e.g., in order to get the correct amount of bottles in the refrigerator the player has to drag the correct number of bottles in the refrigerator). Each task/subgame can be played on four levels, ranging from easy to difficult. Players first have to finish the three subgames in one level before they can proceed to the next level. Each task (on each level) consists of four assignments. The structure of these assignments is the same, but the numbers vary. For example, in one assignment the student is asked to refill a refrigerator in such a way that the ratio between cola and fanta is 6–12. In the next assignment, this ratio can be 16 cola and 4 fanta, etc. (for a more extensive description, see Vandercruysse et al., 2014).

In the *control* condition, all assignments were presented in an identical way and all information required to perform the assignment was available. See Vandercruysse et al. (this volume) for a description of the control condition.

In the *curiosity* condition, two types of curiosity-triggering events (respectively curiosity type 1 and type 2) were implemented in the Refrigerator and the Blender subgames. The main reason to introduce several types is to have variation in curiosity-triggering events. The Jugs subgame did not use curiosity-triggering events because each assignment in the subgame comprised only two jugs which made the implementation of these events less meaningful. As mentioned before, we define curiosity-triggering events as stimuli that present incongruent information which induce curiosity. The operationalization of curiosity type 1 is as follows:

1. The manager character appears and tells that something strange has happened. He does not exactly know what has happened, but he is sure that the current problem (the assignment) can be solved. In this stage, an expectation is created consisting of the assurance that the problem can be solved.
2. When the character has disappeared, the students cannot see bottles or crates with a caption indicating their numerical value, but only large crates (Refrigerator subgame) or shopping bags (Blender subgame) with a large question mark (see Fig. 1a). The students already may have a hypothesis or idea how to solve the problem, but the opportunities in the game environment (the large crates, shopping bags) are incongruent with what was told them before. Consequently, the perceptual information is incongruent with the verbal information provided by the manager.

They have to explore the contents in the crates and bags and decide how they can solve the problem the best. For example, the blackboard in Fig. 1b makes clear that 4 bottles have to be moved into the refrigerator. The learner can hover the crates/shopping bags and reveal their content. The left crate in Fig. 1b contains three smaller packages with 2, 4, and 6 bottles. By exploring the different crates/bags, the learner can decide which crate/shopping bag contains the packages that can best be used to solve the problem. With a mouse click the large crates/shopping bags are unpacked and the smaller packages become available (Fig. 1c).

Fig. 1 The implementation of curiosity type 1. (**a**) (*Upper left*) depicts the initial situation. (**b**) (*Upper right*) shows the content when hovering over the crate with the mouse. (**c**) (*Under left*) shows the situation when the crate is unpacked

The operationalization of curiosity type 2 is as follows:

1. The manager character also appears and tells that something has happened but that the problem can still be solved (creating an expectation).
2. The game environment shows a series of crates (Refrigerator subgame) or bottles (Blender game). The first two crates/bottles have a caption with the amount that they represent; the other crates/bottles have a question mark (see Fig. 2a). Again the opportunities in the game environment (crates/bottles with a question mark) are incongruent with what was told them before. So again there is an incongruency between perceptual and verbal information.

The learner can hover the crates/bottles and reveal their content (Fig. 2b). By exploring the content, learners can discover and decide which option best fits the solution of the problem. A crate/bottle can be activated with a mouse click and then be moved to the refrigerator or blender used (Fig. 2c). The crates/bottles always represent an arithmetic relationship (e.g., 12, 18, 24, 30, 36, 42, 48).

Fig. 2 The implementation of curiosity type 2. (**a**) (*Upper left*) depicts the initial situation. (**b**) (*Upper right*) shows the content when hovering over the crate with the mouse. (**c**) (*Under left*) shows the situation when the crate is selected and dragged to the refrigerator

In each level, two curiosity type 1, one curiosity type 2, and one normal assignment were presented in a random order.

Tests. Proportional reasoning skill was measured with a test consisting of 12 open questions: four questions for each problem type. The questions were comparable with the assignments in the game. An example (missing value) is:

"For a banana milkshake you have to use 28 bananas and 48 units of ice. How many units of ice do you need if you are going to use 56 bananas and you want to remain the same proportion?"

There were two versions of the test. The structure of these versions was the same, but the numbers were different. The comparability of both versions was tested in pilot study.

Motivation was measured with the enjoyment subscale (7 items) from the Intrinsic Motivation Inventory (Ryan, 1982) with a 7-point Likert scale (ranging from "strongly disagree" to "strongly agree"). All items were translated into Dutch and tested in a pilot study (reliability Cronbach's alpha = .74).

Procedure

The experiment was run on the computers of the schools. The experiment took 150 min divided into three sessions of 50 min. In the first session, the experiment was introduced and the pretest was administered (40 min). When participants had finished the pretest, they could do their homework. The second and third sessions, a week later, were two successive lessons with a break of 10 min. In the second session, the participants played the game (40 min) and filled in the motivation questionnaire (10 min). At the beginning of the session, the participants were seated at a designated computer and received a login code. All actions of the players during playing the game were logged. After the break, the posttest was administered in the third session (40 min). One version was used in the pretest, the other version in the posttest.

Scoring

Skill test. Each answer of the pretest and posttest was coded as 0 (wrong answer or no answer) or 1 (correct answer). For the analysis, we focused on the performance on the three problem types (4 questions each) and on the overall performance (12 questions).

Motivation questionnaire. For each participant, a mean score was calculated.

Game performance. Due to technological problems during logging, the data of six participants was removed from the dataset. Two variables were calculated for each participant:

1. The total time they spent in a subgame to perform the assignments.
2. The number of assignments they correctly solved in a subgame.

Results and Conclusion

For all statistical tests, a significance level of .05 was applied. Effect sizes will be expressed in Cohen's *d*. Table 1 shows the results for each condition on proportional reasoning skill and motivation.

A paired-samples *T*-test on the pretest and posttest scores confirms hypothesis 1 arguing that playing the game improves learning (overall $t(66)=3.31$, $p=.002$, $d=.44$; missing value problems: $t(66)=2.30$, $p=.025$, $d=.32$; comparison problems: $t(66)=.16$, $p>.05$; transformation: $t(66)=4.83$, $p=.000$, $d=.28$).

Table 2 provides an overview of both game performance variables for each subgame.

Table 1 Mean scores and standard deviations on the dependent variables for both conditions in Experiment 1

Experiment 1

	Control		Curiosity	
	Pretest	Posttest	Pretest	Posttest
Proportional reasoning overall [0–12]	3.77 (3.25)	5.00 (3.62)	4.90 (3.07)	6.53 (3.30)
Missing value (Refrigerator) [0–4]	1.42 (1.26)	2.12 (1.56)	2.07 (1.31)	2.59 (1.37)
Comparison (Jugs) [0–4]	1.71 (1.37)	1.61 (1.25)	2.07 (1.26)	2.26 (1.26)
Transformation (Blender) [0–4]	.64 (1.35)	1.27 (1.46)	.77 (1.19)	1.68 (1.51)
Motivation [1–7]	n.a.	3.54 (.38)	n.a.	3.55 (.37)

Note: numbers between [ ] indicate the range of possible scores

Table 2 Mean scores and standard deviations on the game performance variables in Experiment 1

Experiment 1

	Control		Curiosity	
	M	SD	M	SD
Missing value (Refrigerator)				
Correct assignments	5.67	3.50	6.81	3.52
Time on task (s)	641	355	596	245
Comparison (Jugs)				
Correct assignments	4.42	2.55	5.07	2.94
Time on task (s)	135	102	140	87
Transformation (Blender)				
Correct assignments	5.33	3.60	6.28	3.59
Time on task (s)	651	252	818	417

To test the hypothesis that game performance (correct assignments and time on task) predicts posttest performance, we used a hierarchical regression with two blocks. The first block consisted of the pretest score. In the second block, correct assignments and time on task were entered stepwise. By using two blocks, the effect of the pretest score on the posttest can be isolated. From Table 3 can be concluded that hypothesis 2 is partly confirmed: when the variance caused by the pretest score and both game performance variables is accounted for, only the number of correct assignments and pretest score are predictive for posttest performance. In the control condition, number of correct assignments explains 25 % of the variance extra, in the curiosity condition 20 %.

At face value, it seems that hypothesis 3 can be (partly) confirmed because the curiosity condition benefits more from playing the game than the control condition (see Table 1). However, a series of ANCOVAs (condition as fixed factor and pretest score as covariate) reveals no statistical differences: proportional reasoning all: $F(1, 60) < 1$; missing value: $F(1, 60) = 2.57$, $p = .11$; comparison: $F(1, 60) = 1.5$, $p = .22$ and transformation: $F(1, 60) = 1.70$, $p = .20$. Since motivation was only measured after playing the game, a T-test was conducted $(t(65) = -.18, p = .86)$, indicating no difference in reported motivation.

Table 3 Hierarchical regression on game performance variables in Experiment 1

Experiment 1			
	B	SE B	β
Control			
Step 1: Constant	2.64	.92	
Pretest score	.56	.19	.51*
Step 2: Constant	−.25	1.10	
Pretest score	.39	.16	.35**
Correct assignments	.22	.06	.53*
Curiosity			
Step 1: Constant	3.28	.93	
Pretest score	.60	.16	.58*
Step 2: Constant	1.03	1.04	
Pretest score	.34	.16	.33**
Correct assignments	.19	.06	.51*

Note: * $p < .005$, ** $p < .05$
Control: $R^2 = .26$ for step 1, $\Delta R^2 = .25$ for step 2
Curiosity: $R^2 = .33$ for step 1, $\Delta R^2 = .20$ for step 2

Discussion

Although playing the game yielded learning (hypothesis 1) and game performance was positively related to posttest performance (hypothesis 2), we did not find a beneficial effect of curiosity-triggering events in posttest performance nor in motivation (hypothesis 3).

Interviews conducted after the experiment revealed that some students did not immediately understand the intention behind the curiosity-triggering events. This was especially true for the curiosity 1 type assignments. For instance, students raised here their hand and told that they could not solve the problem because there were no bottles with a number (e.g., a bottle with a numerical value) that they could use to perform the assignment. We had expected that this would trigger them to find ways in the game to solve the problem, but they did not make this connection. In the first level of the game, we also observed that some students did not know what to do in the game (also in the control condition). Despite a tutorial, it took these students time to understand what they had to do in an assignment and the actions that were needed to perform the assignment. The log files indicated that most students neglected the tutorial. Based on these findings, we adapted the game.

Experiment 2

In this experiment, we adapted the GBL environment. The most important rationale to conduct Experiment 2 is that the curiosity implementation in Experiment 1 was not clear for all students. Some of them could not make a connection between what was told by the NPC character at the beginning of the curiosity event and what they could do in the game world. In Experiment 2, we have made this link more prominent by introducing a dialogue which refers to the situation in the game world. In addition, the curiosity type 2 events were replaced by curiosity type 1 events (see the "Method" section for more detailed information). Finally, the tutorial was redesigned in order to support students during game play. The same hypotheses were tested.

Method

Participants and Design

Again a pretest–posttest design was used. Students from two small classes were randomly assigned to the control ($N = 11$) and curiosity ($N = 14$) condition.

Materials

Domain. The same domain was used as in Experiment 1.

Game environment. The same game was used as in Experiment 1 with major adaptions. First, the passive tutorial was replaced by an interactive learn-while-you play tutorial which is more in line with contemporary games. Second, the graphics were redesigned in order to limit the size of the game. The game used in Experiment 1 was quite large (40 MB) and sometimes caused long download times. Figure 3 gives an impression of the new visual design (size of the game is 1.2 MB).

The *control* condition was exactly the same as in Experiment 1. The *curiosity* condition was different from the curiosity condition in Experiment 1 on two points:

First, the expectation is now created by a short dialogue between the manager and the aunt character. For example, "Manager: What a strange situation! Yet I know for sure that it is possible to perform the task!" <aunt appears> "Aunt: But how then? .... I only see crates with question marks. Where are the bottles?" It puts more emphasis on the fact that something strange had occurred but that the assignment is still solvable.

Secondly, experts criticized that the arithmetical relationship in the curiosity type 2 events was in fact an additional instructional aid which could confound with the curiosity intervention. Both the curiosity intervention and the (arithmetic) instructional aid can potentially explain a positive effect of the curiosity type 2 events. Therefore, the curiosity type 2 events were replaced by curiosity type 1 events.

Tests. The pretest and posttest were the same as used in Experiment 1. Due to time constraints, the motivation questionnaire was omitted.

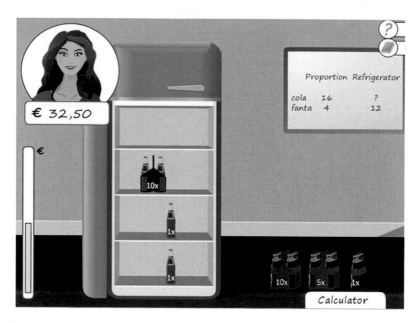

Fig. 3 The new design of the GBL

Procedure

The procedure was the same as used in Experiment 1 with the difference that the posttest was not administered directly after playing the game, but in a third session that took place 3 days later.

Results and Conclusion

The same analyses as in Experiment 1 were conducted. Two participants (one from each condition) were identified as outlier and therefore removed from the dataset.

Table 4 shows the results for each condition on proportional reasoning skill.

Hypothesis 1 is rejected because the paired-samples T-test reveals no learning effect from playing the game (overall $t(22) = 1.01$, $p > .05$). Also tests on subgame level did not reveal differences (missing value problems: $t(22) = .92$, $p > .05$; comparison problems: $t(22) = 1.15$, $p > .05$; transformation: $t(22) = 1.35$, $p > .05$).

Table 5 gives an overview on game performance.

The hypothesis that game performance (correct assignments and time on task) predicts posttest performance (H2) can be partly confirmed: when the variance caused by the pretest score and both game performance variables is accounted for, only the number of correct assignments and pretest score are predictive for posttest performance. The number of correct assignments explains 46 % and 62 % of the variance extra in the control and curiosity condition, respectively (see Table 6).

Table 4 Mean scores and standard deviations on the dependent variables for both conditions in Experiment 2

Experiment 2	Control		Curiosity	
	Pretest	Posttest	Pretest	Posttest
Proportional reasoning overall [0–12]	2.44 (1.01)	2.33 (1.58)	3.71 (1.98)	3.00 (2.38)
Missing value (Refrigerator) [0–4]	.55 (1.01)	.78 (.83)	1.14 (1.34)	1.29 (1.11)
Comparison (Jugs) [0–4]	1.89 (1.17)	1.55 (1.13)	2.28 (.95)	1.42 (1.27)
Transformation (Blender) [0–4]	0 (0)	0 (0)	.25 (.71)	.25 (.70)

Note: numbers between [ ] indicate the range of possible scores

Table 5 Mean scores and standard deviations on the game performance-dependent variables in Experiment 2

Experiment 2	Control		Curiosity	
	M	SD	M	SD
Missing value (Refrigerator)				
Correct assignments	4.93	2.66	4.09	2.26
Time on task (s)	632	323	602	238
Comparison (Jugs)				
Correct assignments	4.50	3.23	3.00	1.84
Time on task (s)	168	77	122	100
Transformation (Blender)				
Correct assignments	3.93	2.84	3.09	2.47
Time on task (s)	672	331	444	343

Table 6 Hierarchical regression on game performance variables in Experiment 2

Experiment 2	B	$SE\ B$	β
Control			
Step 1: Constant	2.07	.93	
Pretest score	.11	.26	.15
Step 2: Constant	.37	.99	
Pretest score	.12	.21	.16
Correct assignments	.11	.05	.68*
Curiosity			
Step 1: Constant	1.36	1.93	
Pretest score	.30	.40	.29
Step 2: Constant	−1.35	1.48	
Pretest score	−.19	.30	−.19
Correct assignments	.41	.13	.92*

Note: * $p < .05$
Control: $R^2 = .02$ for step 1, $\Delta R^2 = .46$ for step 2
Curiosity: $R^2 = .08$ for step 1, $\Delta R^2 = .62$ for step 2

Hypothesis 3 indicating that the curiosity condition will yield higher learning gains than the control condition must be rejected. Neither on the overall game nor on the different problem types (subgames) the ANCOVAs revealed differences between both conditions (all $F(22) < 1$, $p > .05$).

Despite the modifications in the game environment, we found no learning effect after playing the game (hypothesis 1). The regression analysis on the other hand provides some evidence that game play improves proportional reasoning skills: 46 % and 62 % of the variance in the posttest score (respectively, the control and curiosity condition) can be attributed to the number of correct assignments. This implies that better performance on the posttest can be explained by a higher number of correct assignments which indicates that effective game play improves learning (hypothesis 2). We did not find evidence that curiosity-triggering events improved learning more than a game without these events (hypothesis 3).

The absence of a learning effect can be the result of a lack of motivation during the administration of the posttest. The comparison of the pretest and posttest scores provides some support for this assertion. We found that three participants with rather high scores on the pretest (8, 8, and 7 where the maximum score could be 12) scored very low on the posttest (respectively 2, 0, and 3). It is possible that the game has such a strong negative learning effect, but this is not in line with the results of the control condition in Experiment 1 which was comparable with the control condition in Experiment 2. In Experiment 1, the participants scored significantly higher on the posttest then on the pretest. In our view, it is more likely that these differences arise from low motivation during the administration of the posttest in Experiment 2.

Another explanation may be that the posttest was administered 3 days after the game (in Experiment 1, this was immediately after the game), but there is some evidence that learning effects of GBL environments do not decrease with delayed testing, at least not after 3 days (Wouters et al., 2013).

General Discussion

The goal of the experiments was to investigate whether the use of a GBL environment for proportional reasoning enhances learning. In addition, we examined whether our implementation of curiosity in the GBL environment would further increase the learning effect. Our operationalization of curiosity was based on Loewenstein's information-gap theory (1994). It views curiosity as a reference-point phenomenon, with the reference point being the information that the player wants to know. We concur with Jirout and Klahr (2012) that the information-gap theory combines elements from Gestalt psychology, Social psychology, and behavioral decision theory.

The operationalization involved two phases. First, the student was told that a strange situation had occurred but that the current problem could still be solved. In this way, we created an expectation in the student. Second, the student was confronted with a game environment in which it was not immediately clear how this problem could be solved. Taken together we regard this as a cognitive conflict namely the conflict between the expectations of the learner and the affordances in the learning environment. Our assumption was that students had to explore the game environment and find the objects (crates/bottles) that would enable them to implement the solution that they had conceived.

In Experiment 1, we found that playing the game had a learning effect. In Experiment 2, game play did not yield learning, though in both studies performance on the game assignments contributed strongly to off-line posttest performance (see the results of the regression analyses). In both experiments, we failed to find a beneficial effect of the curiosity-triggering events. Based on Loewenstein's (1994) and Berlyne's (1960) ideas, we hoped that these situational determinants would induce curiosity. The game environment however had a strong repetitive character which made it perhaps difficult to maintain a curiosity effect. Our implementation of curiosity depended on an incongruity between what players were told and what they saw. Some remarks can be made regarding this implementation. Firstly, can an incongruity that is materialized in two different modalities (verbal and visual) evoke the intended cognitive conflict? It was difficult for some students to make a connection between what was told in the verbal channel and what was shown in the visual channel. This may also explain the confusion that some students experienced when they were confronted with the curiosity-triggering events. It is worth to investigate the impact of the curiosity-triggering events when they occur in only one modality. For example, by focusing on an incongruity within the verbal mode. An additional character can be introduced in the game who challenges the actions of the student or who provides information that is incongruent with the information that is already mentioned. Malone discerned cognitive and perceptual curiosity (Malone, 1981). An interesting addition to cognitive curiosity as we included so far is to implement also some form of pure perceptual curiosity, for example, by hiding bottles in the room in such a way that students have to "collect" the bottles that they want to use.

Secondly, we also don't know if players experienced a cognitive conflict or that they were just confused. For this reason, an obvious next step might be to understand what players think or experience when the curiosity-triggering events occur. Interesting methods in this respect are the use of think aloud protocols and/or eye-tracking.

Thirdly, our interpretation of information gap neglected cognitive conflict as a strategy to promote conceptual change. According to the theory, this can be achieved by presenting new information that challenges preexisting knowledge of the learner.

Whether a cognitive conflict can induce conceptual change depends on various (meta)cognitive factors. The learner must have sufficient prior knowledge in order to identify the gap with the incongruent information. This means that the gap should not be too big and that the learner must feel confident that the knowledge conflict can be reconciled (see Limón, 2001; Merenluoto & Lehtinen, 2004). In GBL environments, such as a math game, this requires a student model with reliable information about a student's prior knowledge and self-confidence. In the current generation of GBL environments, this is still difficult to implement. An application of cognitive conflict to promote conceptual change that we currently investigate starts with a set of proportional reasoning problems that are designed in such a way that one strategy is the most obvious to solve the problem. We assume that this strategy will become prior knowledge because students have to apply it repeatedly. Then, an event in the game changes the characteristics of the problem that the student is working on. The strategy that was used in the preceding problems is now less appropriate so that the student will have to devise a different strategy, which all together could enhance learning.

Some clear limitations adhere to the studies reported here. First, the number of participants in Experiment 2 is very low so the results should be interpreted with care. In addition, we were not able to administer a motivation questionnaire. Second, the comparison of both studies is complicated because in Experiment 1 not only another curiosity-triggering event is used but also because of the changes in the game environment.

Besides the proposals for future research that we have already mentioned, there is another interesting point for further research. Our curiosity manipulation is an example of an added-value comparison in which the effect of a specific game characteristic is investigated (Mayer, 2011; Wouters & Van Oostendorp, 2013). It is possible that the control condition is already effective and that additional curiosity manipulation has no added-value. For future research, we propose research which combines a curiosity and a control condition with a non-game condition. The comparison of the latter two is a media comparison which may give an understanding of the efficacy of the game control condition (see also Girard, Ecalle, & Magnan, 2013).

Acknowledgment This research is funded by the Netherlands Organization for Scientific Research (project Number No. 411-00-003).

References

Anderson, J. R. (1990). *Cognitive psychology and its implications.* New York, NY: WH Freeman.

Berlyne, D. E. (1960). *Conflict, arousal and curiosity.* New York, NY: McGraw-Hill.

Cameron, B., & Dwyer, F. (2005). The effect of online gaming, cognition and feedback type in facilitating delayed achievement of different learning objectives. *Journal of Interactive Learning Research, 16,* 243–258.

de Castell, S., & Jenson, J. (2003). Serious play. *Journal of Curriculum Studies, 35,* 649–665.

Deci, E. L., Koestner, R., & Ryan, R. M. (1999). A meta-analytic review of experiments examining the effects of extrinsic rewards on intrinsic motivation. *Psychological Bulletin, 125,* 627–668.

Dickey, M. D. (2011). Murder on Grimm Isle: The impact of game narrative design in an educational game-based learning environment. *British Journal of Educational Technology, 42,* 456–469.

Girard, C., Ecalle, J., & Magnan, A. (2013). Serious games as new educational tools: How effective are they? A meta-analysis of recent studies. *Journal of Computer Assisted Learning, 29*(3), 207–219.

Graesser, A. C., & McMahen, C. L. (1993). Anomalous information triggers questions when adults solve quantitative problems and comprehend stories. *Journal of Educational Psychology, 85,* 136–151.

Graesser, A. C., & Olde, B. (2003). How does one know whether a person understands a device? The quality of the questions the person asks when the device breaks down. *Journal of Educational Psychology, 95,* 524–536.

Jirout, J., & Klahr, D. (2012). Children's scientific curiosity: In search of an operational definition of an elusive concept. *Developmental Review, 32*(2), 125–160.

Leemkuil, H., & de Jong, T. (2011). Instructional support in games. In S. Tobias & D. Fletcher (Eds.), *Computer games and instruction* (pp. 353–369). Charlotte, NC: Information Age.

Limón, M. (2001). On the cognitive conflict as an instructional strategy for conceptual change: A critical appraisal. *Learning and Instruction, 11*(4), 357–380.

Litman, J. A. (2005). Curiosity and the pleasures of learning: Wanting and linking new information. *Cognition and Emotion, 19*, 793–814.

Litman, J. A., Hutchins, T. L., & Russon, R. K. (2005). Epistemic curiosity, feeling-of-knowing, and exploratory behavior. *Cognition and Emotion, 19*, 559–582.

Loewenstein, G. (1994). The psychology of curiosity: A review and reinterpretation. *Psychological Bulletin, 116*, 75–98.

Malone, T. (1981). Toward a theory of intrinsically motivating instruction. *Cognitive Science, 4*, 333–369.

Mayer, R. E. (2011). Multimedia learning and games. In S. Tobias & J. D. Fletcher (Eds.), *Computer games and instruction* (pp. 281–305). Greenwich, CT: Information Age.

Merenluoto, K., & Lehtinen, E. (2004). Number concept and conceptual change: Towards a systemic model of the processes of change. *Learning and Instruction, 14*(5), 519–534.

Moreno, R., & Mayer, R. E. (2005). Role of guidance, reflection, and interactivity in an agent-based multimedia game. *Journal of Educational Psychology, 97*, 117–128.

Rick, J., Bejan, A., Roche, C., & Weinberger, A. (2012). Proportion: Learning proportional reasoning together. In A. Ravenscroft, S. Lindstaedt, C. D. Kloos, D. Hernández-Leo (Eds.), *Lecture notes in computer science: Vol. 7563. 21st century learning for 21st century skills* (pp. 513–518). Berlin, Germany: Springer.

Ryan, R. M. (1982). Control and information in the intrapersonal sphere: An extension of cognitive evaluation theory. *Journal of Personality and Social Psychology, 43*, 450–461.

Ryan, R. M., Rigby, C. S., & Przybylski, A. (2006). The motivational pull of video games: A self-determination theory approach. *Motivation and Emotion, 30*, 347–363.

Sitzmann, T. (2011). A meta-analytic examination of the instructional effectiveness of computer-based simulation games. *Personnel Psychology, 64*, 489–528.

Tobias, S., Fletcher, J. D., Dai, D. Y., & Wind, A. P. (2011). Review of research on computer games. In S. Tobias & J. D. Fletcher (Eds.), *Computer games and instruction* (pp. 127–222). Charlotte, NC: Information Age.

Tourniaire, F., & Pulos, S. (1985). Proportional reasoning: A review of the literature. *Educational Studies in Mathematics, 16*, 181–204.

Vandercruysse, S., terVrugte, J., de Jong, T., Wouters, P., van Oostendorp, H., & Elen, J. (2015). "Zeldenrust": A mathematical game-based learning environment for vocational students.

Wouters, P., Paas, F., & van Merriënboer, J. J. M. (2008). How to optimize learning from animated models: A review of guidelines base on cognitive load. *Review of Educational Research, 78*, 645–675.

Wouters, P., van Nimwegen, C., van Oostendorp, H., & van der Spek, E. D. (2013). A meta-analysis of the cognitive and motivational effects of serious games. *Journal of Educational Psychology, 105*, 249–265.

Wouters, P., & Van Oostendorp, H. (2013). A meta-analytic review of the role of instructional support in game-based learning. *Computers & Education, 60*(1), 412–425.

Wouters, P., van Oostendorp, H., Boonekamp, R., & van der Spek, E. D. (2011). The role of Game Discourse Analysis and curiosity in creating engaging and effective serious games by implementing a back story and foreshadowing. *Interacting with Computers, 23*, 329–336.

Evaluating Game-Based Learning Environments for Enhancing Motivation in Mathematics

Jon R. Star, Jason A. Chen, Megan W. Taylor, Kelley Durkin, Chris Dede, and Theodore Chao

Abstract During the middle school years, students frequently show significant declines in motivation toward school in general and mathematics in particular. One way in which researchers have sought to spark students' interests and build their sense of competence in mathematics and in STEM more generally is through the use of game-based learning environments. Yet evidence regarding the motivational effectiveness of this approach is mixed. Here, we evaluate the impact of three brief game-based technology activities on students' short-term motivation in math. A total number of 16,789 fifth to eighth grade students and their teachers in one large school district were randomly assigned to three different game-based technology activities, each representing a different framework for motivation and engagement and all designed around an exemplary lesson related to algebraic reasoning. We investigated the relationship between specific game-based technology activities that embody various motivational constructs and students' engagement in mathematics and perceived competence in pursuing STEM careers. Results indicate that the effect of each game-based technology activities on students' motivation was quite

J.R. Star (✉) • C. Dede
Graduate School of Education, Harvard University,
442 Gutman Library, 6 Appian Way, Cambridge, MA 02138, USA
e-mail: jon_star@harvard.edu; chris_dede@gse.harvard.edu

J.A. Chen
The College of William and Mary, Williamsburg, VA, USA
e-mail: jachen@email.wm.edu

M.W. Taylor
Sonoma State University, Rohnert Park, CA, USA
e-mail: ilovemath@mac.com

K. Durkin
University of Louisville, Louisville, KY, USA
e-mail: kelley.durkin@gmail.com

T. Chao
Ohio State University, Columbus, OH, USA
e-mail: chao.160@osu.edu

© Springer International Publishing Switzerland 2015   209
J. Torbeyns et al. (eds.), *Describing and Studying Domain-Specific Serious Games*,
Advances in Game-Based Learning, DOI 10.1007/978-3-319-20276-1_13

modest. However, these effects were modified by students' grade level and not by their demographic variables. In addition, teacher-level variables did not have an effect on student outcomes.

Keywords STEM education • Motivation • Algebraic reasoning • Self-efficacy • Implicit theories of ability

Success in algebra during the middle grades is widely recognized to be a critical gatekeeper that constrains students' decisions about whether to pursue further educational opportunities in Science, Technology, Engineering, and Mathematics (STEM) fields (Adelman, 2006). Unfortunately, during this developmental period many students show significant declines in motivation toward school in general and mathematics in particular (e.g., Archambault, Eccles, & Vida, 2010; Blackwell, Trzesniewski, & Dweck, 2007). One way that researchers have sought to spark students' interests and build their sense of competence in mathematics is through the use of various technological media. These technologies have ranged in complexity and cost from the simple and inexpensive, such as repurposing television programs, to the more complicated and expensive, such as specially designed mathematical experiences based on immersive virtual environments and computer games. We refer to the collection of these various types of technology media that aim to improve learning and motivation in school settings as game-based technology activities.

Despite the widely accepted notion that all game-based technology activities are inherently engaging, the evidence regarding their motivational effectiveness is mixed (Moos & Marroquin, 2010). Part of the reason may be that many different types of technologies are available, and each can be designed well or poorly to leverage various aspects of motivation (e.g., engagement, self-efficacy, tenacity) in different ways. As a step toward improving our understanding of the potential impact of game-based technology activities on students' motivation in mathematics, the goal of this project was to investigate the relationship between (a) specific game-based technology activities that exemplify various motivational constructs, (b) students' engagement in mathematics and perceived competence in pursuing STEM careers, and (c) students' mathematics learning from a short algebra lesson.

Our research questions were as follows. First, what is the impact of the 4-day intervention on students' motivation in mathematics, including interest in pursuing STEM careers? Second, to what extent is this impact influenced by factors such as the type of game-based technology activity the students received and/or students' demographic and academic characteristics (e.g., gender, race/ethnicity, prior achievement)? Third, to what extent is this impact influenced by teacher-level factors such as credentialing in mathematics education, undergraduate major, years of experience, and teachers' beliefs (e.g., teaching self-efficacy)?

We begin by reviewing evidence on how and why game-based technology activities might impact students' motivation in STEM fields.

Motivating Students to Learn STEM

As the National Academy of Sciences (2011) indicated, certain key ingredients are relevant for students who want to pursue STEM careers. These ingredients include a robust confidence in math and science capability (self-efficacy), the ability to see one's abilities in STEM as able to improve over time (implicit theories of ability), and the ability to develop a passion or sustained interest in becoming a scientist or engineer (value beliefs). We discuss each in turn.

Capable students plagued by a loss of confidence about their capacity to succeed in math and science typically avoid careers that require a strong background in those subjects (Lent et al., 2005). Decades of research have shown that students' self-efficacy, defined by Bandura (1997) as "the belief in one's capabilities to organize and execute courses of action required to produce given attainments" (p. 3), is a powerful influence on motivation and achievement. Bandura (1997) hypothesized several sources of self-efficacy, including *mastery experience* (the interpreted results of one's past performance), *vicarious experience* (observations of others' activities, particularly individuals perceived as similar to oneself), and *physiological and affective states* (anxiety, stress, and fatigue)—each of which has been linked to performance in math and science, including students' persistence in STEM fields and choice of STEM majors (e.g., Britner & Pajares, 2001; Gwilliam & Betz, 2001; Lau & Roeser, 2002; Lent, Brown, & Larkin, 1984).

Like self-efficacy, implicit theory of ability (defined as a belief about the nature of intellectual ability (Dweck & Leggett, 1988)) plays an important role in motivation. Some individuals believe that their abilities are a fixed characteristic, and that nothing can be done to change that (i.e., "I'm not smart in math, and there isn't anything I can do about it"). This is referred to as a *fixed theory* of ability. On the other hand, other individuals believe that, with sufficient effort and the proper strategies, one can become more able (i.e., "If I work hard in my math class, I can get smarter in math"). This is known as an incremental theory of ability. A large body of research has shown that implicit theory of ability plays a key role in students' academic motivation, achievement, and career choices (e.g., Blackwell et al., 2007; Good, Rattan, & Dweck, 2012; Grant & Dweck, 2003; Hong, Chiu, Dweck, Lin, & Wan, 1999).

In addition to the self-efficacy and implicit theories of ability, value beliefs are also a significant determinant in students' motivation and achievement (Eccles et al., 1983). Value beliefs in mathematics and science deal with the question, "Do I want to pursue more opportunities in mathematics and science?" Eccles et al. defined values as being composed of several distinct constructs. First, students' *interest* or intrinsic value can affect the activities they pursue—activities that are more enjoyable are more likely to be pursued than are activities that are perceived to be lackluster. Second, students' perceptions of the *utility* of an activity refer to how valuable students perceive an activity to be. If an activity is perceived to be a steppingstone toward students' desired future endeavors, then students are more likely to pursue it. Finally, doing well in mathematics and science may influence students' identity or feelings of self-worth. This *attainment* value describes how important doing well in mathematics and science is to students' identity or feelings of self-worth. Numerous studies have found that interest value predicts STEM career choice (Lent, Lopez, Lopez, & Sheu, 2008; Lent, Paixão, da Silva, & Leitão, 2010), as well as choice in taking STEM courses (Eccles, Midgley, & Adler, 1984; Watt, Eccles, & Durik, 2006).

Motivation and Game-Based Technology Activities

How can the constructs described above be targeted through game-based technology activities to support the motivation of students in mathematics and science? Although the literature on technology and motivation is quite large, relatively few of these studies employ frameworks that are grounded in well-studied psychological theories of motivation (Moos & Marroquin, 2010). Moos and Marroquin noted that the results about the effectiveness of game-based technology activities as a motivational tool are mixed.

With regard to self-efficacy, there is some evidence that engagement with innovative game-based technology activities in academic settings can positively impact self-efficacy toward STEM. For example, Ketelhut and colleagues (Ketelhut, 2007; Ketelhut, Nelson, Clarke, & Dede, 2010) found that students' self-efficacy for scientific inquiry before using a Multi-User Virtual Environment (MUVE) called River City was related to their behaviors within the virtual world. In particular, less self-efficacious students manifested a self-efficacy boost through mastery experiences gained through engagement in the activities of the MUVE (see also Liu, Hsieh, Cho, & Schallert, 2006).

Game-based technology activities also seem to be a promising avenue for impacting implicit theory of ability. In particular, Dweck and her colleagues have developed a web-enabled intervention, Brainology®, which is designed to enhance implicit theory of ability. Students are introduced to two cartoon characters who guide them through the web-based environment, where they learn about the functions of the brain, including that the brain is like a muscle—with conditioning, it can get stronger—an attitude which is linked to an incremental view. Donohoe, Topping, and Hannah (2012) conducted a quasi-experimental study on 33 adolescents (ages 13–14) and found that Brainology® led to a significant increase in students' incremental view of ability.

With respect to value beliefs, researchers have argued that well-designed game-based technology activities can be used to target students' interest value beliefs by making learning goals relevant and meaningful, and by allowing students to identify with characters within the technology environment (Gee, 2003; Squire, 2003). For example, Hickey, Moore, and Pellegrino (2001) showed that the use of *The Adventures of Jasper Woodbury* videodisc activity led to gains in students' mathematics interest, although these gains appeared to result both from the game-based technology activities as well as from teachers' beliefs and instructional practices.

Context of the Present Study

To investigate the potential impact of game-based technology activities on students' mathematics motivation, we designed three different types of game-based technology activities (or "inductions"). The inductions differed along two main dimensions. First, the design of each induction was based on a different motivational construct; in other words, the theory of change underlying each induction differed. Second, the inductions differed in the expense and technical sophistication that were required for their creation and implementation, ranging from the very expensive-to-produce and technically advanced to the modest and inexpensive. Below we describe each induction in more depth.

Induction 1: Virtual Environment

At the core of Induction 1 was an Immersive Virtual Environment (IVE)—a game-based technology activity we designed to introduce students to the mathematical concepts that were to follow in a subsequent lesson. The IVE was professionally produced such that it was similar in look and feel to video games that students may have had experience playing.

For the story line of the IVE, students were provided with the opportunity to explore an outer space environment in the context of a space rescue mission. Various mathematical puzzles were encountered as students moved around the planet; all puzzles related to the generation of and identification of mathematical patterns, similar to what would subsequently be discussed in a mathematics lesson. The initial puzzle was designed to be relatively easy; in later stages of the experience, mathematically related, more complex puzzles were broken down into many smaller steps to scaffold students' progress and to reduce the likelihood that students would be overly frustrated. Similarly, hints were also provided by the IVE for students who requested help in completing any of the puzzles.

Prior to beginning the IVE, each student viewed a short (5-min) video clip of a young STEM professional who talked about the nature of the work they do (e.g., designing astronaut space suits), the difficulties they had encountered in their K-12 math and science classes, and how they were able to overcome these difficulties. Students were provided with a selection of several of these videos, which varied according to the demographic attributes of the STEM professionals (e.g., gender, ethnicity).

Motivationally, Induction 1 was designed to primarily impact students' self-efficacy. In particular, the IVE experience supported mastery experiences by allowing students to experience incrementally more difficult mathematical challenges, and by providing the scaffolds necessary for students to succeed when they were met with obstacles. Vicarious experiences were included in Induction 1 by including real-life, young, STEM professionals who discussed their jobs and the types of obstacles that they faced (and overcame) as they pursued a STEM career. Finally, emotional and physiological states were addressed by ensuring that students felt comfortable and relaxed about solving the mathematical challenges in the IVE. For example, we made the design decision *not* to include a timer that gently reminded students to work more quickly if they were taking too long because such a timer would likely cause a good deal of anxiety—a common experience for many students in mathematics.

Induction 2: Brainology® Web-Based Activity

For the second induction, we used a commercially available series of web-based modules designed to teach students about an incremental view of ability in a game-based manner. These modules are based on the work of Dweck and colleagues and have been shown to be successful at influencing students' motivation and achievement (e.g., Blackwell et al., 2007). Students assigned to Induction 2 were given access to an abridged version of the Mindset Works® StudentKit—Brainology® program (www.mindsetworks.com) described above. The intervention that students experienced was relatively short compared to the entire Brainology® program, which contains over 2 h of online instruction and up to 10 h of additional activities to do over a recommended period of 5–16 weeks.

With respect to motivation, the Brainology® program is explicitly designed to impact students' implicit theory of ability. As noted above, Dweck and her colleagues (Blackwell et al., 2007; Dweck & Leggett, 1988) have shown students possess particular "mindsets" that can influence their motivational and developmental trajectories through the course of school (e.g., fixed theory of ability vs. incremental theory of ability). The Brainology® program activities have been found to encourage students toward an incremental view of ability.

Induction 3: Video on Mathematical Patterns

Induction 3 was intended to provide an off-the-shelf experience for students related to some of the mathematical ideas that were to come in the mathematics lesson. We selected a commercially available PBS NOVA video on fractals because of its engaging story line and graphics, its focus on mathematical patterns, and the accessibility of the content to our target population of students in grades 5–8. The 2009 video, *Fractals*: *Hunting the Hidden Dimension*, is 56 min long and includes visually appealing animations, interviews with mathematicians, and accessible explanations of the mathematics of fractals and their applications to everyday life, such as building smartphone antennas and generating visual effects in movies. However, note that (to contract with the other two inductions), viewing the video on mathematical patterns was intentionally intended not to be game-like.

In terms of motivation, movies have long been used by educators to motivate and engage students in the classroom. Although this movie did not specifically target a particular motivation construct, movies are often used in educational settings as an inexpensive, simple means that teachers can employ to help students see connections between what they are learning and real-world applications.

Mathematics Content Focus

Within the general landscape of STEM, we chose to situate the present study in the content area of algebra. Algebra is widely recognized as a crucial peg in the trajectory of mathematical learning because of the conceptual and procedural groundwork it lays for accessing higher mathematics and because it presents a shift in how students are expected to think mathematically (Kieran, 1992). Algebra is often the first time students are introduced to some of the most important and useful ideas in the field of mathematics, such as the concept of a "variable" or the generalization of patterns in generated data (Star & Rittle-Johnson, 2009). Within the larger landscape of algebra, we focus here on an aspect of algebra that many mathematics educators refer to as algebraic reasoning (e.g., Kaput, 1999), which includes using arithmetic for generalizing, working with patterns to describe functional relationships, and modeling as a way to formalizing generalizations.

Hypotheses

We hypothesized that Inductions 1 and 2 would have the strongest effect on the motivational constructs that they were designed to influence. In particular, we hypothesized that Induction 1 would have the strongest impact on students' self-efficacy and that Induction 2 would have the strongest impact on students' implicit theory of math ability. Because Induction 3 was not designed with a particular theory of motivation in mind, it did not intentionally target any particular motivation variable. However, because of the content in the movie, we hypothesized that this third induction would have an impact on students' value beliefs. Finally, with respect to developmental issues in motivation, the literature is clear that there is a general decline in motivation as students progress through school (Archambault et al., 2010; Eccles et al., 1984). Because the structure of schooling for students in middle school (Grades 6–8) is different from that of elementary school students (Grade 5) and because students conceive of competence differently based on age (Dweck, 1986), we expected the first two inductions to have differential impacts on students depending on their age.

Method

Sample

Data come from all fifth, sixth, seventh, and eighth grade students and their teachers in the Chesterfield County Public School district in Virginia. A total of 18,628 students participated in the study, along with their 476 teachers, from 38 elementary and 12 middle schools.

A number of teachers in our original teacher pool were assistant, ESL, or special education teachers who did not have their own classroom. We removed these teachers from our sample, ending up with 339 teachers in our active teacher sample who participated in random assignment. In the elementary schools, the 163 fifth grade teachers, who taught all subjects to the same group of students each day, implemented the intervention with their homeroom students. In the middle schools, the 60 sixth, 57 seventh, and 59 eighth grade teachers were all math specialists and implemented the intervention in each mathematics classes that they taught.

We removed students who did not have parental consent to be a part of the study, which left us with 16,879 students. In addition, we had to exclude the 8979 students (and their 113 teachers from five schools) who were missing pretest or posttest data used in our analyses, as a result of a miscommunication between the research team and the district relating to the student identification numbers that students were instructed to use at pretest.[1] After removing those students with missing data, we report on the 7900 students and 226 teachers from 44 schools who remained in our analyses. These students were approximately equally divided across grade levels (see Table 1 for demographic information about the sample). We also collected students' most recent scores on the state standardized test in mathematics, the Virginia Standards of Learning (VA-SOL) test; this test is given annually to students in grades 3–8.

Design and Procedure

We used a pretest/posttest[2] experimental design. Prior to the start of the intervention, students and teachers were administered a pretest. After pretest administration, teachers were randomly assigned to one of three inductions described above. Participation in the main part of the intervention occurred over a period of 4

---

[1] Little's (1988) Missing Completely at Random (MCAR) test confirmed that these data were not missing completely at random (χ^2 (1576) = 7162.88, $p < .001$). In particular, students with missing data were more likely to be male, African-American or Hispanic/Latino, with ELL status, and from schools with a high percentage of free or reduced lunch. For a more in depth discussion of the impact of this missing data on our results, see Star et al. (2014).

[2] A delayed posttest was also administered, 2 months after the end of the intervention. However, due to large amounts of missing data, delayed posttest results were not easily interpretable and thus are not included in the present analysis.

Table 1 Student demographic information by condition

Variable		Induction 1		Induction 2		Induction 3		Total	
		n	$\%$	n	$\%$	n	$\%$	n	$\%$
Gender	Male	1373	51	1071	49	1516	50	3960	50
	Female	1308	49	1115	51	1517	50	3940	50
Ethnicity	Native American	11	<1	5	<1	7	<1	23	<1
	Asian	89	3	77	4	91	3	257	3
	African-American	691	26	516	24	647	21	1854	23
	Hispanic/Latino	260	10	194	9	202	7	656	8
	White	1500	56	1309	60	1938	64	4747	60
	Pacific Islander	1	<1	4	<1	4	<1	9	<1
	Multi-race	129	5	81	4	144	5	354	4
Grade	5	768	29	523	24	845	28	2136	27
	6	877	33	370	17	515	17	1762	22
	7	572	21	615	28	898	30	2085	26
	8	464	17	678	31	775	26	1917	24
ELL		125	5	81	4	83	3	289	4

consecutive days. On Day 1, students worked on the induction to which they were assigned. On Days 2 and 3, teachers taught the 2-day mathematics lesson. On Day 4, students again worked on the induction to which they were assigned.

For students in Induction 1, Day 1 of the intervention was spent in the school's computer lab. Each student sat at his/her own computer, with headphones, and watched the short interview of a STEM professional and then played the IVE game for approximately 30 min. On Day 4, students returned to the computer lab and restarted the game-based technology activity, including watching a video of a STEM professional and restarting the IVE game from the beginning—again playing for about 30 min. Similarly, for students in Induction 2, Days 1 and 4 were spent in the school's computer lab, with one student at each computer with headphones, playing the Brainology® program. Finally, Induction 3 students watched the first half of the *Fractals: Hunting the Hidden Dimension* video (about 28 min) on Day 1; on Day 4, these students watched the second half of the video.

Professional Development

All teachers were provided with a 1-day (6.5 h) professional development (PD) workshop, administered within 1 week of the start of the intervention. The PD workshop was designed and implemented by project staff. Most of the PD (approximately 4 h) was devoted to introducing teachers to the 2-day mathematics lesson. Teachers were provided with detailed lesson plans as well as visual aids, handouts, and manipulatives that accompanied the lesson. For the remainder of the PD, we provided teachers with induction-specific training.

Measures

All assessments were administered to teachers and students online, via a password-protected website.

Student motivational measures. All students were administered a pre- and postassessment, in a proctored computer lab in each school, during the regular school day. The pretest, taken between 1 and 3 weeks prior to the start of the intervention, targeted students' motivation, with measures corresponding to the three motivational constructs that were related to the inductions—self-efficacy, implicit theories of ability, and value (see Table 2 for descriptive information on student variables; see Table 3 for sample items and alphas). The posttest was administered on Day 4, after the implementation was completed.

The motivational items on the posttest were identical to the pretest. We assessed self-efficacy students with a 13-item measure that was drawn from Bandura's (2006). The degree to which students endorsed an incremental view of ability (as opposed to a fixed view of ability) was assessed using a 6-item instrument that was adapted from Dweck (1999). Finally, interest, attainment, and utility value beliefs concerning their mathematics class were assessed using scales taken from the Michigan Study on Adolescent Life Transitions (MSALT), which has been used extensively in the past (e.g., Eccles, Barber, Stone, & Hunt, 2003).

Student mathematics learning measure. Assessing students' mathematics learning was not a major focus of the present study, mainly because of the absence of a priori hypotheses related to the differential impact of the three technology inductions on student learning and also the short duration of the math lesson. However, as a manipulative check, we included a short five-item assessment on mathematics learning on both the pre- and posttests. These five items were on algebraic reasoning as related to the 2-day mathematics lesson, specifically data organization, pattern identification, and the ability to make generalizations. The reliability of the math learning measure was low ($\alpha = 0.30$ and 0.40 for the pre- and posttest); as a consequence, the results from this measure must be interpreted with caution.

Teacher measures. Teachers were given a pretest immediately prior to the start of the professional development workshop. The pretest collected background and demographic information about teachers, such as number of years teaching, undergraduate major, advanced degrees held, and national board certification status. In addition, the teacher pretest included items that tapped teachers' own teaching self-efficacy for instruction and student engagement (22 items), technology use (7 items), and mathematics (12 items). Items were drawn or adapted from Bandura (2006). Teachers were also administered a 6-item measure of implicit theory of ability that was adapted from Dweck (1999). See Table 3 for sample items and alphas.

Table 2 Descriptive statistics on student motivation and learning variables

| | Pretest | | | | | | | | | Posttest | | | | | | | | |
| | Induction 1 | | Induction 2 | | Induction 3 | | Total | | | Induction 1 | | Induction 2 | | Induction 3 | | Total | | |
Variable	M	SD	M	SD	M	SD	M	SD	n	M	SD	M	SD	M	SD	M	SD	n
VA-SOL	498	75	491	80	497	78	496	78	7900	–	–	–	–	–	–	–	–	–
Math learning	0.60	0.24	0.61	0.23	0.60	0.24	0.60	0.24	7900	0.68	0.25	0.70	0.24	0.71	0.24	0.70	0.24	6583
Self-efficacy	4.59	0.99	4.49	1.02	4.53	1.00	4.54	1.00	7900	4.60	1.07	4.54	1.08	4.51	1.09	4.55	1.08	7045
Implicit theory of math ability	4.26	1.04	4.17	1.03	4.24	1.03	4.22	1.03	7900	4.09	1.07	4.27	1.08	4.14	1.08	4.16	1.08	7090
Value	4.33	1.00	4.16	1.07	4.23	1.04	4.24	1.04	7900	4.28	1.12	4.14	1.15	4.14	1.15	4.19	1.14	7063

Table 3 Motivational measures

	Construct	Alpha	Measure	Sample question (all on a 6 point scale)
Student measures	Self-efficacy ($n=13$)	0.93, 0.95	General math self-efficacy ($n=4$)	How confident are you that you can master the math skills that will be taught this year?
			Algebraic reasoning self-efficacy ($n=5$)	If you are given five numbers in a sequence, how confident are you that you can figure out the pattern and get the next number in the sequence right?
			Math performance self-efficacy ($n=4$)	How confident are you that you can do well on standardized tests in math?
	Implicit theory of math ability ($n=6$)	0.77, 0.79	Fixed view of math ability ($n=3$)	My math ability is something about me that can't be changed very much
			Incremental view of math ability ($n=3$)	No matter who I am, I can change my math abilities a lot
	Value ($n=6$)	0.83, 0.87	Interest value ($n=3$)	How much do you like math?
			Utility value ($n=2$)	In general, how useful is what you learn in math?
			Attainment value ($n=1$)	For me, how important is being good at math?
Teacher measures	Self-efficacy for instruction and student engagement ($n=22$)	0.96	Self-efficacy for student engagement ($n=4$)	How confident are you that you can motivate students who show low interest in math class?
			Self-efficacy for classroom management ($n=4$)	How confident are you that you can calm a student who is disruptive and noisy?
			Self-efficacy for instructional strategies ($n=4$)	How confident are you that you can use a variety of assessment strategies?
			Self-efficacy for math inquiry teaching ($n=6$)	How confident are you that you can use computer technologies to communicate with your students?
			Self-efficacy for instructional methods ($n=4$)	How confident are you that you can teach well even if you are told to use instructional methods that would not be your choice?
	Self-efficacy for technology use ($n=7$)	0.89		How confident are you that you can facilitate a whole-class discussion?
	Math self-efficacy ($n=12$)	0.92		How confident are you that you can successfully determine the amount of sales tax on a clothing purchase?
	Implicit theory of math ability ($n=6$)	0.86	Fixed view about students' abilities in math ($n=3$)	Students come into math with a certain level of math ability, and it is hard to change that
			Incremental view about students' abilities in math ($n=3$)	Even if students don't initially possess a certain "knack" for math they can develop their math ability

Data Analysis

Given that many students had the same teacher and many teachers were in the same school, we used multilevel modeling (Raudenbush & Bryk, 2002) to account for this nesting of students within teachers and teachers within schools. The first level of the model, the student level, included students' prior knowledge (VA-SOL) scores, pretest math learning scores, pretest self-efficacy scores, pretest implicit theory of ability scores, pretest value scores, and demographic information, including ELL status, grade, gender (male coded as 1 and female coded as 0), and ethnicity.

The second level of the model, the teacher level, measured the effect of experimental condition, teachers' self-efficacy for student engagement and instruction, teachers' self-efficacy for technology use, teachers' mathematics self-efficacy, and teachers' implicit theory of math ability. We specified Induction 1 (the immersive virtual environment) as the referent condition to compare it to the other two inductions. This resulted in the effect of condition being captured by two variables. One variable indicated the difference between Induction 1 and Induction 2, and the other variable indicated the difference between Induction 1 and Induction 3. To test the difference between Inductions 2 and 3, a Wald test (similar to an incremental F test) was used to examine whether the parameter estimates for these conditions were significantly different from one another.

The third level of the model, the school level, measured the percentage of students receiving free or reduced lunch in each school. Finally, we also included two cross-level interactions to test for possible interactions between induction and grade, as well as two cross-level interactions to test for possible interactions between induction and prior math knowledge (VA-SOL). We ran these models to evaluate our four posttest student outcomes: math learning, self efficacy, implicit theory of ability, and value.

Results

We begin by overviewing students' scores on the motivational variables at pretest and posttest and then reporting the effects of condition at posttest.

Student and Teacher Pretest Scores

To begin, we measured whether there were any differences between the inductions on our outcome measures at pretest and on demographic variables (see Table 2). When controlling for other independent variables in the model, there were no significant differences ($p > .05$) between inductions on any of the pretest or demographic variables, with the exception of prior knowledge (VA-SOL). Students in Induction 2 had lower prior knowledge than students in Induction 1, $\beta = -15.76$, $p = .003$, and Induction 3, $\chi^2(2) = 13.63$, $p = .001$. Students in Induction 3 also had slightly lower prior knowledge than students in Induction 1, $\beta=-15.69$, $p=.001$. Prior knowledge was included in all subsequent models, so we controlled for these differences between conditions.

Pre-/Post Gains

Before examining the effects of condition, we first consider whether the intervention generally led to gains in students' motivation (see Table 2). Overall, students did not have statistically significant gains on our measure of self-efficacy ($M_{pre}=4.54$, $M_{post}=4.55$, $t=-1.16$, $p=.246$, $d=-0.01$). For implicit theory of ability, students' incremental view of math ability decreased after the intervention, although this was a small effect ($M_{pre}=4.22$, $M_{post}=4.16$, $t=-6.93$, $p<.001$, $d=-0.07$). For value, students' scores generally decreased after the intervention as well, although the effect was again small ($M_{pre}=4.24$, $M_{post}=4.19$, $t=-8.71$, $p<.001$, $d=-0.06$). For math learning, the intervention led to an average gain on students' scores on the five-item mathematics learning assessment of 10 % points, and this was a moderate effect ($M_{pre}=0.60$, $M_{post}=0.70$, $t=28.60$, $p<.001$, $d=0.40$).

Effects of Condition at Posttest

At posttest, there were significant effects of condition on several of our outcome variables (see Table 4).

Math learning. Comparing Inductions 1 and 2, students in Induction 2 earned similar math learning scores to students in Induction 1, $\beta=0.003$, $p=.872$. There was also no significant interaction between Induction 2 and grade, $\beta=0.01$, $p=.129$. Comparing Inductions 1 and 3, students in Induction 3 had similar math learning scores to students in Induction 1, $\beta=-0.01$, $p=.409$. However, there was a significant interaction between Induction 3 and grade. In particular, students in lower grades benefited more from Induction 1 than from Induction 3. Then as grade increased, Induction 3 became more effective, $\beta=0.02$, $p=.013$. Thus, for students in grade 5, being in Induction 1 led to higher scores on average. For students in grades 6, 7, and 8, being in Induction 3 led to higher scores on average. Finally, post hoc Wald tests comparing Inductions 2 and 3 suggested that there were no significant differences between Inductions 2 and 3 ($\chi^2(2)=1.06$, $p=.589$); however, there was a significant interaction when considering grade ($\chi^2(2)=6.22$, $p=.045$). Essentially, Induction 2 was more effective for lower grades, and as grade increased, Induction 3 became more effective. There were no significant interactions between induction and prior knowledge (VA-SOL) (p's$>.532$).

Self-efficacy. There were no significant differences between any of the inductions on the student self-efficacy variable, nor were there any significant interactions between inductions and grade or inductions and prior knowledge (p's$>.128$).

Table 4 Parameter estimates for student outcomes

Fixed effects	Posttest math learning			Posttest self-efficacy		
	Coefficient	SE	z	Coefficient	SE	z
Intercept	0.67	0.02	41.82***	4.67	0.04	107.55***
Student-level						
VASOL	0	0	11.34***	0	0	1.49
Pretest math learning	0.20	0.01	16.42***	0.14	0.04	3.69***
Pretest self-efficacy	0.02	0	5.87***	0.70	0.01	62.80***
Pretest implicit theory of math ability	0	0	0.44	0.05	0.01	6.20***
Pretest value	0.01	0	3.99***	0.15	0.01	14.11***
ELL status	−0.01	0.01	−0.70	−0.07	0.04	−1.70
Grade	0	0.01	0.08	−0.05	0.02	−2.87**
Gender (male)	−0.02	0.01	−3.61***	0	0.02	0.05
Ethnicity	0	0	0.99	−0.01	0.01	−1.89$^\tau$
Teacher-level						
Induction 2	0	0.02	0.16	−0.01	0.04	−0.18
Induction 3	−0.01	0.01	−0.83	−0.04	0.03	−1.27
Self-efficacy for student engagement and instruction	0.02	0.01	2.18*	0.02	0.02	1.00
Self-efficacy for technology use	−0.02	0.01	−3.07**	−0.02	0.01	−1.58
Math self-efficacy	0	0.01	−0.06	0	0.01	−0.39
Implicit theory of math ability	0	0.01	−0.06	−0.01	0.01	−0.83
School-level						
% free/reduced lunch	−0.11	0.03	−3.90***	−0.06	0.06	−0.92
Cross-level interactions						
Induction 2 by Grade	0.01	0.01	1.52	0.03	0.02	1.52
Induction 3 by Grade	0.02	0.01	2.49*	0	0.02	0.17
Induction 2 by VASOL	0	0	0.62	0	0	0.25
Induction 3 by VASOL	0	0	0.23	0	0	0.94

Random effects	Estimate	SE		Estimate	SE	
Level-1 residual variance	0.21	0		0.66	0.01	
Level-2 residual variance	0.05	0		0.07	0.01	
Level-3 residual variance	0.01	0.01		0	0	

Fixed effects	Posttest implicit theory of math ability			Posttest value		
	Coefficient	SE	z	Coefficient	SE	z
Intercept	4.16	0.05	79.50***	4.28	0.04	96.23***
Student-level						
VASOL	0	0	−0.04	0	0	1.74
Pretest math learning	0.04	0.05	0.86	0	0.04	−0.01
Pretest self-efficacy	0.09	0.01	6.32***	0.09	0.01	7.79***

(continued)

Table 4 (continued)

Fixed effects	Posttest implicit theory of math ability			Posttest value		
	Coefficient	SE	z	Coefficient	SE	z
Pretest implicit theory of math ability	0.60	0.01	56.85***	0.02	0.01	2.76**
Pretest value	0.08	0.01	6.21***	0.83	0.01	79.77***
ELL status	−0.04	0.05	−0.76	0.07	0.04	1.65
Grade	−0.07	0.02	−3.55***	0	0.02	−0.26
Gender (male)	−0.05	0.02	−2.51*	0	0.02	−0.03
Ethnicity	0	0.01	0.32	−0.02	0.01	−2.16*
Teacher-level						
Induction 2	0.09	0.05	2.07*	0.02	0.04	0.43
Induction 3	0.05	0.04	1.17	0.01	0.04	0.26
Self-efficacy for student engagement and instruction	0.04	0.02	1.84	0.01	0.02	0.70
Self-efficacy for technology use	−0.01	0.02	−0.52	−0.01	0.01	−0.56
Math self-efficacy	−0.03	0.01	−1.76	0.01	0.01	0.55
Implicit theory of math ability	−0.03	0.02	−1.88	0.02	0.01	1.39
School-level						
% free/reduced lunch	0	0.08	0	0.03	0.07	0.38
Cross-level interactions						
Induction 2 by grade	0.12	0.03	4.57***	−0.01	0.02	−0.64
Induction 3 by grade	0.03	0.02	1.10	−0.04	0.02	−2.10*
Induction 2 by VASOL	0	0	2.37*	0	0	−1.82
Induction 3 by VASOL	0	0	0.89	0	0	−1.34

Random effects	Estimate	SE		Estimate	SE	
Level-1 residual variance	0.81	0.01		0.66	0.01	
Level-2 residual variance	0.07	0.02		0.08	0.01	
Level-3 residual variance	0.02	0.03		0.03	0.02	

$^{†}p<.06$, $*p<.05$, $**p<.01$, $***p<.001$

Implicit theory of ability. Comparing Inductions 1 and 2, students in Induction 2 had higher implicit view of math ability scores than students in Induction 1, $\beta=0.09$, $p=.039$, meaning that being in Induction 2 led to an implicit theory of math ability score that was 0.09 standard deviations higher than being in Induction 1. There was also a significant interaction between Induction 2 and grade. In particular, students in lower grades had similar implicit view of math ability scores in Induction 2 and Induction 1. Then as grade increased, Induction 2 led to higher implicit view of math ability scores than Induction 1, $\beta=0.12$, $p<.001$. In addition, there was a significant interaction between Induction 2 and prior knowledge (VA-SOL), $\beta=0.001$, $p=.018$; however, as the coefficient indicates, this was a very small interaction.

Students with lower prior knowledge had slightly higher implicit view of math ability scores in Induction 1 than Induction 2. Comparing Inductions 1 and 3, students in Induction 3 had similar scores to students in Induction 1, $\beta = 0.05$, $p = .243$. There was also not a significant interaction between Induction 3 and grade, $\beta = 0.03$, $p = .271$, nor between Induction 3 and prior knowledge (VA-SOL), $\beta < 0.001$, $p = .371$. A post hoc Wald test indicated that overall students in Induction 3 had similar implicit theory of ability scores to those in Induction 2 ($\chi^2(2) = 4.34$, $p = .114$). However, there was a significant interaction when considering grade ($\chi^2(2) = 23.62$, $p < .001$). In lower grades, students in Induction 3 had similar implicit view of math ability scores as students in Induction 2, but as grade increased, students in Induction 2 tended to have higher scores than students in Induction 3. When comparing Inductions 2 and 3, there was also a marginally significant interaction between Induction and prior knowledge (VA-SOL) ($\chi^2(2) = 5.75$, $p = .057$).

Value. For value, in comparing Inductions 1 and 2, overall students in Induction 2 had similar value scores to students in Induction 1, $\beta = 0.02$, $p = .668$. There was also no significant interaction between Induction 2 and grade, $\beta = -0.01$, $p = .520$. When comparing Inductions 1 and 3, students in Induction 3 had similar value scores to students in Induction 1, $\beta = 0.01$, $p = .795$. There was a significant interaction between Induction 3 and grade. In particular, students in lower grades had similar value scores in Induction 3 and Induction 1. Then as grade increased, Induction 1 led to higher value scores, $\beta = -0.04$, $p = .036$. Post hoc Wald tests suggested that there was no significant difference between Inductions 2 and 3 ($\chi^2(2) = 0.19$, $p = .910$). There was also no significant interaction when considering grade ($\chi^2(2) = 4.76$, $p = .093$). Finally, there were no significant interactions between condition and prior knowledge (VA-SOL) (p's $> .069$).

Discussion

Perhaps not surprisingly given the size and complexity of the present study, our results are informative, modest, and not definitive.

RQ1: Impact on Students' Motivation

Our first research question concerned the general impact of the 4-day intervention on students' motivation in mathematics, particularly self-efficacy, implicit theory of ability, and value. Overall, results from the 4-day intervention were mixed. No gains were found in self-efficacy; for implicit theory of ability, a lower incremental view of ability was found; we found modest declines in value beliefs. With respect to math learning, students in all three inductions had modest improvements in their scores on the math learning measure.

RQ2: Influences of Induction Type and Student Characteristics

Second, we were interested in whether the impact of the intervention was influenced by the type of induction that student received and other student-level demographic or academic characteristics. No effects related to self-efficacy were found, and effects related to value were very minor. For implicit theory of ability, there were indications that Induction 2 was more successful than Inductions 1 and 3 in impacting students' views, especially for older students. Induction 2 led to higher incremental views of math ability for students, particularly for students in grades 7 and 8. Induction type also appeared to have a small impact on value, with some evidence that Induction 3 had the strongest impact on utility and attainment value for the younger students, as compared to the other two inductions.

Despite the complexity of these results for our second research question, three clear patterns did emerge.

Absence of effects on self-efficacy. First, Induction 1 did not have the hypothesized impact on students' self-efficacy. Despite the fact that the IVE was designed specifically to foster changes in self-efficacy, there is no evidence that Induction 1 improved self-efficacy any more than the other inductions. There are several possible explanations for this finding. First, given the relatively short intervention, the fact that students in any induction did not experience dramatic gains in a construct as fundamental and multidimensional as self-efficacy is not surprising. Second, Induction 1 was the most complex in terms of cognitive and temporal "overhead" required for students to enact the experience. We hypothesize that, had a longer time period been available for students to shift their focus from learning to enact Induction 1 to reflecting on the content of the experience, effects on self-efficacy would have been greater.

Recall that the three inductions also differed on the expense and technical sophistication required to create and implement them. Does the present finding about Induction 1 and self-efficacy suggest that use of virtual worlds is not worth the trouble and expense? Particularly when inculcating sophisticated knowledge and skills, a substantial body of research suggests that this is not the case (National Research Council, 2011; U.S. Department of Education, 2010). We interpret our results as indicating that this type of complex game-based technology activity with high cognitive overhead may require more instructional "dosage" than short duration provided in the present intervention. Thus, well-designed virtual worlds, which are expensive and technically demanding, can realize their power for engagement and learning only when a sufficient investment of classroom time is made.

Effects linked to students' age. A second pattern that emerges from the complex results of our second research question is that the effects of each induction on students' motivation were influenced by students' age, as evidenced by the frequency of significant induction type by grade interactions. These grade-level interactions held while controlling for prior mathematics knowledge (VA-SOL scores), indicating that the differential impact of the inductions was developmental and not merely the result of differing mathematics ability. Because the structure of schooling for students in middle school (Grades 6–8) is different from that of elementary school students (Grade 5), and because students conceive of competence differently based on age (Dweck, 1986), these findings indicating differential impacts on students depending on their age are confirmatory of prior work and reinforce the importance for practitioners and policy makers of tailoring such interventions to students' developmental level.

Absence of effects for student demographics. Finally, we did not find interactions between induction type and other student demographic variables such as free and reduced lunch, ethnicity, and gender. From a curricular perspective, this is a positive outcome indicating that, in contrast to many educational experiences, these types of intervention may narrow—not widen—troubling achievement gaps. That good design can produce motivational learning experiences effective across the full spectrum of students is very encouraging.

RQ3: Influences of Teacher-Level Factors

Our third research question asked about impact of teacher-level factors on students' motivation, including credentialing in mathematics education, undergraduate major, years of experience, and teachers' beliefs. Based on the extant literature, we had hypothesized that these factors might influence students' motivation. However, teacher-level factors were not significant predictors of student outcomes. Viewing the intervention from a curricular perspective, this is a positive finding suggesting that our design and implementation ensured that all students received a roughly equivalent instructional experience.

With respect to the absence of a relationship between teachers' beliefs and student motivation, although there is good theoretical and empirical evidence to suggest that these variables could predict student outcomes, it is also true that linking teacher-level beliefs to student outcomes is not a clear and straight path (Holzberger, Philipp, & Kunter, 2013; Klassen, Tze, Betts, & Gordon, 2011). In fact, Klassen et al. (2011) noted that there is a lack of evidence that links teachers' self-efficacy to student outcomes, despite the commonly held belief by researchers that this relationship exists. Their review of the literature noted that correlations between teachers' self-efficacy and student achievement were low to modest. Our findings confirm this perspective.

Limitations

There were several limitations to the present study that suggest caution in the interpretation of our results. First and foremost, as noted above, there was a very large amount of missing data—53 % of students were missing demographic, pre-, and/or posttest data. Second, it is important to note that the length of the intervention was relatively short, both in terms of the game-based technology activities, the professional development, and the mathematics lesson. Although we were able to find some influence of the intervention on students' motivation, these effects were quite modest. Further, although a delayed posttest was administered, results were not interpretable; thus, we are not able to report whether or not the effects at posttest were sustained after the end of the intervention. Third, recall that the five-item math assessment had low reliability. Taken together, all of these results raise questions about any attempt to generalize our findings. Future studies—both additional large-scale studies of longer duration, as well as shorter-term studies that afford opportunities for more qualitative exploration—can attempt to address these limitations and continuing moving toward improving our understanding of the relationship between technology, motivation, and STEM learning.

Conclusion

Investigating along a developmental span the relationship between game-based technology activities and student interest in STEM careers is important because much potential talent in STEM is now lost. Our research interweaved alternative motivational activities with effective and authentic mathematics learning, in order to take initial steps toward developing insights about the added value of game-based technology activities for building confidence in math and science capability, seeing one's abilities in STEM as able to improve over time, and developing a passion or sustained interest in becoming a scientist or engineer. Further, we studied the impacts of media with substantially different production costs, providing the basis for a cost-benefit analysis and for articulating contrasting conditions for success.

Our findings highlight the importance of tailoring motivational experiences to students' developmental level. Our results are also encouraging about developers' ability to create instructional interventions and professional development that can be effective when experienced by a wide range of students and teachers. Further research is needed to determine the degree, duration of, and type of instructional intervention necessary to substantially impact multidimensional, deep-rooted motivational constructs, such as self-efficacy.

Acknowledgments The research was supported by a grant from the National Science Foundation (DRL #0929575) to Chris Dede and Jon R. Star. The ideas in this chapter are those of the authors and do not represent official positions of the National Science Foundation.

Portions of this chapter were adapted from: Star, J. R., Chen, J., Taylor, M., Durkin, K., Dede, C., & Chao, T. (2014). Evaluating technology-based strategies for enhancing motivation in mathematics. *International Journal of STEM Education*, 1:7. doi: 10.1186/2196-7822-1-7. http://www.stemeducationjournal.com/content/1/1/7

Thanks to Adam Seldow, Greg Jastrzemski, and the faculty, administration, and students of Chesterfield County Public Schools for their enthusiastic participation in the project. Thanks to Stephanie Fitzgerald for her assistance with all aspects of the project, and to Kinga Petrovai, Bharat Battu, Kevin Reeves, Arielle Niemeyer, Joy Casad, Chad Desharnais, Maisy Suslavich, Lauren Schiller, and Amy Venditta for their assistance with data collection and analysis.

References

Adelman, C. (2006). *The toolbox revisited: Paths to degree completion from high school through college*. Washington, DC: United States Department of Education.

Archambault, I., Eccles, J. S., & Vida, M. N. (2010). Ability self-concepts and subjective value in literacy: Joint trajectories from Grades 1 through 12. *Journal of Educational Psychology, 102*, 804–816.

Bandura, A. (1997). *Self-efficacy: The exercise of control*. New York, NY: W.H. Freeman.

Bandura, A. (2006). Guide for constructing self-efficacy scales. In F. Pajares & T. Urdan (Eds.), *Self-efficacy beliefs of adolescents* (pp. 307–337). Greenwich, CT: Information Age.

Blackwell, L. S., Trzesniewski, K. H., & Dweck, C. S. (2007). Implicit theories of intelligence predict achievement across an adolescent transition: A longitudinal study and intervention. *Child Development, 78*, 246–263.

Britner, S. L., & Pajares, F. (2001). Self-efficacy beliefs, race, and gender in middle school science. *Journal of Women and Minorities in Science and Engineering, 7*, 271–285.

Council, N. R. (2011). *Learning science through computer games and simulations*. Washington, DC: National Academy Press.

Donohoe, C., Topping, K., & Hannah, E. (2012). The impact of an online intervention (Brainology) on the mindset and resiliency of secondary school pupils: A preliminary mixed methods study. *Educational Psychology, 32*, 641–655.

Dweck, C. S. (1986). Motivational processes affecting learning. *American Psychologist, 41*, 1040–1048.

Dweck, C. S. (1999). *Self-theories: Their role in motivation, personality, and development*. Philadelphia, PA: Psychology Press.

Dweck, C. S., & Leggett, E. L. (1988). A social cognitive approach to motivation and personality. *Psychological Review, 95*, 256–273.

Eccles (Parsons), J. S., Adler, T. F., Futterman, R., Goff, S. B., Kaczala, C. M., Meece, J. L., & Midgley, C. (1983). Expectancies, values, and academic behaviors. In J. T. Spence (Ed.), *Achievement and achievement motivation* (pp. 75–146). San Francisco, CA: W. H. Freeman.

Eccles, J. S., Barber, B. L., Stone, M., & Hunt, J. (2003). Extracurricular activities and adolescent development. *Journal of Social Issues, 59*, 865–889.

Eccles, J. S., Midgley, C., & Adler, T. (1984). Grade-related changes in the school environment: Effects on achievement motivation. In J. Nicholls (Ed.), *Advances in motivation and achievement: The development of achievement motivation* (Vol. 3, pp. 283–331). Greenwich, CT: JAI Press.

Gee, J. P. (2003). *What video games have to teach us about learning and literacy*. New York, NY: Palgrave MacMillan.

Good, C., Rattan, A., & Dweck, C. S. (2012). Why do women opt out? Sense of belonging and women's representation in mathematics. *Journal of Personality and Social Psychology, 102*, 700–717.

Grant, H., & Dweck, C. S. (2003). Clarifying achievement goals and their impact. *Journal of Personality and Social Psychology, 85*, 541–553.

Gwilliam, L. R., & Betz, N. E. (2001). Validity of measures of math- and science-related self-efficacy for African Americans and European Americans. *Journal of Career Assessment, 9*, 261–281.

Hickey, D. T., Moore, A. L., & Pellegrino, J. W. (2001). The motivational and academic consequences of elementary mathematics environments: Do constructivist innovations and reforms make a difference? *American Educational Research Journal, 38*, 611–652.

Holzberger, D., Philipp, A., & Kunter, M. (2013). How teachers' self-efficacy is related to instructional quality: A longitudinal analysis. *Journal of Educational Psychology, 105*(3), 774–786. doi:10.1037/a0032198.

Hong, Y. Y., Chiu, C. Y., Dweck, C. S., Lin, D. M. S., & Wan, W. (1999). Implicit theories, attributions, and coping: A meaning system approach. *Journal of Personality and Social Psychology, 77*, 588–599.

Kaput, J. (1999). Teaching and learn in a new algebra. In E. Fennema & T. Romberg (Eds.), *Mathematics classrooms that promote understanding* (pp. 133–155). Mahwah, NJ: Erlbaum.

Ketelhut, D. J. (2007). The impact of student self-efficacy on scientific inquiry skills: An exploratory investigation in River City, a multi-user virtual environment. *Journal of Science Education and Technology, 16*(1), 99–111.

Ketelhut, D. J., Nelson, B. C., Clarke, J. E., & Dede, C. (2010). A multi-user virtual environment for building and assessing higher order inquiry skills in science. *British Journal of Educational Technology, 41*(1), 56–68.

Kieran, C. (1992). The learning and teaching of school algebra. In D. Grouws (Ed.), *Handbook of research on mathematics teaching and learning* (pp. 390–419). New York, NY: Simon & Schuster.

Klassen, R. M., Tze, V. M. C., Betts, S. M., & Gordon, K. A. (2011). Teacher efficacy research 1998–2009: Signs of progress or unfulfilled promise? *Educational Psychology Review, 23*, 21–43.

Lau, S., & Roeser, R. W. (2002). Cognitive abilities and motivational processes in high school students' situational engagement and achievement in science. *Educational Assessment, 8*, 139–162.

Lent, R. W., Brown, S. D., Sheu, H.-B., Schmidt, J., Brenner, B. R., Gloster, C.,…Treistman, D. (2005). Social cognitive predictors of academic interest and goals in engineering: Utility for women and students at historically black universities. *Journal of Counseling Psychology, 52*, 84–92. doi:10.1037/0022-0167.52.1.84.

Lent, R. W., Brown, S. D., & Larkin, K. C. (1984). Relation of self-efficacy expectations to academic achievement and persistence. *Journal of Counseling Psychology, 31*, 356–362.

Lent, R. W., Lopez, A. M., Lopez, F. G., & Sheu, H. (2008). Social cognitive career theory and the prediction of interests and choice goals in the computing disciplines. *Journal of Vocational Behavior, 73*, 52–62.

Lent, R. W., Paixão, M. P., da Silva, J. T., & Leitão, L. M. (2010). Predicting occupational interests and choice aspirations in Portuguese high school students: A test of social cognitive career theory. *Journal of Vocational Behavior, 76*, 244–251.

Little, R. J. A. (1988). A test of missing completely at random for multivariate data with missing values. *Journal of the American Statistical Association, 83*(404), 1198–1201.

Liu, M., Hsieh, P., Cho, Y., & Schallert, D. L. (2006). Middle school students' self-efficacy, attitudes, and achievement in a computer-enhanced problem-based learning environment. *Journal of Interactive Learning Research, 17*, 225–242.

Moos, D. C., & Marroquin, E. (2010). Multimedia, hypermedia, and hypertext: Motivation considered and reconsidered. *Computers in Human Behavior, 26*, 265–276.

National Academy of Sciences. (2011). *Expanding underrepresented minority participation: America's science and technology talent at the crossroads*. Washington, DC: National Academies Press.

Raudenbush, S., & Bryk, A. (2002). *Hierarchical linear models: Applications and data analysis methods* (2nd ed.). Thousand Oaks, CA: Sage.

Squire, K. D. (2003). Video games in education. *International Journal of Intelligent Games & Simulation, 2*, 49–62.

Star, J. R., Chen, J., Taylor, M., Durkin, K., Dede, C., & Chao, T. (2014). Evaluating technology-based strategies for enhancing motivation in mathematics. *International Journal of STEM Education, 1*:7. doi:10.1186/2196-7822-1-7. http://www.stemeducationjournal.com/content/1/1/7

Star, J. R., & Rittle-Johnson, B. (2009). Making algebra work: Instructional strategies that deepen student understanding, within and between representations. *ERS Spectrum, 27*(2), 11–18.

U.S. Department of Education. (2010). *Transforming American education: Learning powered by technology* (National Educational Technology Plan 2010). Washington, DC: Office of Educational Technology, U.S. Department of Education. Retrieved from http://www.ed.gov/technology/netp-2010

Watt, H. M. G., Eccles, J. S., & Durik, A. M. (2006). The leaky mathematics pipeline for girls: A motivational analysis of high school enrolments in Australia and the USA. *Equal Opportunities International, 25*, 642–659. doi:10.1108/02610150610719119.

Formal and Informal Learning Environments: Using Games to Support Early Numeracy

Hedwig Gasteiger, Andreas Obersteiner, and Kristina Reiss

Abstract Learning environments created to support children's development of early numeracy often use games. This applies to both formal and informal learning environments. However, there is hardly any empirical research on the effectiveness of games being used in such learning environments. Moreover, it has rarely been discussed whether the games are appropriate from a mathematics educational perspective. In this article, we first describe quality criteria for mathematical learning games and provide an overview of studies that investigated the effectiveness of using games to support young children's learning of early numeracy. We suggest that games for mathematical learning can differ significantly in their roles. Some games are intentional, structured, and with clear learning objectives, others have been designed for entertainment purposes, but nevertheless offer opportunities to learn mathematics. We then discuss in more detail the results of an intervention study as an example of a study on using games in informal learning environments. In this study, kindergarteners played conventional board games with classic dice. Although these games were not specifically designed to support numerical learning, the intervention effects were relatively high. However, the number of studies with systematic evaluation is very limited, so that more research is needed. More generally, we suggest that the term "game" should be used carefully and only for learning environments in which playing in its original meaning is an essential aspect.

Keywords Game-based learning • Number games • Play situations • Early numeracy • Mathematical learning environments

H. Gasteiger (✉)
Department of Mathematics, Ludwig-Maximilians-Universität München,
Theresienstr. 39, Munich 80333, Germany
e-mail: hedwig.gasteiger@mathematik.uni-muenchen.de

A. Obersteiner • K. Reiss
TUM School of Education, Technische Universität München, Munich, Germany
e-mail: andreas.obersteiner@tum.de; kristina.reiss@tum.de

J. Torbeyns et al. (eds.), *Describing and Studying Domain-Specific Serious Games*,
Advances in Game-Based Learning, DOI 10.1007/978-3-319-20276-1_14

Research has shown that early numerical learning is crucial for the development of mathematical abilities (e.g., Desoete, Ceulemans, De Weerdt, & Pieters, 2012). In particular, important developmental stages of numerical learning such as estimation of quantities, verbal counting, exact quantification, and subitizing (Krajewski & Schneider, 2009; Resnick, 1989) have been identified. Interventions to support early numerical learning often make use of games, because playing is an appropriate form of learning for children at a young age. However, it has rarely been discussed whether the games being used are actually appropriate for early numerical learning. The purpose of this article is to discuss from a mathematics educational perspective the appropriateness and effectiveness of games used in formal and informal learning environments to foster young children's numerical abilities, and to propose quality criteria for game-based mathematical learning environments.

In the first section, we discuss the use of the terms game and play, the rationale behind using games for early learning of numbers, as well as quality criteria of such games. Based on this section, we suggest that it could be helpful for a well-founded discussion of scope and effectiveness of game-based learning environments to consider a continuum ranging from games designed for the purpose of entertainment only to targeted instruction with only few entertaining features. In the second section, after specifying the contents included in early learning of numbers, we provide an overview of studies that investigated the effects of number games on young children. In the third section, we discuss in more detail the results of an intervention study using games that can be located close to the former end of the "mainly entertainment"–"mainly instruction" continuum. The study examined mathematical learning in kindergarteners who played conventional board games with classic dice in an everyday play situation. In the fourth section, we provide conclusions from these analyses and suggestions for further research.

Early Learning of Numbers with Games

What Is a Game and Why Are Games Used in Learning Environments?

Using games is one approach to support children in their learning of numbers. A game can generally be defined as "a physical or mental activity or contest that has rules and that people do for pleasure" (Merriam-Webster, 2015), but different authors have used a variety of characterizations. Habgood and colleagues (Habgood & Ainsworth, 2011; Habgood & Overmars, 2006) argue that it is more reasonable to define games by describing how they differ from other forms of entertainment rather than by specifying the commonalities of all things that are referred to as games. For these authors, an essential aspect is that games provide an interactive challenge, which distinguishes them from films (which are not interactive) and toys (which do not include an inherent challenge). In the context of early learning, the torm "play" has been used as a key term to describe learning situations, and it includes more than playing games (Gasteiger, 2012; Van Oers, 2010). Play can be described as a joyful activity, determined and possibly made up by the child, which focuses on the process rather than on the product (Fröbel, 1838; Oerter & Montada, 2008; Wood & Attfield, 2005). This description includes engaging in games with clearly defined rules as well as other forms of play activities, such as constructive play (e.g., building blocks) or role-play (e.g., playing shop keeper). Accordingly, games can be seen as those joyful, interactive, and challenging play activities that follow specific rules. As we will discuss in some detail below, not all activities that are labelled as (learning) games are actually joyful and challenging activities, and the focus does not always lie on the process rather than the product.

But why should we use games for early numerical learning? We know that learning requires motivation (Boekaerts, 1997) and learning activities are more effective when they are embedded in meaningful contexts (Cordova & Lepper, 1996). Games can create motivation through several aspects. For example, the player is constantly and actively involved in the progress of the game. Many games also include the element of competition, which can be engaging and challenging, and which can result in a feeling of success. When games are played together with other players, playing is a highly social experience (Huizinga, 1949; Pramling & Carlsson, 2008; Wood & Attfield, 2005). All these reasons are generally believed to increase motivation (Ryan & Deci, 2000). Play situations should be utilized as learning opportunities especially for younger children, because they occur naturally in their everyday lives, they provide a meaningful context, and they are a developmentally adequate form of learning. Playing allows children to discover themselves and their environment actively—in other words: to learn—in a kind of protected space (Fröbel, 1838).

While games and play situations have the potential to support early learning, it will certainly depend on the specific content, whether or not we would consider them as suitable for children's mathematical learning.

Quality Criteria of Games from a Mathematics Education Perspective

Good games for mathematical learning necessarily meet quality criteria for mathematics education in general. Although there is no universally accepted list of such criteria, important aspects can be derived from research in early mathematics education and related fields (see Gasteiger, 2015). We consider four of these aspects particularly relevant for discussing the quality of games to support early numerical learning from a mathematics education point of view: First, the mathematical content needs to be closely linked to the mechanics of the game. As outlined by Habgood and Ainsworth (2011), many educational games have used a "chocolate-covered broccoli" (Bruckman, 1999, as cited in Habgood & Ainsworth, 2011) approach, which means that the game element is only used as a separate reward for engaging in the learning content, but it is not actually linked to this content. In such a case, the game mechanics, although motivating, does not provide a meaningful context for mathematical learning. Such approaches have been identified in the context of early mathematics education, when learning tasks are simply embedded in a colourful environment or surrounding story (Gasteiger, 2012; Wittmann, 2006). An indicator for a close link between the learning content and the game mechanics is that the learning task could not easily be replaced by another task.

A second quality criterion is that the mathematical content needs to be presented correctly in order to enable continuous mathematical learning. This seems self-evident, but reducing the mathematical content for children at a very young age, and presenting it in a comprehensible and yet mathematically correct way can be challenging. It might often be necessary to transform or simplify the mathematical learning content to implement it in a learning game, and it is then important to keep the basic structure of the mathematical content so that it is compatible with the mathematics learned later on (Bruner, 1999).

As a third criterion, the learning content should be essential for further mathematical learning. So-called big ideas of mathematics, such as numbers, operations, or spatial relations (Sarama & Clements, 2009), can provide some orientation particularly for early mathematics education. For example, one would not consider a game as a high-quality mathematical learning game, if the learning content would not be relevant for further mathematical learning.

A fourth criterion is that the game needs to be appropriate for children's individual learning processes (Siraj-Blatchford, Sylva, Muttock, Gilden, & Bell, 2002). This means that the game environment should be comprehensible and motivating for children at a particular age and somehow address the needs of children at that age. Moreover, a good game for mathematical learning should be tailored to children's individual stage of mathematical development and be adjustable to this stage if necessary. Obviously, individual development does not necessarily follow the hierarchical structure of the mathematical content (see the second criterion above).

The criteria suggested here can help to evaluate how suitable a game is for supporting mathematical learning. To discuss the suitability of a game, it is also necessary to take into account the specific role that a game has within a specific learning environment.

Games in Formal and Informal Learning Environments: Two Poles of a Continuum

Children acquire knowledge about numbers long before they receive systematic instruction in kindergarten or school. For example, almost all children have been found to be able to count up to ten at the time they enter school and many children can solve addition or subtraction tasks, when tasks are presented in a real-life context (e.g., Van den Heuvel-Panhuizen, 1996). Obviously, children develop such early numerical abilities in informal or natural learning contexts (Gasteiger, 2012) nearly everyday, for example, through counting stairs or plates. Furthermore, children play various games that involve numbers and offer opportunities to learn mathematics. Many of these playful activities have not been designed for the purpose of learning but children are informally involved in mathematical learning processes.

On the other hand, learning environments for children can also be more formal. This means that a teacher provides the environment, and learning is structured and intentional (Commission of the European Communities, 2001, p. 32). Therefore, there is a strong focus on the learning content in these environments. For example, for practicing calculation, children might work on a set of calculation tasks, thereby improving their calculation abilities.

Games that provide opportunities to learn in informal learning environments differ considerably from games intentionally used in formal learning environments. To analyse games in game-based learning environments, we propose a continuum that specifies the more general "pure play–non-play continuum" described by Wood and Attfield (2005, p. 6, referring to Pellegrini, 1991) in the context of learning games. Focusing on play activities in young children, Wood and Attfield locate these activities along a continuum. On one end of this continuum, there are purposeless play activities initiated by the child. On the other end, there are playful activities that a child is engaged in under the guidance of an adult person for particular purposes other than pure play (e.g., learning).

We adopt this continuum to learning games by focussing on the purpose for which a game was initially designed.[1] On the one end of our continuum, there are games which are not specifically designed for the purpose of learning but for the purpose of entertainment, and which are not really instructive, but still offer the possibility to learn mathematics in an informal way. On the other end of this continuum, there are purposefully designed instructive mathematical tasks or learning activities which can be considered as games if they meet some of the above-mentioned aspects of a joyful, rule-governed, and challenging activity. So-called serious games are located at this end of the continuum, because they are designed for the purpose of education or instruction (Zyda, 2005, p. 26) and not primarily for amusement (Abt, 1987, p. 9).

This continuum is the basis for our discussion in the following section. For learning activities placed at the "mainly instruction" side of the continuum, the main question is whether such activities can actually be considered as games (in terms of the definition specified above). For games placed at the "mainly entertainment" end of the continuum, the main question is whether such games can actually foster mathematical learning.

---

[1] Note that Ritterfeld and Weber (2006) describe education and entertainment as two orthogonal dimensions to discuss the extent to which these dimensions are involved in individual activities. In contrast to this approach, we do not focus on the activities on the part of the individual, but rather on the intended purposes on the part of game designers.

Game-Based Intervention Studies to Support Early Numerical Learning

The structure of this section is guided by the continuum ranging from games that are designed for early mathematical learning in formal learning environments to games that are originally designed for the purpose of entertainment and can therefore be considered as informal learning environments. The two following subsections reflect the two ends of this continuum. In each subsection, we discuss selected intervention studies in light of the criteria for good mathematical learning games (see above). Rather than providing a systematic review, we summarize important theoretical ideas underlying these studies and discuss the games being used and their potential for mathematical learning. Before that, it is necessary to clarify the content of early numerical learning.

Contents of Early Numerical Learning

There is concurrent evidence from developmental psychology, numerical cognition, and mathematics education that early numeracy is the basis for the acquisition of arithmetic abilities. Being able to quickly recognize small sets of numerosities ("subitizing"; Mandler & Shebo, 1982) and to approximate larger sets is thought to be at the core of numerical development (Feigenson, Dehaene, & Spelke, 2004). According to Dehaene (1992) and Von Aster (2000), these non-verbal representations of numerical information become linked to verbal representations, such as number words, and symbolic representations, such as Arabic number symbols. Linking these representations is most important for the acquisition of elementary school mathematics (Krajewski & Schneider, 2009), and counting seems to be an important procedure in this process, because counting objects helps children link number words to quantities and eventually understand the relations between numerical quantities. Several studies have shown that impaired performance on any of the aspects described above (subitizing, approximating, counting) is related to lower mathematical performance (e.g., Dornheim, 2008; Krajewski & Schneider, 2009; Landerl, Bevan, & Butterworth, 2004; Siegler & Opfer, 2004).

Formal Learning Environments with Games Designed for Learning Purposes

Several studies investigated the effects of game-based learning environments with games specifically designed for early numerical learning. These games are located at the "mainly instruction" end of our continuum. Aiming at supporting the development of a mental number line, Kucian et al. (2011) used a computer game in which children had to navigate a landing rocket onto the correct position on a horizontal number line. The target position was indicated on the rocket (by numerals or simple calculation tasks). Obviously, the mathematical content was not closely related to the mechanics of the game, because there was no logical reason why the rocket had to land on a certain position or why simple arithmetic was used for landing a rocket. However, the mechanics of the game was related to the content in the sense that the numbers (or the results of the calculation tasks) corresponded to a certain position on the number line. The mathematical content was presented correctly, it was highly relevant (understanding of numerical magnitudes and simple calculation), and the game content was certainly appropriate for young children. In an evaluation study, pre-schoolers with and without diagnosed dyscalculia used this game for 15 min on five days a week, over five weeks. All participants improved their performance not only on number line estimation tasks, but also on specific arithmetic problems, such as elementary addition and subtraction.

Other studies focused on the development of an approximate understanding of numbers as an important part of early mathematical learning (see above). They used number comparison tasks in addition to linear number representations. Wilson, Dehaene, Dubois, and Fayol (2009) trained pre-schoolers from families with low-socio-economic status in comparing two numerical values, which were presented as sets of dots, Arabic number symbols, or simple addition or subtraction problems. They used the computer game "The Number Race" (Wilson et al., 2006), in which the player has to solve such comparison tasks and to move the game characters on a linear board. The tasks are embedded in an underwater world where the game characters are fish, crabs, or other sea animals. These animals collect treasure that enables them to proceed in a number race. The game environment has no logical connection to the mathematical tasks, because there is no logical reason why sea animals would collect treasure in order to compete in a race. While the number comparison tasks could easily be replaced by any other non-numerical task and the game would still work, the mechanics of the number race itself is linked to mathematical content, because—like in other board games—counting is necessary to move the game character on the board. Moreover, the content of the game (comparing numbers, counting) is important for mathematical learning, and is presented in an age-appropriate way. After six intervention sessions of 20 min each, the children's performance improved on symbolic number comparison tasks, but not on non-symbolic number comparison tasks or on addition tasks. Thus, there were positive effects only on some tasks that were directly trained, but no transfer effects.

Only small intervention effects were also found by Räsänen, Salminen, Wilson, Aunio, and Dehaene (2009), who compared the effects of the games "Number Race" and "Graphogame-Math". In the latter game, the player has to select the correct visually presented number that corresponds to an auditory probe. Visual numbers are represented in organized dot patterns (requiring subitizing skills), number symbols, or additions and subtractions. In this study, pre-schoolers with low numeracy played either the "Number Race" or the "Graphogame-Math" in a daily training session over a three-week period. While there were specific improvements on number comparison tasks compared to a control group of typically performing children, no significant training effects were found for other measures of arithmetic skills, such as object counting, addition, or subtraction.

Obersteiner, Reiss, and Ufer (2013) investigated the specific effects of fostering early mathematical learning in a game-based learning environment with children who were in their first year of primary school. To contrast the relevance of the two main basic skills for numerical development—exact and approximate number processing—they used two modified versions of the "Number Race", which were identical in their overall design but differed in the relevant aspects: One version required exact and the other approximate number processing. In this study, the computer games were used in order to implement the intervention conditions in a highly controlled manner rather than because of their game characteristics as such. As in the previous studies with the Number Race, the modified versions used in this study did not meet all the criteria of good games described above, since there was not always a logical connection between the mathematical content (number comparison, simple calculation, number recognition) and the mechanics of the game (collect diamonds in an underwater world). However, the mathematical content was presented correctly and in an age-appropriate way, and the content was highly relevant for future mathematical learning. The authors found effects on different aspects of numerical abilities, but these effects were restricted to those tasks directly trained during the intervention. In particular, training in quickly and precisely recognizing of number sets did not improve approximate number processing, while training in approximate number processing (number comparison, estimation on a linear board) did not improve exact number processing. The transfer effects on other numerical tasks that were not directly trained during the intervention were very small.

All in all, studies analysing short-term training on very specific numerical skills seem to show relatively small intervention effects, which are for the most part restricted to the tasks that were directly trained. In all these studies, the effects on mathematical competence in a broader sense were either not investigated or these effects were low.

Informal Learning Environments with Games Designed for the Purpose of Entertainment

In contrast to the above-mentioned studies with games specifically designed for the purpose of learning, there are studies that investigated the use of conventional games in their original or in a slightly modified version in more informal game-based learning environments. Some of these intervention studies assessed the effectiveness of playing linear number board games to support the development of a mental number line in children. In these games, the player had to roll the dice and to move a token on a game board the number of spaces indicated on the dice. While passing each square, children had to name the numbers of the squares in question to link verbal and symbolic representations of numbers. Siegler and Ramani (2009; see also Ramani & Siegler, 2008, 2011; Siegler & Ramani, 2008) showed that after just live intervention sessions of 15—20 min each, pre-schoolers from low-income families improved their performance on number comparison and number identification tasks. Furthermore, these children benefited more from subsequent learning of addition problems than children of a control group.

Whyte and Bull (2008) also reported positive effects of the same linear number board game play on counting abilities, number understanding, and approximation in pre-schoolers after four intervention sessions of 25 min each. Concerning the criteria mentioned earlier, the mathematical task in these games is closely related to the mechanics of the game—children count and move their token forward, respecting the one-to-one correspondence. The structure of the game correctly represents the structure of the mathematical content (the counting numbers). Furthermore, the content of the game (reading numbers, subitizing dot patterns on dice, counting) is highly relevant, and the game is appropriate for children at a young age. What can be questioned is the issue of challenge. Although the participants in the study were pre-schoolers, it can be assumed that many of them become familiar with the number line from 1 to 10 fairly quickly, so that it is not really challenging any more to simply move the character on the board.

A study by Young-Loveridge (2004) analysed how number games and storybooks can improve the numeracy of five-year-old children. Over a seven-week period, lower achieving children attended daily intervention sessions (30 min each) in school. Two children played (modified) commercial dice and card games with a teacher, heard a number story, and talked about the numbers in the accompanying pictures. The teachers were advised to engage the children in mathematical activities and to support them in their individual development. Compared to a control group, the intervention group had significantly higher learning effects, even 15 months after the intervention. Children of the intervention group had greater gains in knowledge of number, number patterns, numeral identification, in making small collections of objects, and in adding the numbers of two sets of objects.

Rechsteiner, Hauser, and Vogt (2012) compared the mathematical achievement of kindergarteners (aged 6.3 years) who played games with mathematical content in an informal learning environment with that of children who were given an instructional training and with that of children in a control group with no intervention. Children in the game-based learning environment played three times a week (30 min per session) over an eight-week period, using commercial and specifically designed card and board games. They played on their own in small groups. Children in the instructional training group were given a commercial training program for the same period of time and with the same timetable. The control group did not receive any explicit training. Children in the game-based learning environment showed significantly higher learning gains in mathematics than children in the control group, whereas children in the instructional training group did not perform significantly better or worse than children in the two other groups. The game-based learning-environment seemed to be comparable with the instructional training, but considerably more effective than the regular daily work in kindergarten.

Rechsteiner et al. (2012) and Young-Loveridge (2004) used modified and original conventional games. The mechanics of the games (e.g., rolling the dice and moving a token forward, sorting or ordering cards) offered many opportunities for mathematical learning. The mathematical content was inherent and therefore presented correctly. Furthermore, the content of the games (subitizing dot patterns on the dice, linking verbal and symbolic representations by sorting numerals on cards, counting, one-to-one correspondence) was highly relevant, and the games were appropriate for children at a young age. These games were designed for the purpose of entertainment. Therefore, it is to be expected that these games allow joyful, interactive, and challenging activities in which the process of playing is more important than a product.

The results from the studies discussed above do not generalize to all children and all kinds of informal game-based learning environments, because these studies often focused on children from low socio-economic-status families or with low numeracy development. Furthermore, the games used in these studies were often modified to highlight the mathematical content or specifically designed with a mathematical idea. These games were not conventional games, which limits the practical implications of these studies, because kindergarten teachers and parents often make use of conventional games that are easily available. When conventional board games were used, they were sometimes combined with other material, such as picture books, card games, or other games (Rechsteiner et al., 2012; Young-Loveridge, 2004). Additionally, the intervention conditions were not highly controlled.

Therefore, we explored in a controlled setting whether playing conventional games with classic dice in "real" play situations—that is, in situations without a specific focus on learning—can result in sustainable, continuous mathematical learning processes for children.

A Study on the Effectiveness of Conventional Board Games with Classic Number-Dice

Following the idea of early mathematics learning in natural learning situations, this study focused on conventional board games and their potential for mathematical learning in informal learning environments. We expected to find positive effects on children's mathematical learning, because although not instructive and located on the "mainly entertainment" end of our continuum, games with classic number-dice (i.e. dice with dot patterns from 1 to 6 on the sides) offer opportunities for informal practice of numerical activities such as counting.

Participants and Design

We used a pre-posttest design with an experimental and a control group. Ninety-five children 1½ years prior to school enrolment (52 female, mean age: 4.8 years) were randomly assigned to an experimental or a control group. Children in the experimental group played conventional board games with classic dice (number-dice), children in the control group played games using dice with colours (colour-dice) or non-numerical symbols (symbol-dice) (see game descriptions below). We chose this control group to ensure that all children were active under highly comparable conditions. This way, they all engaged in a common play activity, carried out similar actions during the game, and received the same attentiveness of an adult person. Moreover, colour- and symbol-dice games are often played in kindergartens in Germany, because many teachers consider number-games as too demanding for young children. Over a 3½-week period, the children participated in seven 30-min play sessions in groups consisting of two or three children and an adult. The main focus of our study was to prove the potential of conventional number-dice games for informal mathematical learning. Therefore, the adults were instructed not to give any explicit hints concerning the mathematical contents, but to play alert to children's reactions. This means they were asked to intervene if, for example, a child did not move correctly, by saying, for example: "Look, your token was here!" and to encourage he or she to think about the play situation (e.g., "Oh, you can catch someone!"). Moreover, they were instructed to serve as a role model by verbalizing the action they were carrying out, such as counting when moving their token or naming the number, colour, or symbol of the dice. To measure direct effects of the intervention, children were tested individually with the TEDI-Math test (Kaufmann et al., 2009), a standardized test for children between kindergarten and third grade. This test contains the subscales counting principles, enumeration, numeral identification, number word identification, and calculation. In addition, we used items to measure children's ability to subitize and to quickly recognize dot patterns as they appear on dice (Gasteiger, 2010). The reliability of pre- and posttest was high (Cronbach's $\alpha = .91$ for pretest and .92 for posttest). To control for children's intelligence, we used the Wechsler Preschool and Primary Scale of Intelligence (Petermann & Lipsius, 2011).

Intervention Games

In the following, we describe the ideas and the rules of the games used in this study. For the experimental condition we chose conventional number-dice games with a high potential for early mathematical learning, which can be played by children at an early age. Children in the experimental group played Ludo in a slightly modified version (Bee-Game), Coppit and Collecting Treasures. To parallelize both conditions, we chose dice games also for the control condition, but these games were played with colour- or symbol-dice. We decided to use the Mole's Favourite Game because it is similar to Ludo, and the very popular Worm Game. In addition to the game description, for each game, we provide some information on its potential for mathematical learning.

Ludo—Bee Game. "Ludo" (German version: "Mensch ärgere dich nicht", Schmidt-Spiele) is a very traditional conventional game. Playing this game with young children can take quite some time, because each player has to move four tokens on a game track of 40 squares in order to reach the finishing line. To make the game more appropriate for younger children, we used a slightly modified version to reduce playing time. Instead of four tokens, each player only had three tokens and the number of steps from start to finish was reduced to 24. To realise this, we designed a new game board (Fig. 1).

The Bee Game is played with the same rules as Ludo. Each player has three tokens in his bee hive (see Fig. 1). To start, a player must roll a 6 on the dice. If a player has no token in active play, he is allowed to roll the dice three times when it is his turn. If a player has one or more tokens in active play, he can decide which token he would like to move. Whenever a player rolls a 6, he must enter one of his tokens into active play. If there is no more token in one's bee hive, a token in play has to be chosen to advance it. Rolling a 6 allows an additional roll. If a player moves his token to an occupied square, the opponent's token has to be returned to its owner's bee hive. This token can be returned to play, when its owner rolls a 6. The game is finished after one player has entered all his tokens into his finishing line—the three dots in the middle of the game board of the respective colour.

When playing the Bee Game, children carry out many mathematical activities: After rolling the dice, they have to count or subitize the number of dots on the dice. When moving their token forward, they have to count verbally and make use of the one-to-one correspondence. When a player has more than one token in play, he might be in the situation to make strategic decisions, because he could choose to enter a new token into play, send an opponent's token back to its owners bee hive, or bring a token across his own finishing line. These decisions require numerical thinking.

Fig. 1 Game board of the "Bee Game"

Fig. 2 Board of the game "Coppit" (Copyright Ravensburger Spieleverlag GmbH)

Coppit. "Coppit" (German version: "Fang den Hut", Ravensburger) is also a traditional game. Each player has four caps as tokens and starts on his home space. When it is his turn, a player rolls the dice and moves his token forward. If he rolls a 6, an additional roll is allowed. If a player reaches a square where an opponent's token is placed, the player can catch the opponent's token by placing his cap on top of the opponent's. He has to try to reach his home space as soon as possible in order to place the opponent's cap there. If he manages to do so, the cap is lost for the opponent. The grey spaces are "safe squares" (Fig. 2). It is not permitted to catch tokens of the other players on these squares. The aim of the game is to collect as many tokens of the opponents as possible and to return them back to the own home space. When a player's last token is caught, he is out of the game.

Coppit offers mathematical learning opportunities that are similar to those of the Bee Game. Children have to count or recognize the number of dots on the dice, count and use the one-to-one correspondence while moving their token forward, and make decisions between reaching the grey space, catching an opponent's token, or reaching the own home space to place the opponent's cap. Each of these decisions requires comparing the number of squares with the number of dots shown on the dice.

Collecting Treasures. The game "Collecting Treasures" is part of a collection of playful activities that offer opportunities for early mathematical learning (Dolenc, Gasteiger, Kraft, & Loibl, 2005). In this game, children roll the dice and move their token forward. Some squares show a number of dots (Fig. 3). If the token lands on one of these squares, the child has to collect the right number of coloured treasures. When the first player reaches the last square—the den of thieves—the game is over. Each player counts his treasures, and the player who has most is the winner of the game.

While playing Collecting Treasures, children are engaged in all the counting activities mentioned in the analysis of the Bee Game. Additionally, they have to count the treasures when their token lands on one of the dot-squares. At the end, all children count their treasures. This can be done in different ways. Children can count out loud, beginning with "one" and respecting the one-to-one correspondence or they can structure the set of treasures in groups of ten or five in order to count quickly and avoid counting mistakes. In case the collected treasures differ

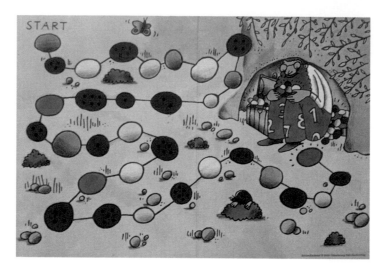

Fig. 3 Board of the game "Collecting Treasures" (Dolenc, Gasteiger, Kraft, & Loibl, 2005)

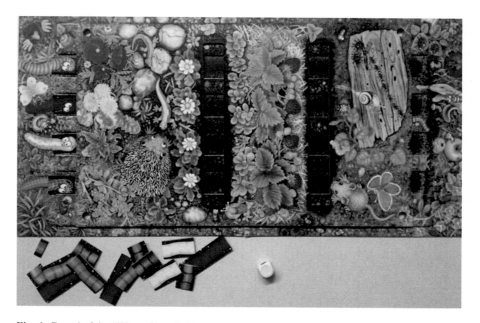

Fig. 4 Board of the "Worm Game" (Zoch)

considerably in number, children can also identify the winner through approximation rather than counting.

Worm Game. The "Worm Game" ("Da ist der Wurm drin", Zoch-Spiele) is a very popular game in Germany. The players use colour-dice. Each player chooses a worm and places the head of the worm at the starting point of the game board (see Fig. 4, left side of the board). If it is a player's turn, he rolls the dice. The colour shown on

Fig. 5 Board of the game "The Mole's Favourite Game" (Copyright Ravensburger Spieleverlag GmbH)

the dice decides which piece the player can add to his worm. The pieces are of different length, according to the colour. By adding worm pieces, the head of the worm moves forward. The player whose worm reaches the end of the game board first, wins the game.

Playing the Worm Game, children need neither to count, nor to subitize, or to use the one-to-one correspondence. As they use colour-dice, they only need to match the colour of the dice to the correct piece of the worm. Winning this game is a matter of chance, because the player cannot make strategic decisions. The Worm Game offers nearly no arithmetic learning activities, but children can get experience in comparing the lengths of the worms or of their pieces.

The Mole's Favourite Game. "The Mole's Favourite Game" ("Der Maulwurf und sein Lieblingsspiel", Ravensburger) has the same rules as Ludo (see above), with the only difference being that the dice show symbols, such as, e.g. a sun, a tree, or a heart, rather than numbers. The symbols correspond to the squares in the game track. Rolling a tree allows a player moving the token forward to the next tree (Fig. 5). Rolling a flower corresponds to rolling a 6 in the Ludo game, that is, rolling a flower is necessary to move the token out of the starting square and it allows an additional roll. If a player moves his token to a square occupied by an opponent, the opponent has to return his token to the starting square. The game is over if one player—the winner—has crossed his finishing line with all his tokens.

Dice with non-numerical symbols are used in The Mole's Favourite Game. Therefore, children practise neither counting nor subitizing or enumeration while playing this game. Instead, children can—as in all of the games described here—learn to follow rules, to act one after the other, or to strategically prepare their next move.

Results

To investigate intervention effects, we used an analysis of covariance, with pretest-results as a covariate and posttest scores as the dependent variable. Table 1 displays the test scores of the experimental and control group for both tests. In pretest, both

Table 1 Mean scores in pretest and posttest for the experimental group and the control group

	N	M (SD)	
		Pretest	Posttest
Experimental group	48	.60 (.16)	.72 (.14)
Control group	47	.61 (.15)	.67 (.16)

groups performed nearly equally, but in posttest, the experimental group showed significantly higher scores than the control group, $F(1, 92) = 13.57, p < .001$, partial eta squared $= .13$. The results indicate that children who played games with number-dice showed significantly higher learning gains from pre- to posttest than children in the control group who used dice with colours or symbols.

In the subscale enumeration, children of the experimental group performed substantially better than children of the control group, $F(1, 92) = 9.96, p = .002$, partial eta squared $= .10$.

Discussion

The games used in this intervention study were conventional board games, as available for example in toyshops, and they were not specifically designed for the purpose of targeted intervention. However, the effects on numerical abilities were considerably high. This is a remarkable result, considering that effects of intervention studies on game-based learning environments are often very small or even absent (see above; for an overview of computer-assisted interventions, see Räsänen et al., 2009). Although the intervention condition included numerical activities, there was no explicit focus on these activities, and the children did not receive any systematic instruction in mathematics. They just played a conventional game which nevertheless offered opportunities for numerical learning and which met the quality criteria outlined above. Compared to children in the control group, children of the experimental group improved especially their ability to enumerate. This was expected because the children—while playing the games with number-dice—practiced important quantifying skills such as counting and respecting the one-to-one correspondence when they moved their tokens forward. Although conventional number-dice games are not designed for the purpose of mathematical learning, important prerequisites for mathematical learning (see above), such as subitizing (dot patterns on dice), verbal counting, and exact quantification (moving a token forward), were trained. Children's mathematical development can benefit from playing these games. An interesting question for further research is whether the positive intervention effects persisted over a longer time period. This question will be addressed by analysing the scores of a delayed posttest (not analysed yet), which the children took one year after the intervention and just before they entered school.

General Discussion

The purpose of this article was to discuss from a mathematics education perspective the appropriateness and effectiveness of using games to support early numerical learning in formal and informal learning environments. To get a better overview of the available studies, we made a distinction between studies that used games specifically designed for the purpose of learning or a specific intervention in formal learning environments on the one hand, and studies that investigated the effectiveness of informal learning environments with conventional games originally designed for the purpose of entertainment on the other hand. We further discussed the use of the term "game" for mathematical learning environments.

With regard to specifically designed games for the purpose of learning, the results suggest that the intervention effects are for the most part restricted to those numerical abilities that were directly trained during the intervention (Obersteiner et al., 2013; Räsänen et al., 2009; Wilson et al., 2009). Transfer effects on other numerical tasks—which have often not been considered—seem to be very limited. A possible explanation for the limited effects could be that the use of various types of tasks may be more beneficial than the repeated use of a very specific task such as number comparison, because even simple arithmetic requires the integration of several basic numerical skills. From the perspective of game development, our discussion has shown that games specifically developed for the purpose of intervention rarely meet every quality criterion of good games for mathematical learning. Frequently, the content of a game is not directly linked to its mechanics. Moreover, in controlled research studies, the participants often play the games in artificial settings rather than in informal play situations. The defining aspects of games—a joyful, interactive, and challenging, rule-based activity in which the process of playing is more important than a product—can often not be realized in games that are designed for specific learning purposes. Therefore, we suggest that the term "game" should be used carefully when playing is not an essential aspect and the learning activity is located closer to the "mainly instruction" end of our continuum.

With regard to games that were not originally designed for the purpose of learning, it is quite surprising that there is only little systematic research on their effectiveness on children's learning. In many of the existing studies the intervention conditions were not well controlled, because the games were played in normal play situations in school or kindergarten. This limits their significance, because strictly controlled intervention conditions are necessary for a systematic analysis. As the results of our own study have shown, conventional games designed mainly for entertainment can have surprisingly large effects on basic numerical abilities such as counting, even though these games were not designed for the purpose of learning mathematics. This is important to know, because games such as conventional board games with classic (number-)dice are inexpensive and can easily be played in children's homes together with friends or family members.

In view of the available intervention studies, the use of board games with number-dice seems to be most promising. Moreover, explicitly training number concepts with a focus on the relationships between different aspects of numbers in formal learning environments could contribute to a deeper conceptual understanding. As of yet, the cognitive link between lower-order numerical abilities and higher-order arithmetical achievement is not sufficiently understood.

Considering the variety of game-based learning environments, instructional approaches, and intervention contents, there is still a grave lack of empirical studies. Two aspects of early numeracy seem to be particularly worthwhile to be further investigated: On the one hand, we need more knowledge on the specific effects that interventions with different theoretical approaches—game-based or not—have. This would contribute to a better understanding of early numeracy. In particular, this would clarify which aspects are most relevant for further development and how they can be fostered. On the other hand, from a more practical perspective, we need more systematic, well-controlled evaluations of low-cost intervention games. Such evaluations could give valuable advice to parents and kindergarten teachers how to effectively support their children's learning processes.

References

Abt, C. (1987). *Serious games*. Boston, MA: University Press of America.

Boekaerts, M. (1997). Self-regulated learning: A new concept embraced by researchers, policy makers, educators, teachers, and students. *Learning and Instruction, 7*, 161–186. 10.1016/S0959-4752(96)00015-1.

Bruckman, A. (1999, March). *Can educational be fun?* Paper presented at the Game Developers Conference 1999, San Jose, CA.

Bruner, J. (1999). *The process of education*. 25th printing. Cambridge, MA: Harvard University Press.

Commission of the European Communities. (2001). *Making a European area of lifelong learning a reality*. Brussels, Belgium: COM 678.

Cordova, D. I., & Lepper, M. R. (1996). Intrinsic motivation and the process of learning: Beneficial effects of contextualization, personalization, and choice. *Journal of Educational Psychology, 88*, 715–730.

Dehaene, S. (1992). Varieties of numerical abilities. *Cognition, 44*, 1–42.

Desoete, A., Ceulemans, A., De Weerdt, F., & Pieters, S. (2012). Can we predict mathematical learning disabilities from symbolic and non-symbolic comparison tasks in kindergarten? Findings from a longitudinal study. *British Journal of Educational Psychology, 82*, 64–81. doi:10.1348/2044-8279.002002.

Dolenc, R., Gasteiger, H., Kraft, G., & Loibl, G. (2005). *ZahlenZauberei. Mathematik für Kindergarten und Grundschule*. München, Düsseldorf, Stuttgart: Oldenbourg.

Dornheim, D. (2008). *Prädiktion von Rechenleistung und Rechenschwäche: Der Beitrag von Zahlen-Vorwissen und allgemein-kognitiven Fähigkeiten*. Berlin, Germany: Logos.

Feigenson, L., Dehaene, S., & Spelke, E. (2004). Core systems of number. *Trends in Cognitive Sciences, 8*, 307–314. doi:10.1016/j.tics.2004.05.002.

Fröbel, F. (1838). Ein Ganzes von Spiel- und Beschäftigungskästen für Kindheit und Jugend. Erste Gabe: Der Ball als erstes Spielzeug des Kindes. In E. Blochmann (Ed.), *Fröbels Theorie des Spiels I* (2nd ed., pp. 16–38). Langensalza, Germany: Thüringer Verlagsanstalt.

Gasteiger, H. (2010). *Elementare mathematische Bildung im Alltag der Kindertagesstätte. Grundlegung und Evaluation eines kompetenzorientierten Förderansatzes*. Münster, Germany: Waxmann.

Gasteiger, H. (2012). Fostering early mathematical competencies in natural learning situations. Foundation and challenges of a competence-oriented concept of mathematics education in kindergarten. *Journal für Mathematik-Didaktik, 33*(2), 181–201. doi:10.1007/s13138-012-0042-x.

Gasteiger, H. (2015). Early mathematics in play situations: Continuity of learning. In B. Perry, A. Gervasoni, & A. MacDonald (Eds.), *Mathematics and transition to school. International perspectives* (pp. 255–272). Singapore, Singapore: Springer. doi:10.1007/978-981-287-215-9_16.

Habgood, M. P. J., & Ainsworth, S. E. (2011). Motivating children to learn effectively: Exploring the value of intrinsic integration in educational games. *The Journal of the Learning Sciences, 20*, 169–206. doi:10.1080/10508406.2010.508029.

Habgood, M. P. J., & Overmars, M. (2006). *The game maker's apprentice: Game development for beginners.* Berkeley, CA: Apress.

Huizinga, J. (1949). *Homo ludens.* London, England: Routledge.

Kaufmann, L., Nuerk, H.-C., Graf, M., Krinzinger, H., Delazer, M., & Willmes, K. (2009). *TEDI-MATH. Test zur Erfassung numerisch-rechnerischer Fertigkeiten vom Kindergarten bis zur 3. Klasse.* Bern, Switzerland: Hans Huber, Hogrefe.

Krajewski, K., & Schneider, W. (2009). Early development of quantity to number-word linkage as a precursor of mathematical school achievement and mathematical difficulties: Findings from a four-year longitudinal study. *Learning and Instruction, 19*, 513–526. doi:10.1016/j.learninstruc.2008.10.002.

Kucian, K., Grond, U., Rotzer, S., Henzi, B., Schönmann, C., Plangger, F., et al. (2011). Mental number line training in children with developmental dyscalculia. *NeuroImage, 57*, 782–795. doi:10.1016/j.neuroimage.2011.01.070.

Landerl, K., Bevan, A., & Butterworth, B. (2004). Developmental dyscalculia and basic numerical capacities: A study of 8–9-year-old students. *Cognition, 93*, 99–125. doi:10.1016/j.cognition.2003.11.004.

Mandler, G., & Shebo, B. J. (1982). Subitizing: An analysis of its component processes. *Journal of Experimental Psychology: General, 11*, 1–22.

Merriam-Webster. (2015). *Game.* http://www.merriam-webster.com/dictionary/game

Obersteiner, A., Reiss, K., & Ufer, S. (2013). How training on exact or approximate mental representations of number can enhance first-grade students' basic number processing and arithmetic skills. *Learning and Instruction, 23*, 125–135. doi:10.1016/j.learninstruc.2012.08.004.

Oerter, R., & Montada, L. (2008). *Entwicklungspsychologie.* Weinheim, Germany: Beltz.

Pellegrini, A. D. (1991). *Applied child study: A developmental approach.* Mahwah, NJ: Lawrence Erlbaum.

Petermann, F., & Lipsius, M. (2011). *Wechsler preschool and primary scale of intelligence III, German version.* Frankfurt, Germany: Pearson Assessment.

Pramling, I., & Carlsson, M. A. (2008). The playing learning child: Towards a pedagogy of early childhood. *Scandinavian Journal of Educational Research, 52*(6), 623–641. doi:10.1080/00313830802497265.

Ramani, G. B., & Siegler, R. S. (2008). Promoting broad and stable improvements in low-income children's numerical knowledge through playing number board games. *Child Development, 79*, 375–394. doi:10.1111/j.1467-8624.2007.01131.x.

Ramani, G. B., & Siegler, R. S. (2011). Reducing the gap in numerical knowledge between low- and middle-income preschoolers. *Journal of Applied Developmental Psychology, 32*, 146–159. doi:10.1016/j.appdev.2011.02.005.

Räsänen, P., Salminen, J., Wilson, A. J., Aunio, P., & Dehaene, S. (2009). Computer-assisted intervention for children with low numeracy skills. *Cognitive Development, 24*, 450–472. doi:10.1016/j.cogdev.2009.09.003.

Rechsteiner, K., Hauser, B., & Vogt, F. (2012). Förderung der mathematischen Vorläuferfertigkeiten im Kindergarten: Spiel oder Training? In M. Ludwig & M. Kleine (Eds.), *Beiträge zum Mathematikunterricht 2012* (pp. 677–680). Münster, Germany: WTM.

Resnick, L. B. (1989). Developing mathematical knowledge. *American Psychologist, 44*(2), 162–169.

Ritterfeld, U., & Weber, R. (2006). Video games for entertainment and education. In P. Vorderer & J. Bryant (Eds.), *Playing video games—Motives, responses, and consequences* (pp. 399–413). Mahwah, NJ: Lawrence Erlbaum.

Ryan, R. M., & Deci, E. L. (2000). Intrinsic and extrinsic motivations: Classic definitions and new directions. *Contemporary Educational Psychology, 25*(1), 54–67. doi:10.1006/ceps.1999.1020.

Sarama, J., & Clements, D. H. (2009). *Early childhood mathematics education research. Learning trajectories for young children.* New York, NY: Routledge.

Siegler, R. S., & Opfer, J. E. (2004). Development of numerical estimation in young children. *Child Development, 75*, 428–444.

Siegler, R. S., & Ramani, G. B. (2008). Playing linear numerical board games promotes low-income children's numerical development. *Developmental Science, 11*, 655–661. doi:10.1111/j.1467-7687.2008.00714.x.

Siegler, R. S., & Ramani, G. B. (2009). Playing linear number board games—But not circular ones—Improves low-income preschoolers' numerical understanding. *Journal of Educational Psychology, 101*, 545–560. doi:10.1037/a0014239.

Siraj-Blatchford, I., Sylva, K., Muttock, S., Gilden, R., & Bell, D. (2002). *Researching effective pedagogy in the early years.* Norwich, England: Queen's Printer.

Van den Heuvel-Panhuizen, M. (1996). *Assessment and realistic mathematics education.* Utrecht, The Netherlands: Freudenthal Institute.

Van Oers, B. (2010). Emergent mathematical thinking in the context of play. *Educational Studies of Mathematics, 74*(1), 23–37. doi:10.1007/s10649-009-9225-x.

Von Aster, M. (2000). Developmental cognitive neuropsychology of number processing and calculation: Varieties of developmental dyscalculia. *European Child & Adolescent Psychiatry, 9*, 41–57. doi:10.1007/s007870070008.

Whyte, J. C., & Bull, R. (2008). Number games, magnitude representation, and basic number skills in preschoolers. *Developmental Psychology, 44*, 588–596. doi:10.1037/0012-1649.44.2.588.

Wilson, A. J., Dehaene, S., Dubois, O., & Fayol, M. (2009). Effects of an adaptive game intervention on accessing number sense in low-socioeconomic-status kindergarten children. *Mind, Brain, and Education, 3*, 224–234.

Wilson, A. J., Dehaene, S., Pinel, P., Revkin, S. K., Cohen, L., & Cohen, D. (2006). Principles underlying the design of "the number race", an adaptive computer game for remediation of dyscalculia. *Behavioral and Brain Functions, 2*, 19. doi:10.1186/1744-9081-2-19.

Wittmann, E. C. (2006). Mathematische Bildung. In L. Fried & S. Roux (Eds.), *Handbuch der Pädagogik der frühen Kindheit* (pp. 205–211). Weinheim, Germany: Beltz.

Wood, E., & Attfield, J. (2005). *Play, learning and the early childhood curriculum.* London, England: Sage.

Young-Loveridge, J. M. (2004). Effects on early numeracy of a program using number books and games. *Early Childhood Research Quarterly, 19*(1), 82–98. doi:10.1016/j.ecresq.2004.01.001.

Zyda, M. (2005). From visual simulation to virtual reality to games. *Computer, 38*(9), 25–32. doi:10.1109/MC.2005.297.

Index

© Springer International Publishing Switzerland 2015
J. Torbeyns et al. (eds.), *Describing and Studying Domain-Specific Serious Games*,
Advances in Game-Based Learning, DOI 10.1007/978-3-319-20276-1